THE CROSS
AND
THE SELF

— Expanded Edition —

by
Bill Freeman

MINISTRY
PUBLICATIONS
Scottsdale, Arizona

www.NormanGrubb.com

First Edition 1994
Expanded Edition 1998

Library of Congress Catalog
Card Number: 98-67789

ISBN 0-914271-97-0

Ministry Publications

PO Box 48255
Spokane, WA 99228
(509) 466-4777 / (800) 573-4105
Email: ministry@thechristian.org
www.thechristian.org

Printed in the United States of America

CONTENTS

Chapter   **Page**

PREFACE

In the beginning man was created to live by the life of God. This means man was created as a dependent creature. More specifically, the soul of man was designed by God to be in a dependent position, drawing its supplies from God's life as its source and expressing God's image through its faculties of mind, emotion, and will.

With the fall of man, however, the soul left its dependent position. The result was that the dependent soul of man degenerated into an independent "self." Thus, by the fall the same soul that was intended to express the image of God became an independent, autonomous, and sinful self, alienated from the life of God.

God's answer to fallen man's disarranged being is the cross. By the cross God reconciles man back to Himself. This reconciliation includes justification, termination, identification, and regeneration. In other words, man is now right with God (justification), finished with self (termination), joined to the Lord (identification), and inwardly supplied in his spirit with the life of God (regeneration). Such a full reconciliation by the cross brings man's soul back to its original position of dependency.

Now God's great work in our lives is to transfer us experientially and practically out of the self-life into Himself. He wants to daily take the *self* out of the soul and replace it with *Himself*. This transfer is summarized by the Lord's words in

Matthew 16:24-25 when He speaks of denying the self, losing the soul-life, taking up the cross, and following Him.

In the process of this transfer, the same light that shines in our heart to expose the subtleties of the independent self also shines to turn us away from all our own efforts to change ourselves. It keeps us dependent — living a life "beholding the glory of the Lord." By this beholding we are spontaneously being "transformed into the same image from glory to glory, even as from the Lord, the Spirit" (2 Cor. 3:18).

The Cross and the Self was ministered out of a burden from God's Word concerning the transfer of our source. All the chapters were spoken messages given in the setting of a practical church life, and are best understood in that context.

May the Lord use these messages to further our spiritual understanding of the Bible's basic revelation concerning man — that we would see that man was created to live a life dependent upon God as his source and supply, and also see that God's way to accomplish this dependency is by the cross dealing with the self. This is all a work of the grace of God.

— Bill Freeman
Scottsdale, Arizona

DEEPER, DEEPER, IN THE CROSS OF JESUS

Words: Bill Freeman

Music: C. P. Jones

1. Deep-er, deep-er, in the cross of Je - sus; Deep-er let me go;

Death and life, they al - ways go to-geth-er; Deep-en, Lord, the flow.

Chorus

Oh, deep - er yet we pray, Do work in us each day; Go deep - er through and through, Till in Thee we're whol - ly new,

(continued)

2. Higher, higher, in the life of Jesus;
       Lord, we are too low.
   By Thy life we all can go much higher —
       Higher let us go.

           Oh, higher yet we pray —
           Transform us every day —
           And richer in the flow;
           May Thy life be all we know.

3. Growing, growing, in us He is growing,
       More and more each day.
   Into all our living He is flowing —
       This is now His way.

           For growth, O Lord, we pray;
           Increase in us each day.
           It's not enough to know;
           Now Thy life in us must grow.

4. Living, living, Christ is all our living;
       He's so practical:
   Small things, big things, anything and
           all things —
       He's involved in all.

           Live Christ in every way;
           Oh, live Him out today.
           His name you now must call,
           And give Him your all for All.

5. Person, Person, Jesus is our Person,
       Living now in us.
   He's our tastes, our attitudes and actions;
       Oh, how glorious!

           Our Person, Lord, Thou art;
           Make home in all our heart.
           As life in every way
           Be our Person, Lord, each day.

6. Churches, churches, meeting with the churches
     We all find the flow:
   Deeper, higher, Christ as all our living,
     For the church we grow.

         The churches are today
         Just Christ in every way.
         For this, from self we cease,
         For Thy Body, Thine increase.

7. Building, building, we will see the building
     Of the church this way:
   Christ experienced will produce the building —
     He's the only way.

         Oh, build us, Lord, we pray,
         By growth of life each day.
         Oh, make us now such men
         For the New Jerusalem.

8. Coming, coming, Jesus soon is coming
     For His chosen Bride.
   In the churches we are all preparing
     To be glorified.

         Lord Jesus, come again —
         This cry is deep within.
         We'll praise Thee to the end,
         Oh, come back! Come back! Amen!

S cripture quotations are taken from a combina-
tion of translations including *The New King
James Version,*[†] *The King James Version, The
New American Standard Version,*[§] etc.   Minor
changes have been made in the various versions
from time to time to give a better rendering of the
Hebrew and Greek texts.

Throughout the Scripture quotations, words
are italicized for added emphasis.

This book is composed of messages given in
Seattle, Washington, and Scottsdale, Arizona.
The spoken form of the messages has been
preserved, with some editing for publication.

One having died for all, *His death was their death,* and…He died for all in order that the living may *no longer live to themselves, but to Him* who died for them and rose again.

❖ *2 Corinthians 5:14-15* ❖

Weymouth Version

The Positive Significance of the Soul

To understand the meaning of the cross and the self, we need to see the positive significance God has assigned to man's soul. The Bible reveals this significance by showing us the original position of the soul in God's creation. In Genesis 2:7 God created man with a body and a spirit so that man could become "a living soul." Because God created man with a soul, we need to know the soul's position and function according to God's original thought.

God made man in such a way that man's soul would be a faculty dependent upon Him moment by moment. In other words, God gave man's soul the position of always remaining as a dependent faculty. The spirit was not to be dependent upon the soul, but the soul was made to be dependent upon the spirit. Thus, our soul was created to live according to God's life in our spirit.

To properly understand the meaning of living dependent upon God in our spirit, we need to see the three parts of man according to 1 Thessalonians 5:23: "Now may the God of peace Himself sanctify you completely; and may your whole *spirit*, and *soul*, and *body* be preserved blameless at the coming of our Lord Jesus Christ." The diagram of three concentric circles on the following page helps us to visualize our whole being according to God's creation. Our *body* is the outermost part of our being. Our *soul* is composed of our mind, emotion, and will. And our *spirit* is the deepest part of our being. In regeneration, when we receive Christ, He enters into our spirit. We are born of the Spirit in our spirit (John 3:6).

The parts of man's soul
(Heb. 4:12; Psa. 139:14;
Job 7:15; Matt. 26:38-39)

The Lord's life of dependency

The Lord Jesus as the last Adam was a complete man with a spirit, soul, and body. The Gospels, which describe the Lord's human life, are filled with references of how He was related to His spirit and His soul (cf. "spirit" = Matt. 26:41; Mark 8:12; Luke 2:40; John 11:33; "soul" = Matt. 26:38; Mark 14:33-34; John 12:24-25, 27). During His 33 1/2 years on earth, His soul was in a dependent position. He depended on the Father who was dwelling in His spirit. He did nothing from Himself (John 5:19). He did not do His own will, seek His own glory, or speak from the source of Himself. He never acted on His own. Moment by moment, He was a man living wholly out of the Father (John 6:57).

In the wilderness the devil tried to remove the Lord from His dependency upon the Father by saying, "If You are the

Son of God, command that these stones become bread" (Matt. 4:3). Here the devil was attempting to remove the Lord from His dependency upon the Father *in His humanity* by getting Him to exercise His equality with God *in His divinity* (cf. Phil. 2:5-8). However, when Satan tried this, the Lord responded as a man, saying, "*Man* shall not live by bread alone, but by every word that proceeds out of the mouth of God" (Matt. 4:4). In other words, the Lord took the position of man and spoke concerning the way man should live. Christ spoke as a man with a soul-life that was positioned to feed upon the Father through the Word. In essence, the Lord was saying, "My soul is living from My Father. I am not living by bread alone, but by every word that is proceeding out of the mouth of God. I am dependent upon that proceeding word." So the Lord was telling the devil, "I'm a dependent creature. In My humanity I'm dependent."

Because the Lord lived dependent in all His human living, His mind, emotion, and will became so saturated and permeated with the Spirit that His total humanity as the last Adam became a life-giving Spirit (1Cor. 15:45). That is, in resurrection He brought man fully into God. He glorified humanity in Himself. Now, as a life-giving Spirit, He can impart Himself into our spirit, giving us the kind of life He lived — a dependent life.

This dependent life is the life in our spirit crying "Abba, Father" (Mark 14:36; Gal. 4:6; Rom. 8:15). To cry "Abba" is to express our dependency and child-like trust in the Father. It ushers us into a dependency upon the Father for everything.

When I'm crying "Abba, Father" from my spirit, His Spirit witnesses with my crying spirit in the form of an inward consciousness of a child-like dependency. I'm dependent upon Him for all my living. For example, I'm dependent upon Him in suffering. I'm suffering with Him. My spirit is engaged with Him. I'm being led as a son of God by participating in the very life and nature of the Son of God.

The primary leading of the Spirit in my life is the leading to put to death everything of my independent, natural life (Rom. 8:13-14). I don't trust in anything proceeding out of myself. I don't trust the way I make my decisions, the way I handle my money, the way I think about my future, the way I interact with my problems, the way I cope with things within me. Rather, I just SINK into God. I sink into God in order to live out of Him. By this I keep the proper position of my God-created soul — dependency upon God.

Man before the fall

Genesis 2:7 says, "And the LORD God formed man of the dust of the ground, and breathed into his nostrils the breath of life; and man became a living soul." The Hebrew word for soul is *nephesh*. This word is equivalent to the New Testament Greek word *psuche,* which should be translated "soul" or "soul-life." The first step God took in making man was to create him out of the dust of the ground, forming his body. The second step was to breathe into man the breath of life. The word "breath" is the Hebrew word *neshamah,* which is also translated "spirit" in Proverbs 20:27: "The spirit of man is the lamp of the LORD, searching all his innermost parts" (RSV). Thus, the "breath of life" that God breathed into man was man's spirit. This is also confirmed by Zechariah 12:1, a verse that summarizes God's creative work. It speaks of God forming the spirit of man within him. Because God is spirit, He made man with a spirit in order that man could correspond with Him. Now man can be born of the Spirit in his spirit, and can worship and correspond with God according to what God is in His spirit-nature (John 3:6; 4:24).

This is a crucial matter. As a human being, knowing how God made you can change your life and change your understanding of how to relate to yourself. When God made us, He made us in a particular way and in a certain order. We need to realize that man "works," or functions properly, only when he lives according to the way God made him. God did not begin in His creation of man by forming the soul in man's body. The soul did not come into being before man's spirit was formed. God's order was first to make a body, and then to breathe the spirit into the body. The result of the spirit being breathed into the body was that "man became a living soul." In other words, the soul is a direct result of the spirit. In God's created order, the soul was not positioned ahead of the spirit. It is the spirit that underlies the soul. It is the spirit that is the means of supply to the soul. It is the spirit that gives life to the soul.

The soul is a dependent faculty

God never intended that the soul of man with its mind, emotion, and will would be an independent faculty of man's being. According to God's created order, the soul of man was never to take the initiative on its own. God's thought is revealed in the way He created man. He first breathed a human spirit into man; and then, and only then, did man become a living soul. Thus, the soul is a *manifestation* of the spirit. The soul is the effect, not the cause. The spirit is the cause; the soul is the result. The spirit is the source, and the soul is the expression of the source (cf. Luke 1:46-47; Phil. 1:27; 2:1-2; Eph. 5:18-20 with 6:6; Heb. 4:12).

Man's spirit, not his soul, is to be the source of his living. This is because God's dwelling place in man is the spirit. Therefore, God Himself in man's spirit is the source of man's being. The soul is not the source, but rather remains in a dependent position. When the soul is dependent and drawing from the source of the spirit, then God is expressed in the soul.

When the spirit is the source in our lives, we find the true meaning and function of our soul — to express God. But when we reverse the order of our being and seek to save our soul, making it the source, we lose it as a faculty to express God. This is the meaning of the Lord's words in the Gospels related to seeking to save our soul-life *(psuche)* and losing it, or losing our soul-life and then finding it (Matt. 10:38-39; 16:24-26; Mark 8:35; Luke 9:23-25). When we seek to save and preserve the independence of our mind, emotion, and will, the soul loses its reason to exist.

Recovering the order of man's being after the fall

The soul is only to be a result and expression of its proper source, the spirit. That was the divine order in creation. However, when the fall occurred in Genesis 3, this order was lost because man's spirit died (Eph. 2:1). That means fallen man now had a soul without a source to live by. The soul lost its dependency on the spirit and became an independent faculty in itself. The Bible calls this condition of independency "death" (Gen. 2:17). We remain in a condition of death until the Lord washes, justifies, redeems, and reconciles us back to Himself, and then imparts His life into our spirit. This impartation is called *regeneration* in the New Testament (1 Pet. 1:3). God recovers the order of man's being after the fall by regenerating his spirit (John 3:6).

Now we have a regenerated spirit so that we can function properly as a human being. We are not functioning properly if we are not living by the source of our regenerated spirit (cf. 1 Cor. 2:11). God's purpose in redeeming us is to reestablish the proper order of our humanity, with the spirit as the source and supplier of our soul. Thus, the moment we live from our soul as the source, in that moment the soul becomes the *self*, and we cease to exist as a proper God-created human being.

The nature of the first sin

In 2 Corinthians 11:3 the apostle Paul describes the nature of man's first sin. He shows how the devil came to Eve to tempt her to take an independent step with her mind, that is, to act out of her soul as the source. Paul says, "But I fear, lest somehow, as the serpent deceived Eve by his craftiness, so your minds may be corrupted from the simplicity that is toward Christ." This reveals that the devil's primary area of attack was Eve's mind, the leading part of her soul. He came to draw her out of her spirit and into the thoughts and reasonings of her mind. He came with a suggestion that she would be like God. The underlying subtlety of Satan's temptation was to get Eve to think and reason independent of God. He suggested thoughts that made her question God. He brought a little bit of complication into her thinking. By this she lost her child-like simplicity and dependence upon God. She acted on her own.

Acting on our own is the root cause of all sin. This is what is so devastating about sin. It is not just the evil thought or the evil practice in and of itself, but that these things originate from acting on our own. This was the nature of the first sin — independence from God. Thus, the account of the first sin of man reveals that God created the soul to be in a position of utter dependency upon Him (cf. James 4:13-17).

Dependency maintained by the cross

It is always so life-giving to meet persons who live dependent upon God. They talk differently. They fellowship differently. They have a different flavor. There is an ease in which there can be openness and genuine fellowship. This is altogether different from relating to the kind of person who has an inward structure supported by an independent self. A person who lives independent of God in the affairs of his daily life lives as a soulish person, using his soul rather than his spirit.

When you meet this kind of person, you meet a fortified self-life, and there is no way to fellowship and work things out together in the Lord. This is because the things of the Spirit are foolishness to a person who lives from the soul (1 Cor. 2:14).

In contrast to this, when you meet a believer in whom there is a pliableness and an openness, there is genuine fellowship in spirit (Phil. 2:1). He is not someone outwardly agreeing with you while inwardly disagreeing, but he is one who is open and dependent upon God, one who knows his source is not himself. To meet this kind of person is to find fellowship (1 John 1:3).

This openness and dependency characterized the Lord as He prayed in the garden of Gethsemane, "My Father, if it is possible, let this cup pass from Me; nevertheless, not as I will, but as You will" (Matt. 26:39). That little word "nevertheless" reveals volumes about His dependent relationship with the Father. "Nevertheless" means that He was fully dependent, even in those moments when He was making a proposal to the Father to let the cup pass from Him. This shows us that a dependent person thinks, makes proposals, and has suggestions, but all the while he is a person submissive to God.

The Lord lived a life of sinking into the Father, with His soul wholly dependent upon Him (cf. John 1:18). And now our soul is to be permanently dependent upon our spirit, which is joined to the Lord (1 Cor. 6:17). In this way our soul becomes a faculty to express Christ, not an organ to express the self-life. Thus, there is the need to experience the cross in our daily lives. It is by *the cross* terminating *the self* that our dependent position is maintained, the divine life is continuously imparted into us, and God gets His expression through man. This is the positive significance of the soul.

2

THE GOAL IN DEALING WITH THE SELF

Having a subjective transfer from soul to spirit

The positive significance of man's soul is to be found in its dependency upon God. God wants to reestablish that dependency by becoming man's source in spirit. Thus, we can see that the goal of all God's dealings is to transfer our source from soul to spirit. God does this by the dealing of the cross. God does not leave us to ourselves. He deals with us. Hebrews 12:7 says, "If you endure chastening, *God deals with you* as with sons; for what son is there whom a father does not chasten?" The basic dealing for all God's sons is the dealing of the cross.

What does God want to accomplish in us as we pass through the dealings of the cross? What goal does He have in view? His unique goal is that we would have a transfer of our source, that is, that we would be transferred from the realm of living in our soul to the realm of living in our spirit. This transfer means that subjectively we begin living from a different source, or place. We relate to ourselves from a different place. We listen and hear others from a different place. We hear and read the Bible from a different place. Instead of coming from the source of our self, we come from the source of our regenerated spirit.

Having this subjective transfer from our soul to our spirit is the goal of all dealings with the self. The experience of the cross is the means for God to reach this goal in us. Our environment always aims at experientially terminating the self in order to effect a progressive transfer of our source from soul to spirit.

When we are born again, a new source is established within our being. In John 3:6 Jesus said, "That which is born of the flesh is flesh, and that which is born of the Spirit is spirit." This statement reveals that there are two sources for our being, that is, two places we can "come from" in the way we interact with things. We can come from the flesh or we can come from the spirit. To come from the flesh means we live out of our fallen self. In fact, if you drop the "h" in the word "flesh" and reverse the order of the letters, you have the word SELF. Both of these words, the *flesh* and the *self*, refer to another source for man's being other than the spirit.

These two sources for man to live by are revealed at the beginning of the Bible. In Genesis 2:8-9 God put man in a garden in front of two trees: the tree of life and the tree of the knowledge of good and evil. These two trees show that man can live by one of two sources. The tree of life represents dependence upon God in the realm of the spirit. To live by the tree of life is to live by God as our source. It is to take God Himself as our life, living in fellowship with Him and relying upon Him moment by moment. It is to live a life believing and trusting in the Lord. It is a life of learning to draw from God as our supply, and then following the impulses of that supply.

It is a life that can be described as "living out of God." It is a life of not making our own decisions anymore or leaning on our own understanding (Prov. 3:5-6). It is a life of filtering everything through the divine life. It is a life of not making a move or doing anything apart from compatibility with the Lord. It is a life of abiding in the Lord. It is a life in which we can do nothing apart from Him (John 15:5).

In contrast to the tree of life is the tree of the knowledge of good and evil. This tree represents independence from God in the realm of knowledge. It represents living apart from God in the source of the self, behaving "as gods" by making our own decisions according to what *we* think is good and evil (Gen. 3:5). It is a life of going our own way according to the dictates of our mind, emotion, and will. Thus, our own thoughts, feelings, and choices become the source from which we live. It is a life of doing things out of the accumulation of knowledge, apart from conferring with God. Isaiah 47:10 describes this kind of person: "For you have trusted in your wickedness; you have said, 'No one sees me'; your wisdom and *your knowledge have warped you; and you have said in your heart, 'I am, and there is no one else besides me.'* "

The two trees in Genesis 2 and 3 represent two different ways we can live and function as human beings. One way is to live and operate in the realm of our spirit, with God as our source. The other is to live and operate in the realm of our independent self, with Satan as our source. Thus, there is a desperate need to have a subjective transfer from the realm of our soul to our spirit. All of the cross's dealings with the self should effect in us a transfer from living out of our self into living and dwelling in our spirit, with God Himself as our source.

A new base of operation

One of the main reasons that Christ died on the cross was to give us a new base of operation in our spirit, so that we would no longer live to ourselves. We see this in 2 Corinthians 5:15-17: [15] "And He died for all, that those who live should live no longer to themselves, but to Him who died for them and rose again. [16] Therefore, from now on, we regard no one according to the flesh. Even though we have known Christ according to the flesh, yet now we know Him thus no longer. [17] Therefore, if anyone is in Christ, he is a new creation; old things have passed away; behold, all things have become new." Thus, the practical issue of the cross in our lives is that we no longer live to ourselves but to Him. This means we have a new center, a new point of reference, a new base from which we operate, a new source from which we draw our resources.

In Galatians 2:20 our new base of operation is described: "It is no longer I who live, but Christ lives in me." Our base of operation is no longer our self. The cross has freed us from ever again having to take the self as the source from which we live. Now we can deal with everything *from* the Lord, *in* the Lord, and *with* the Lord.

We have to worship the Lord for coming to us *by* His mighty hand in our environment, *through* the members of the

Body, and *through* the supply from the Word — all of which are to deal with our self to effect a transfer of source. This transfer to a new base of operation means that we no longer operate out of the self. When we deny the self, we become a person who enjoys the Lord as our source. This denying of the self is not the practice of asceticism; rather, it issues from our enjoyment of Christ as the Spirit in our spirit. By the Spirit we are putting to death all the practices of the body (Rom. 8:13). In this way we are operating out of a new base.

However, the less we allow the Lord to deal with our self, the more we will crowd Christ out, not allowing Him to be our source and center from which we handle everything. If the self is not denied, we are just little "gods," doing our own thing, operating our own lives. Then our base of operation and understanding is just the self. Thus, we can see that the goal of dealing with the self is to effect a subjective transfer of source, giving us a new base of operation.

To change our source of living

To fully appreciate the significance of having a change in the source of our living, we need to consider the example of the Lord Jesus. John 5:19 says, "Then Jesus answered and said to them, Most assuredly, I say to you, the Son can do nothing from Himself, but what He sees the Father do; for whatever He does, the Son also does in like manner." Consider the source from which the Lord lived, from which He did everything. His base of operation was constantly the Father. This means that the Lord Himself in His humanity did not take His soul as His source. Rather, He was one with the Father. This oneness came out of His continual fellowship with the Father in the Word (Matt. 4:4), in prayer (Luke 5:16-17), and in crying "Abba, Father" (Mark 14:36). As He lived a life of fellowship with the Father, He lived a life of absolute dependence. The source of His life was exclusively the Father. He denied and terminated His soul-life, and He lived out the Father's life.

To make us dependent

Now the Lord wants to reproduce in us this same dependent relationship. This dependent relationship is for the transferring of our source out of our self into our spirit, for the building of the church, for the shutting of the gates of Hades, and for the crushing of Satan. So it is crucial for us to see the goal — that we no longer operate out of the base of our independent self. Rather, we are dependent, relying on the Lord, trusting Him moment by moment for everything — our thought-life, our reactions, our fears, our problems, our way of living (2 Cor. 1:9; 3:4-5). We are a person who is depending upon God and living out of Him as our source (2 Cor. 5:18).

May the Lord grant that more of us would actually experience this transfer and begin coming from a different place. Then when others meet us, they would not meet our mind or our emotion, but they would meet Christ. We are coming from the Spirit, coming from Another life, because we are living dependent on the Lord. This is the goal of all our dealings with the self — to effect a real transfer of source.

Getting into our situation with light and life

Now we need to consider a basic principle of dealing with the self, that is, having someone get into our situation with light and life. For example, Paul got into the situation of the saints in Rome. The kind of self that was there in Rome could be characterized as an *ignorant* self — the self without light, without proper revelation. Paul was dealing with a self whose chief characteristic was ignorance about the truth. In Romans, Paul uses the word ignorant a number of times: "Are you ignorant?" (6:3; 7:1); and "I would not have you ignorant" (1:13; 11:25). He was touching something of the undealt-with self in its ignorance of the truth. The ignorant self does not know how to relate to the truth concerning sin, the flesh, and the law.

We need a transfer into the Spirit in order that we could be a person who relates to the truth about sin, about the flesh, and about the law. We need to know the objective truth — that our old man was crucified (Rom. 6:6) and that we died to the law (Gal. 2:19-20). Then we become a person who relates to our self according to the truth. So we need to know the truth, have the revelation of the truth, and have our mind renewed by the truth. When we see the truth, we spontaneously declare, "Praise the Lord! My old man was crucified! I do not live by the old man. I live by Christ." The fact is that many things have already transpired in the Lord's finished work. We need to know these *objective* truths so that we can properly relate to everything in our *subjective* experience.

An ignorant self does not know how to relate to the truth in the middle of reactions. When we have a reaction of sin in our flesh, we just need to speak to it, saying, "Listen, reaction, you are terminated! You have nothing in me (John 14:30). You have no ground in me." But instead we may listen to that reaction, pay attention to it, worry about it, sink into it, and even indulge in it because we do not know how to relate to it in the truth at the time it surfaces.

To have a proper church life we need to relate to one another according to the truth. The truth tells us that we are one Body. The truth says that there is no division. The truth reveals that we have an organic relationship with one another in life as the Body of Christ. It is crucial that we relate to one another according to this truth. For this we need the renewing of the Word of God.

Not only do we need to relate in the truth, but we also need to relate properly in the realm of life. An ignorant self does not know how to relate in this realm with the saints. Do we know how to relate in life with one another? What does it mean to relate in life? Romans 8:6 says, "The mind of the flesh is *death;* but the mind of the Spirit is *life* and *peace*" (ASV). This can also be translated, "The mind set on the flesh is *death,* but the mind set on the Spirit is *life* and *peace*" (NASV). An ignorant self will not know how to relate to the feelings or consciousness of life identified in this verse as "death" and "life and peace."

In the realm of life there are feelings and sensations of life (Eph. 4:18-19). These sensations may also be identified as the consciousness of life. For example, when you are talking with someone out of the source of your self, you may have a consciousness of feeling awkward, restless, uneasy, and uncomfortable. There is something within you forbidding. If you do not know the realm of life, you will just ignore those sensations and proceed with your thought, your view, your argument, your words. This means you are living out of the wrong source. Instead of coming from the source of the spirit and being sensitive to the feelings of life, you override the realm of the spirit by the self. So the undealt-with, ignorant self does not know how to relate in life.

To be a person in the realm of life is to be one who progressively learns to take care of the spirit and the spirit registrations of life and peace. It is not to pay attention to right and wrong according to the self, but to pay attention to life and peace according to spirit. This is to take care of an inner consciousness in our being. It is the same as paying attention to the registrations of the Spirit written on our heart and mind (Heb. 8:10). It is the same as taking care of the flow of life coming from our innermost being (John 7:38-39), and it is the same as recognizing peace and joy in the Holy Spirit (Rom. 14:17). This is how we relate in life.

Brothers and sisters, how much of our daily experience is in life? How much are our relationships in life? If our self is ignorant and undealt with, we are a person who does not know how to relate in life. Then you may ask, "How can I get help?" Let us answer with the Word of God. How did the Romans get help? How did the Corinthians get help? How did the

Philippians get help? How did the Galatians get help? They all got help by a member getting into their situation with light and with life, speaking the truth in love to them (Eph. 4:15).

Paul did not come to the saints with politics. He brought them to the Spirit, where the self gets terminated. He brought them to the experience of Christ. For example, to the Colossian believers who were in danger of being cheated through philosophy and empty deceit, Paul declared, "We preach [Christ], warning every man and teaching every man in all wisdom, that we may present every man full grown in Christ Jesus" (Col. 1:28). This means Paul got into the saints' situation. Also, to the Ephesian elders he testified, "You know...how I kept back nothing that was helpful, but proclaimed it to you, and taught you publicly and from house to house" (Acts 20:18-20). From these words we realize that Paul freely ministered to the saints, even in their homes, getting into their situation to help them.

Praise the Lord for the members in the Body who get into our situation with light and life. We are not preserving or protecting the self; neither do we desire to save it. It is a mercy from the Lord that we could remain open to hear the Body even when the fellowship is transparent (Gal. 4:16). The result of such fellowship is that the Lord can do something over us. By our being open to the Body and not preserving our self, we can receive help from the saints. We are helped to be a person who relates in life rather than relating from the tree of the knowledge of good and evil. So this is our prayer — that the Lord would bring us out of the realm of knowledge and into the realm of life.

With the realm of life there is a flow and a consciousness supplied into our very being. This supplied consciousness is God Himself as life (John 14:19-20). This is also the way the Lord manifests Himself to us (John 14:21). In other words, life is experienced in the form of a consciousness. Life is God Himself in our very being.

When we fellowship with the Lord, it brings in the consciousness of His life (Rom. 8:16), and we treasure that consciousness because it is God Himself operating within us (Phil. 2:12-13). Out of this fellowship the Lord may restrain us from speaking something that may seem so right, so logical, so good. We are restrained by a feeling within, a consciousness. If we follow that life-consciousness and obey it, we relate in the realm of life, not in the realm of knowledge. By this kind of experience we are led out of the ignorant self that does not know how to relate in the realm of life.

The ignorant self in environments

The ignorant self also does not know how to properly relate to environments. It blames circumstances. It blames the wife, the husband, the boss — whomever. This is the ignorant self. But let us see how Paul related to his environments. In Romans 8:28 he affirms, "And we know that all things work together for good to those who love God, to those who are the called according to His purpose." And in verses 36-37 of the same chapter he further interprets all his environments: [36] "As it is written: For Your sake we are killed all day long; we are accounted as sheep for the slaughter. [37] Yet in all these things we are more than conquerors through Him who loved us." These verses all reveal that Paul was living out of another source, and from that source he gathered up all his environments as raw material for the self to be terminated, for the self to be crossed out once again, so that resurrection life could come forth.

The ignorant self does not properly relate to environments. Rather, it is confused. It is frustrated. It is hurt. It blames. It is hoping for a better day. It does everything but deal with the Lord. It does everything but allow itself to be terminated. In its ignorance it does not know how to relate to environment in the realm of life and truth. These are all characteristics of an ignorant and undealt-with self and expose that we still come from the wrong place, and do not come from the experience of life to meet our environments with God's view.

God's view of our environment is that all day long we are just being led to put to death the practices of the body (Rom. 8:13-14). This means we are being led into a new kind of reaction — led to put to death, led to react with the cross. We are being led into another circumstance for more of the self to surface so that it can be interrupted and terminated. Hallelujah! In this way all things are working together for good — for our conformity to Christ (Rom. 8:28-29).

Learning how to relate in the Body by life

The ignorant self also does not know how to relate in the Body. In Romans 12, in the context of revealing the Body of

Christ, Paul describes a person who is not consecrated (v. 1), not renewed (v. 2), and does not receive all the members (vv. 3-5, 16). These are characteristics of the ignorant self that does not know how to relate in the Body. But Paul tells us in verse 2 how to be brought out of our ignorance: "And do not be conformed to this age, but be transformed by the renewing of your mind." The ability to relate in the Body comes by having a thorough dealing with the world and not being conformed to this age.

How do you relate in the Body? The Body is one hundred percent a matter of life. It is organic and it only responds to life. It only receives life. It rejects anything that is not life. So if there is anything of the world in us, any conformity to the age, then to that degree we will not know how to relate in the Body. The Body is not something organized. It is not something we mentally grasp. We apprehend the reality of the Body by experiencing Christ as life. The Body is a matter of life.

To relate in the Body by life, our mind needs to be renewed. Our thoughts need to be renewed. This renewal of our mind and our thoughts is related to our dealing with the world and not being conformed to this age. This is why through the years in the church life, whenever there have been dealings with the world, dealings with this present evil age, dealings over what our hearts were riveted to, there has been a quickening among us concerning the reality of the Body. On the other hand, if the Body is not that real to us, and we do not relate in life in the Body, it may be due to our lack of dealing with the world. If we have not dealt with the things that possess our hearts, but rather have closed out light and life, the Body will not be that real to us.

So we can see our need to relate (1) in life, (2) to the truth, (3) to our environment, and (4) to the Body. Dealing with the self will issue in properly relating to all these things. Dealing with the self also issues in the Lord's building of the church. May the Lord do His work of exposing this self so that we can deny it and terminate its tyranny over us (Matt. 16:23-24). By this dealing we shut the gates of Hades and cast Satan out so that the Lord has a way to build us together and spread His economy on the earth (Eph. 1:10; 3:9; 1 Tim. 1:3-5).

While the Lord is building the church, there is also a goal being realized within each of us subjectively. More and more as this self is being dealt with, we are experiencing a transfer, we are coming from another source. We do not come from our mind or our emotions — from our self. We begin to come from our spirit. We hear in the spirit. We speak from the spirit. We consider from the spirit. We do not have any rights to live apart from the Spirit. We have lost every right. We no longer have the choice to live from ourself (2 Cor. 5:15). We are actually living from the tree of life, dependent upon God. This is the goal of all the dealing with the self — to effect a real inward transfer from the soul, from the self, into the spirit, so that we handle things, do things, and relate to ourselves in an altogether different way.

How can the self be dealt with for the building and spread of the church? The way the self is dealt with is by someone getting into our situation with light and life. The underlying principle of the New Testament Epistles is simply that someone is getting into the situation of the saints and the churches with light and life. Virtually every locality in the New Testament represents some undealt-with aspect of the self. So all the Epistles written to the churches were simply brothers getting into the situation of the saints in a specific way with light and life, ministering the truth in a transparent way.

Unless the Lord performs a special miracle, there is no way that a local church that is having problems can be recovered without someone getting into the situation in a specific way to have fellowship. Just consider the Epistles from this viewpoint. What are the Epistles? They are simply light and life getting into all the situations of the saints in a specific way. How could the Corinthians be helped without someone getting into their situation and ministering the truth and fellowshipping in life? How could the Galatian situation be helped apart from Paul getting into it? So all the Epistles show us a basic principle concerning dealing with the self, that is, the principle of allowing someone to get into our situation.

But we preserve our self. Often we hide from the Lord's dealing. We even close light out in our experience, sometimes consciously, other times unconsciously. We suppress the inner speaking of the Lord and close ourself to light. We may go on for years preserving and protecting ourself, not allowing ourself to be dealt with. Then one day, by the Lord's mercy, a member, or members, of the Body get into our situation, bringing in light and life; and we open ourself to the Body, just as Saul opened to Ananias. Ananias got into Saul's situation. As a result of allowing this member of the Body to minister something of the Lord's economy to him, Saul was changed into another man. This is a basic principle in dealing with the self — we must allow the Body to get into our situation to fellowship with us in light and life.

Consider how Paul fellowshipped with the churches, getting into the situation of the saints in a specific way. This shows us that dealing with the self is not merely an individual matter but a Body matter. Because dealing with the self is for the building up of the church, it becomes a Body matter. This is crucial to having the church life in a practical way.

Christ Himself and the building of the church

Let us look at the Lord's words in Matthew chapter 16 when He was speaking about the church. Peter confessed in verse 16 that the Lord Jesus as the Son of Man was "the Christ, the Son of the living God." Then immediately the Lord said to him, "And I also say to you that you are Peter, and on this rock I will build My church, and the gates of Hades shall not prevail against it" (v. 18). Here the Lord reveals that the building of the church is upon "this rock," which is Christ. And this rock is not only Christ Himself, but it is also Peter's revelation and confession of Christ. So for the building of the church there must be the revelation and confession of Christ Himself as our person, as our reality, as our source. This shows us that the self can have nothing to do with the building of the church.

Christ is the essence, the substance, and the reality of the building. Out from Him the whole Body is built together. In Ephesians 4:15-16 Paul says that we "may grow up in all things into Him who is the Head — Christ — out from whom the whole Body, joined and knit together…" This shows us that the reality of this building is out of the source of Christ Himself and out of our growing up into Him in all things.

The church comes one hundred percent
from the revelation and experience of Christ

The church comes fully from the source of revelation and the experience of Christ. When the building of the church is out of Christ as the source, it is just Christ enlarged and increased. Anything other than Christ is not the church. Anything of the self is not the church. Only Christ experienced is the church.

In Genesis 2:22 Eve, typifying the church, was "builded" out of the rib of Adam, typifying Christ. Just as Eve, in every aspect, was out of the element and substance of Adam, so the church is built altogether out of the resurrection life of Christ. Apart from Christ there is no church. The Lord said, "Upon this rock I will build My church." In other words, He was saying, "I am this rock. The rock is the revelation and confession of Me." This makes it clear that the building of the church is just Christ. This is not mere doctrine or teaching. Christ experienced by us *is* the building of the church. It is one hundred percent Christ. This fact reveals how important it is to have a transfer of our being from soul to spirit.

*Being processed with the crucified
and resurrected Christ*

The kind of Christ who is building the church is the crucified and resurrected Christ. This is revealed in Matthew chapter 16. Immediately after the Lord speaks of building the church, verse 21 says, "From that time Jesus began to show to His disciples that He must go to Jerusalem, and suffer many things from the elders and chief priests and scribes, and be killed, and be raised again the third day." This was the first time the Lord announced His crucifixion and resurrection, and He did it following the revelation of the building of the church. This shows us that the kind of Christ that builds the church is the crucified Christ and the resurrected Christ. It is not the kind of Christ often propagated today even in Christianity — merely a kind of religious figure. Rather, the Christ that builds the church is the crucified and resurrected Christ.

This crucified and resurrected Christ has joined us to Himself organically. Thus we are joined to His death and His resurrection. In Galatians 2:20 Paul testified, "I have been crucified with Christ; it is no longer I who live, but Christ lives in me." It was the crucified and resurrected Christ that Paul was joined to and experienced. So when we experience Christ, we experience Him as the crucified and resurrected Christ.

The Christ who was processed in incarnation, human living, crucifixion, resurrection, and ascension is living in us to process us. That is, this Christ is now processing us with all the elements of His own process. For example, He is processing us in crucifixion. Not only were we terminated objectively on the cross two thousand years ago, but subjectively, day by day, we are being terminated. Our whole being is now being processed in crucifixion. That means our mind, our emotions, our will — our whole being with the practices of our body — are being processed day by day in crucifixion in order to be processed in resurrection.

Our whole being is under a divine process of crucifixion and resurrection. Because we have been joined together in the likeness of His death, we will also be in the likeness of His resurrection. Our whole being is under the process of crucifixion and resurrection for the building of the church.

The hindrances to the building of the church

In Matthew 16:18-21 we see the Lord prophesying about building the church and about being crucified and resurrected. Then in verses 24-25, He speaks about the hindrances to the building of the church: 24 "If anyone desires to come after Me, let him deny himself, and take up his cross, and follow Me. 25 For whoever desires to save his soul-life will lose it, and whoever loses his soul-life for My sake will find it." So in the context of the building and of the crucified and resurrected Christ, the Lord immediately begins to talk about dealing with the self — denying the self, taking up the cross and following Him, and losing the soul-life. He even speaks of "whoever desires to save his soul-life," warning us not to preserve our self, or our soul-life. The soul-life is not to be preserved. It is not worth it. It is dung (Phil. 3:8). Do not save your self in any way, in any dimension; but as the Lord says, deny the self, lose it. By our losing the soul-life, there is a way for the building of the church.

Why is it so crucial to deal with the self when we come to the matter of the building of the church? Why does the Lord relate dealing with the self to the building in these verses? The context makes it clear. To talk about the building of the church, the Lord has to talk about the dealing with the self. Why is it so crucial for the self to be under the dealing of the cross for the Lord's building? It is because the self is the gateway for Satan into the church. Through the self the gates of Hades come out to prevail against the church. Practically speaking, the Lord equates the self with Satan in these verses. When Peter tried to prevent the Lord from going to the cross by saying, "Far be it from You, Lord; this shall not happen to You!" the Lord turned and said to Peter, "Get behind Me, Satan! You are an offense to Me, for you are not minding the things of God, but the things of men" (Matt. 16:22-23). Here the Lord identified Peter's undealt-with self as Satan. This shows that the undealt-with self becomes the gates of Hades trying to prevail against the building of the church.

So we can see why it is critical for the self to be dealt with by the Lord. The undealt-with self is the ground that Satan takes to destroy the church. Thus, the self becomes the expression of Satan. By dealing with the self, we deal practically with Satan. We shut the gates of Hades and prevent Satan from attacking the church. It is in this way that the enemy, Satan, is cast out of the church.

Satan does not merely come against us by his oppression felt in the atmosphere of a church meeting, but he subtly comes out through the undealt-with self. Peter expressed his good opinion, yet that good opinion turned out to be Satan hiding in the self. So the reason the Lord needs to deal with our self-life in the church is because it is the same as dealing with the enemy himself. The revelation in Matthew 16 clearly shows us the relationship between the building of the church, dealing with the self, and defeating the enemy. Thus, the goal in dealing with the self is to transfer us out of the soul into the spirit for the sake of the building of the church.

3

THE EXPRESSION OF THE SELF — OPINION

No longer living to ourselves

The Christian life is not merely a matter of receiving Christ and knowing that we have eternal life and are going to heaven. Although none of these matters are wrong, they are short of the divine thought. God's thought when we receive Christ is that a new source would be established within us for our entire being. This new source is our regenerated human spirit (John 3:6). Thus, having a change of source is the most central thing in our regeneration.

To have a source-change means that we no longer live to ourselves, but to God. We no longer live by the self, but by His life. What naturally follows the initial birth of our spirit is a progressive transfer of our source in our daily life. For this transfer to happen, it is necessary to pass through experiences with the Lord in which the old source, the self, is dealt with, and the new source, our spirit, gains the ascendancy (cf. 2 Cor. 4:16).

According to 1 Thessalonians 5:23, man is a being composed of spirit, soul, and body. Before we are regenerated, although our spirit exists within us as a potentiality, it is in a dead condition. So the source of our living is not our spirit, but our soul, which includes our mind, emotion, and will. In Ephesians 2:1-3 Paul clearly defines our unregenerate state:

[1] "You...who were dead in trespasses and sins, [2] in which you once walked according to the age of this world, according to the ruler of the authority of the air" — that is, according to Satan. And then Paul says, "the spirit who is now operating in the sons of disobedience, [3] among whom also we all once conducted ourselves in the lusts of our flesh, fulfilling the desires of the flesh and of the thoughts." "The desires of the thoughts" means that we have lived out Satan in our independent thoughts. We have been one with Satan in the realm of our thoughts. This characterizes our old life before we are regenerated.

But when the Lord enters into us, our spirit is born and we have an inner rearrangement of our being. The mind, emotion, and will are no longer to take the lead to determine our living. The leading part of our being now becomes our regenerated spirit, where we are joined to the Lord (1 Cor. 6:17). It is from this Christ-indwelt center that all the parts of our soul will find their proper place and function. Formerly, we were an independent self that did its own things, thought its own thoughts, made its own decisions. But once our center changes, all this is altered. Christ comes in to make home and rearrange all our inward parts (Eph. 3:16-17).

Now the Lord wants us to become familiar with our spirit — to discover our spirit, release our spirit, and learn to take initiative with our spirit. But because our soul has taken the initiative for so many years, we have been flooded with our own thoughts and enmeshed with our own feelings and choices. So even after we are regenerated, we may not live one spirit with the Lord that much. We may still live out of the source of our self in many things. But we have to see that in regenerating our spirit, the Lord intends that all our living be permeated with the Spirit. So we need to practice living out of this source, actually being one spirit with the Lord in our experience.

God's dealings effecting a transfer of our source

The Lord wants us to know that all the dealings with our self, all the many blows it receives, are to effect a transfer of our source experientially. Everything He allows is for the process of bringing us into this wonderful transfer of our source. By this transfer we become persons actually living one spirit with the Lord. For example, at home with your husband or wife, you live one spirit with the Lord practically — regulated and controlled by the Spirit. You are living out of the source of Another life, rather than living loosely, freely, and independently. Rather than rebelliously speaking what we want to speak, we actually experience a transfer. Praise the Lord!

Second Corinthians 5:15 reveals the experiential result of our transfer: "And He died on behalf of all, that those who live should live…to Him." To "live" here means not just to humanly exist on this earth, but to live in union with the Lord. This is how we live. We live joined to this crucified, resurrected Christ. This is the truth. The fact is that in regeneration we have been joined and married to Christ (Rom. 7:4). And because we have been crucified with Him and raised together with Him, the very nature of our spirit is crucifixion and resurrection — *crucifixion* for the flesh, the self, the old man; and *resurrection* for us to live one spirit with Him.

Then Paul continues in 2 Corinthians 5:15, "that those who live should live no longer to themselves, but to Him." You can see that this is experiential. The cross is a fact that transfers the source of our lives. Now we are joined to Christ through regeneration. What is the issue of this? What is the purpose of it all? It is that we no longer live *to* ourselves, that we no longer take ourselves as the point of reference for anything! We no longer consult with ourselves or debate with ourselves. To "live no longer *to* themselves, but *to* Him" means that we have a new center, a new source, a new base of operation. From this new source, we live "to Him who died for them and has been raised."

Based upon this transfer and its experiential effect of no longer living to ourselves, verse 16 begins, "Therefore, from now on…" In verse 15 it is "no longer." And in verse 16 it is, "from now on, we know no one according to the flesh." This means we do not interpret people or relate to one another in the way we did in the past. "From now on" is the outcome of "no longer" living to ourselves. Because we have a new base of operation, our whole attitude about one another and how we relate to one another is changed. We no longer know each other according to the flesh.

This knowing even includes the way we are related to the Lord, to Christ. Paul testifies, "Even though we have known Christ according to the flesh, yet now we know Him thus no longer" (v. 16). We do not remain in our human concepts, ideas, views, and imaginations about Christ. But now, as we are firmly, solidly established in spirit — our new base, our new source — we know Him as the life-giving Spirit and as the Head filling the members of His Body (Eph. 1:22-23). Then 2 Corinthians 5:17 says, "Therefore, if anyone is in Christ, there is a new creation; the old things have passed away; behold, all things have become new." So, brothers and sisters, we can see from these verses that Paul is speaking about a transfer of source in which we no longer live to ourselves.

We see this same precious transfer in Romans 14:7-8: [7] "For none of us lives to himself, and no one dies to himself. [8] For if we live, we live to the Lord; and if we die, we die to the Lord. Therefore, whether we live or die, we are the Lord's." This simplifies everything. This makes everything uncomplicated. This keeps us in the enjoyment of Christ hour after hour. Then we no longer handle the self, consult with it, debate with it, or live it out. We just know one thing — how to enjoy Christ, how to fellowship with Him, handle everything with Him, and relate to our environment with Him.

In this transfer we find ourselves no longer living an independent, self-trusting life. But increasingly we live dependent on the Lord, just as He lived dependent on the Father. In John 8:28 He describes His own living: "I do nothing from Myself." He neither spoke nor acted from Himself. It is this dependent life that the Lord supplies to us in our spirit. This grace-wrought dependency is the goal of all the dealings with the self. It is the result of a genuine transfer of source that takes place in us so that we live one spirit with the Lord.

In Romans 8:4 Paul explains the transfer of our source in still another way: "...the righteous requirement of the law might be fulfilled in us who do not walk according to the flesh but according to spirit." This phrase "according to" signifies the standard by which we live. We no longer live according to the standard of the flesh. The flesh is not our standard or point of reference anymore. We do not live out from the flesh, or according to flesh. This is synonymous with saying "not according to self." Our standard now is to walk "according to spirit," which means to do things, conduct ourselves, and live according to spirit. This requires a new spirit-source.

In Romans 8:5 Paul says, "Those who live according to the flesh mind the things of the flesh." This means that you take yourself as your source and live according to it. Experientially, you are absorbed in yourself. You live out of yourself, considering your condemnation, your shortage, your condition, your situation. This is to mind the things of the flesh. Minding the things of the flesh means your tendency is to bring up your whole history — your failures, your inability, your conflicting thoughts. When you begin thinking in this way, you get bent in that direction, and soon you are possessed with yourself again. Actually, it means that you are just taken over by the devil and his thoughts (2 Cor. 2:11). You are susceptible to thinking the devil's thoughts. Indeed, your soul-life is enmeshed with the demonic realm (James 3:15). You entertain demonic thought patterns. Why? Because you have lived out of the wrong source — not according to spirit but according to flesh.

Romans 8:5 continues, "Those who live according to the spirit mind the things of the Spirit." We enter into another realm here. This is merging with Christ and participating in His life (John 14:19). We begin to enjoy an all-inclusive Christ who is everything to us. As we enjoy all that He is in "the law of the Spirit of life," we are being freed continuously from the bondage of this self (Rom. 8:2). So we can see how crucial it is for us to be transferred out of our self and into the spirit.

4-21-08

The primary expressions of the self

Now let us fellowship about the expression of the self so that we can more practically know the meaning of being transferred out of the self. There are three primary expressions of the self. By defining them, the self will not be abstract to us, but we will be able to grasp what it means to live out of the self.

The first expression of the self is opinion. To live in our opinion is to live in the self and express the self. In other words, self and opinion are two sides of one thing. Opinion is the manifestation of the self, and the self is embodied in opinion.

The second expression of the self is reasoning. The reasoning of our mind refers to our thinking process. By this process we evaluate things and make decisions according to our own concepts, logic, proofs, and rationalizations, and even according to our imaginations and fantasies. To live according to reasoning is to live according to the self.

The third expression of the self is subjectivity. What does it mean to be subjective? It is the opposite of being objective.

To be subjective means that we are a person who is prone to evaluate our personal situation, our present condition, and our relationships with others entirely on the basis of our own feelings and our own thoughts. We have no objective base. The Word of God is not our base. The truth is not our base. And the fellowship of the Body is not our base.

The Word is objective and the Body is objective. If I am objective, I am a person who opens up to the Word and to the members of the Body. I fellowship with others and hear the Body (Matt. 18:15-17). But if I am subjective, I analyze everything according to my own feeling, regardless of what others say and regardless of what the Word says. The deciding factor is how *I feel*, how *I think*. So a subjective person is a self-centered person — one who has no other way of seeing things but from himself, making it very difficult to hear and understand others properly.

Subjective persons are totally wrapped up in themselves, taking themselves as the standard by which they measure others and interpret or understand situations. This destroys the ability to live Christ and have a proper church life. Being subjective also makes it very difficult to receive the impressions of the Spirit — to be touched by the Lord, to hear and know what the Lord is speaking, and to be shined upon by Him.

WHAT OPINION IS

We have seen that opinion, reasoning, and subjectivity are three practical expressions of the self. Though the word *self* is quite abstract, we can identify these three concrete expressions — opinion, reasoning, and subjectivity. Now let us consider the first expression of the self — opinion. First we need to ask, What is opinion? In the dictionary *opinion* is defined in several ways. First, opinion is "a view, a judgment, or an appraisal formed and found in the mind about a certain matter." Something formed in our mind can also be called a *concept*. We may have a concept about our husband or wife. We may have a concept about the church in a certain place. This concept, view, or judgment formed in our mind is our opinion. From experience we know that opinion controls and dictates how we relate to one another. Proverbs 23:7 says, "As he *thinks* in his heart, so is he." What is formed in our heart, what we think, what our concept is, dictates how we relate to others.

Another definition of opinion is "a settled judgment in regard to any point." Opinion is something that is settled. This is what is most damaging about opinion. When we have settled thoughts about each other, the Lord has no way to break down the barriers in our relationships. In 2 Corinthians 10:4-5, Paul shows us that settled thoughts are strongholds. There is no way for us to be properly related to others because of the stronghold of settled judgments we have about them.

A third definition of opinion is "notions, beliefs, or convictions based upon probable evidence." Often we form a notion or a belief about someone which does not have any basis in fact. "Probable evidence" and "suspicion" are the soil in which opinion grows.

Just consider these definitions before the Lord. How do you feel about others? Do you have an opinion about them? Is there something formed, a settled judgment, in your mind?

These things dictate how you relate to the brothers and sisters. To live by these settled judgments, these views, these concepts, is to live in opinion.

4-28-08

WHAT OPINION DOES

Opinion divides us

Having defined what opinion is, let us fellowship about what it does. In the Body opinion divides us. Wherever there is opinion, there is division. In 1 Corinthians 1:10 Paul says, "Now I plead with you, brethren, through the name of our Lord Jesus Christ, that you all speak the same thing, and that there be no *divisions* among you, but that you be perfectly joined together in the same mind and in the same opinion." Paul is burdened for the saints to be of the same mind and of the same opinion. We know that they were of different opinions because each was saying, "I am of Paul" or "I am of Apollos" or "I am of Cephas" or "I am of Christ" (1 Cor. 1:12). So division existed among the believers in Corinth due to their opinions about the superiority of certain brothers.

There was division in the church, but it was not denominational division at that juncture. It had not developed to that degree. But Paul calls it division. Division due to what? Due to their opinion — their judgments, their concepts, and their settled views about the brothers. They were even speaking out their opinion. So Paul diagnoses that locality as being in division, by saying, "that there be no divisions among you." These verses in 1 Corinthians show us that opinion produces division in the church.

We cannot be so confident as to say that we are without division. In the church there may be much opinion. There may be settled views, judgments, and concepts about the saints, about our relationship to other churches, about our relationship to certain brothers, and about the way to practice the church. There may even be opinions about what it means to experience Christ as life. Some saints may have an opinion, a settled view in their mind, that others are walking according to the flesh, when actually they are genuinely following the Lord (2 Cor. 10:2). For example, there may be saints who are dealing with the Lord about getting rid of some worldly items in their house. They are before the Lord, and they are having specific experiences of Christ. But others may think, "This is too much. The Lord does not care what we do with our possessions. We will wait and see if this is really the Spirit." To stay in this realm and entertain thoughts like this is to be in the realm of opinion. It is this kind of opinion that causes division.

Opinion insulates us

Opinion not only causes division, but it also insulates us from one another. By holding opinion, we cut off the organic flow of life between us, insulating ourselves from the other members of the Body. What is left is just an outward existence together. You and I may meet under the same roof, sing the same songs, and read the same Bible, but there is no organic reality of life, due to the insulation. And the insulation is due to opinion — the expression of the self.

Ephesians 2:14 says, "For He Himself is our peace, who has made both one, and has broken down the middle wall of partition, the enmity." The insulation is the middle wall of partition. And the middle wall of partition is the enmity. So the insulation is the enmity. And what is the enmity? It is this little bad feeling I have toward you and the little bad feeling you have toward me. These ill feelings, this enmity, is in apposition to the middle wall in this verse. Thus, the middle wall equals the enmity.

Then verse 15 says, "Having abolished in His flesh the enmity, that is, the law of commandments contained in ordinances, that He might create the two in Himself into one new man, so making peace." According to this verse, the factor producing the enmity is the ordinances. Ordinances are the concepts we hold dear, the things that we feel strongly about. Wherever there is an ordinance, it will always breed some enmity and bad feelings. Holding ordinances and having strong opinions go hand in hand. They damage the organic relationships in the Body and keep the members insulated from one another.

We not only have opinions about the church or the brothers, but many of us have a deep-seated opinion about our husband or wife. If we live with such an opinion about each other, there will constantly be bad feelings and reactions. Why are there so many reactions in your marriage? Why are you always angry? Why is your temper always on the surface? It is only because the self is alive through opinion. This is not a normal way to exist. Temper is a symptom of the self-life that lies beneath the surface in the form of ordinances and opinion.

When the Lord deals with the self by dealing with opinion, temper is killed, as well as all that insulates and divides us. The cross is the only answer for opinion (Matt. 16:22-24).

Opinion disintegrates the reality of the Body

Where opinion exists, it not only divides and insulates us, but it also disintegrates the reality of the Body. Furthermore, it prevents us from discerning the Lord's Body. In 1 Corinthians 11:18 Paul says, "There are divisions among you." There were opinions, choices, and preferences among the saints, and in that condition they presumptuously took the Lord's table, "not discerning the Lord's body" (v. 29). So the reality of the oneness of the Body was disintegrated through division caused by opinion. Satan works through opinion to divide, insulate, and disintegrate.

Opinion immobilizes us

Ultimately, opinion immobilizes us as members of the Body. In getting into the saints' situation at Philippi, Paul's burden was that the opinion existing in the church and causing the dissension would be dealt with. Then they all would think the same thing and be joined together in soul. In Philippians 4:2 Paul implores two sisters, Euodias and Syntyche, "to be of the same mind in the Lord." Then in verse 3 he addresses another saint, saying, "I beseech you also, true yokefellow, help these women" (ASV). This means that Paul wanted someone to get into the situation of these two sisters. They could not deal with the self and experience Christ by themselves. Their self, expressed in their opinion, needed someone to get into their situation.

Through the book of Philippians, Paul's burden was to get into the situation of the saints and help them to deal with the opinion among them that was causing the disharmony. He realized that opinion had immobilized the church. This is why he exhorts the saints in Philippians 1:27, "Only let your conduct be worthy of the gospel of Christ, so that whether I come and see you or am absent, I may hear the things concerning you, that you stand firm in one spirit, with one soul striving together in the faith of the gospel." This means that for the Lord's move on the earth to be a shining testimony that holds forth the word of life (2:15-16), and for the church to be aggressive for the gospel, the saints needed to be standing "in one spirit, with one soul striving together." The words "striving together" come from the compound Greek word συναθλέω *(sunathleo)*. The root word is rendered "athlete," and the prefix means "with" or "together with." So this word gives you the sense of a team of athletes moving together, *mobile*, for the advancement of the gospel.

But opinion will immobilize and even completely stop this genuine coordination, this "striving together." There cannot be genuine fellowship and openness when opinion is in the air, because there is actual division and insulation among us. As a result, the reality of the Body is disintegrated and we are just immobilized. This is why it is crucial to deal with the self and its expression of opinion. Without this dealing, the Lord cannot obtain a proper expression of His Body.

We have seen what opinion does — it divides, insulates, disintegrates, and immobilizes. For example, if there is opinion existing between a husband and wife, they are immobilized as parents from properly and adequately handling and dealing with the children. So when parents live in their opinion, the children receive the brunt of it.

If opinion immobilizes on the smaller scale of the family, consider its effects on the larger scale of the church, the Body of Christ. No wonder Paul exhorts the Philippians to "stand firm in one spirit." Stand firm, because it is so easy to be pulled out of your spirit by your opinion or consideration. When Paul speaks of standing firm in one spirit with one soul, practically it means praying together (1:19; 4:6), emptying yourself (2:7), laying aside your thought, and not grasping for anything out from yourself (2:6). This standing together in one spirit issues in having one soul. The soul simply follows as long as we stand together in one spirit. This is how Paul got into the situation of the saints in Philippi with light and life, ministering to them in a transparent way. Because of this, they could deal with opinion and continue in the Lord's work together.

THE EXAMPLES OF OPINION

5 - 5 - 08

Secret pride and "I know better"

We can see another example of opinion with Peter in Matthew chapter 16. In verse 21 the Lord speaks about His crucifixion and resurrection. Then verse 22 says, "Then Peter took Him aside and began to rebuke Him, saying, Far be it from You, Lord; this shall not happen to You!" By analyzing this verse, we can see that this was Peter's opinion concerning what the Lord had just said. Peter immediately had a strong view, a settled judgment; and taking the Lord aside, he rebuked Him, telling Him that this should not happen to Him. This is the way opinion expressed itself in Peter — he held the view that he knew better.

This is the way opinion works in your mind — you think you know better. You think your view is better, your judgment is better, your interpretation is better. This is secret pride, hidden pride. Opinion is the expression of this self that is filled with secret pride and says, "I know better." How could Peter make such an absolute statement to the Lord if beneath it all he did not hold the view that he knew better than the Lord? The Lord was talking about being killed, about being put to death. But Peter thought he knew better: "This shall not happen to You!" This would be like my saying to a saint who is dealing with the Lord concerning some possessions, "You have gone too far; that is too much." For me to say this would mean that I think I know better. This is exactly what Peter did, and this is what we may unwittingly do in the church life.

What does it mean to think you know better? It means you are living out the self. You are living in opinion. You are living by your own view, which is "better" than everyone else's. Through the years in fellowship with the saints, we have discovered in the Lord's light that all of us, some to a greater degree than others, have this feeling that we know better. We feel our judgment is better, our view is better. Just like Peter, we inwardly hold this view — "This shall not happen to you."

How could we speak in that way if we did not have such an underlying feeling of knowing better?

Opinion fed by spiritual successes

Opinion that expresses itself in "I know better" is also fed by our spiritual successes. Our spiritual successes support our opinion and feed it. Consider Peter's experience. He had just had a tremendous spiritual success. In front of all the disciples he was the one who spoke out and said to the Lord, "You are the Christ, the Son of the living God." He was in the forefront, so to speak. And the Lord responded to him, "Blessed are you, Simon Bar-Jonah, for flesh and blood has not revealed this to you, but My Father who is in heaven" (Matt. 16:16-17). So Peter was a success in being the vehicle of divine revelation. And the Lord Himself confirmed the whole experience. Immediately, that spiritual success did one thing — it fed Peter's self. He became self-confident. And in the next moment his opinion came out. Then the Lord said to him not "blessed" but "Satan." This shows us that Satan was expressed through Peter's opinion.

It is quite sobering to see the way opinion was expressed through Peter, and to see that the Lord identified it as Satan. Spiritual success can become a means for you to support your self-confidence. For example, you spent an hour with the Lord, or you preached the gospel and ten people were saved, or the Lord answered your prayer, meaning God heard you — you have a "line to heaven" — so you cannot be wrong. Or from the Spirit you succeeded in overcoming the flesh. You by the Spirit put to death the practices of your body. All day long you were in the spirit, and then you came home with your spiritual success. Now you feel you are really on top of everything. Then you talk to your wife about something, and your view comes out, your opinion comes out — you are so "right," so confident in your rightness, because of your earlier spiritual success.

Even our spiritual successes — praying, reading the Word, following the Lord — can become the soil in which our self grows bigger and bigger and our opinion becomes reinforced. By Peter's example, we see that spiritual success can feed our self and fortify opinion. So we should not trust in anything but our present, living contact with the Lord. Apart from Him we can do nothing (John 15:5). We do not trust our thoughts. We do not trust our past experience. We only trust in this Person who is living in us and anointing us moment by moment.

Opinion is based upon man's views and principles

After identifying Peter's opinionated self as Satan, the Lord said to him, "You are not setting your mind on the things of God, but on the things of men" (Matt. 16:23). Peter was in the realm of "the things of men." He had a settled view about the Lord being crucified and resurrected. This settled view, or opinion, was based upon man's principles, man's wisdom. This is the way opinion works with us. We form human views according to human principles.

When Peter was setting his mind on the things of man, he was living by principles, not by God. Sometimes when saints come to us for fellowship, we may merely give them good advice based on human principles, rather than bringing them into contact with the Spirit to know God. If our fellowship is in the realm of principles, we can only give advice to others. The Lord needs to transfer us out of the realm of the things of man into the realm of God and the things of God.

So another characteristic of opinion is that it is based upon certain principles that we live by. Consequently, we have a particular view, and we judge ourselves and others according to this view. It is possible as a Christian to live by principles for years and completely miss God. Can we not say that Peter expressed a good principle — "Far be it from You, Lord; this shall not happen to You." Peter had the revelation of who the Lord was — the Son of God, the Son of Man, the Christ. But then he left the realm of revelation and entered the realm of good human principles. Now, based on principle, he forbade the Lord to be crucified. At that point, he was setting his mind on the things of man.

All these characteristics of opinion in Matthew 16 are identified by the Lord in verse 24 as the expression of the self: "Then Jesus said to His disciples, If anyone desires to come after Me, let him deny *himself,* and take up his cross, and follow Me." Here the Lord specifically names what needs to be denied — the self. And then in verse 25 He speaks of losing the soul-life. When Peter said to the Lord, "This shall not happen to You," this was his opinion coming from an unde-nied self-life. So again, we see that opinion is an expression of the self.

4

DEALING WITH OPINION

By exposure

Now that we have identified what opinion is, how do we deal with it? Peter's dealing was first through exposure. The Lord turned directly to him and said, "Get behind Me, Satan!" Thus, the Lord's way of dealing with opinion in Peter was by calling it what it was — "Get behind Me, Satan." This is how opinion is dealt with — by a frankness that can thoroughly expose the real nature of what has been said. To deal with our opinion, we first need to know that expressing our opinion is the way Satan is expressed.

As long as we coddle or indulge our opinion, holding a reservation that it may be okay to preserve it a little bit, it will not get dealt with. So just as the Lord did, we have to call it what it is — "Satan"! Humanly or ethically speaking, and according to the standards of etiquette, the Lord broke all the rules. Just consider, Peter had confessed such a good word, "This shall not happen to You." In other words, "Pity Yourself, Lord!" Peter was "protecting" the Lord. Though it seemed good, it came right out of the self. That good opinion coming out of the source of his self-life was just Satan.

The greatest help we could ever receive is by someone getting into our situation, listening to us talk, listening to us express our opinion, and then in spirit saying to us, "Do you realize that you are just speaking Satan? that your opinion is the embodiment of Satan because it comes out of the source of your undenied self?" This exposure disarms us. We are unable to defend ourselves. We must agree, "My opinion is the embodiment of Satan." So the first step in dealing with opinion is exposure.

Through failure

Another help to experience this transfer out of ourself and opinion is failure. We are so fortified with self-confidence that we live out the self just as Peter did. Peter was so full of the self, so full of self-confidence, so full of his opinion, that God allowed him to have a big failure. Immediately after his spiritual success, he had a big failure. So failure is part of the process of dealing with our opinion. This principle is brought out in Watchman Nee's book *The Messenger of the Cross,* in the chapter entitled "Knowing the Self." Of course, to know the self is part of knowing the Lord. If we do not know the self, we cannot adequately know the Lord. And when we adequately know the Lord, we know ourself — we know that we are untrustworthy, that there is nothing good in us. So experientially, the more we get to know the Lord, the more we know ourself in God's light (Psa. 36:9).

In his chapter "Knowing the Self," Watchman Nee uses Deuteronomy 8:2 as the text: "And you shall remember that the LORD your God led you all the way these forty years in the wilderness, to humble you and test you, to know what was in your heart, whether you would keep His commandments or not." This verse shows us that the Lord humbled the children of Israel and tested them. Their being humbled came about through many testings and failures. It was not that the Lord needed to learn more about them or get to know them; but they needed to get to know themselves. It was the same with Peter in the Gospels. It is obvious that he was a person full of self-confidence, because he had so many opinions. So the Lord allowed him to fail the most.

We may express our opinion to our husband or wife, or to other saints. We are so strong. We feel we are so right. We are convinced the other person is wrong and we are right. But then in some area of our personal life, we sin. We live in the flesh. We fail. Yet we may not connect our opinion with this failure. But this failure is intended to cause us to open ourself to the Lord and tell Him, "Lord, I do not know anything. I cannot do anything. I just open to You, Lord, to cast down not only the sin, but all of my opinion." Through dealing with failures in this way we are brought more and more to the place of having no confidence in ourself but in the Lord Himself.

Exposure and failure are both part of dealing with the self to effect a subjective transfer of our being into the spirit. By this transfer we are living one spirit with the Lord and not in our settled opinions, which come out of our self. Then you might ask, Are we not to have any opinions? Are we not to think? Are we not to have any views? What about when we coordinate and fellowship? We have to make a decision. Do we just sit there and say nothing? Can no one offer a view or any kind of feeling? Of course, we know that the main point in answering this kind of question is, What is our source? If we are a person whose self is undealt with, even when we offer a legitimate view and feeling, the self is enmeshed with it and taints it with impurity. In other words, the view and feeling may not be wrong in and of itself, but the source from which it comes is wrong. This shows us why it is important to have a transfer of our source from the self to the spirit.

You may think, "We need *some* views. We need *some* concepts." But when we are dealing with the stronghold of opinion, because it is connected with the self, we have to throw everything out. That means our right opinion must go. When the opinion goes, the self goes with it, because opinion and self are attached to one another. It may seem like I have to cut off my head. If I lose my opinion — if I drop my opinion, if I do not live by my opinion — that means I am nobody! I have no way to live, because I have lived by opinion all my life. Watchman Nee describes this realization in his book *Spiritual Authority*. He says that it is like losing your very life when the Lord begins to deal with your reasoning and opinionated mind. You feel like you are losing what you have operated from your whole life.

So we have to see that the self must be dealt with. The source must be dealt with. Then, when we are transferred into the realm of the spirit, yes, we have views, we have feelings, we fellowship, but everything is liquid. Everything is flexible and subject to the Spirit. We can move with the Lord, one spirit with Him, and not hold on to anything. We do not live by settled and formed thoughts in our mind. We are just living in fellowship with the Lord and are free to follow Him wherever He goes (Rev. 14:4). Our only desire and thought is to abide in Him.

By getting into another realm

We deal with opinion by exposing it, by calling it what it is — Satan. The Lord also uses failure to deal with opinion. And a third way we can deal with opinion is by getting into another realm. The Lord was talking about realms when He said to Peter, "You are not setting your mind on the things of God, but the things of men" (Matt. 16:23). So what Peter needed to do was get into another realm! He needed to set his mind on the things of God. To set our mind on the things of God, we have to do what Colossians 3:2 says: "Set your mind on things above." This happens by spending time with the Lord, opening to Him, seeking Him. Then, by being supplied in fellowship with Him, we are enabled to set our mind on the things of God. So we deal with opinion by getting into another realm.

To get into another realm is to get into the spirit and touch the cross. When we touch the Spirit, the Spirit is composed of a crucifying power that puts the soul-life to death, cuts off the opinion, denies the self, and does not allow the self to make any provision for itself. The Spirit ushers the cross in to deal with our opinion, to execute crucifixion over our opinion. We need the exposure and the failures to humble us and open us up to the Lord, so that we will lose all confidence in the self and simply trust in the Spirit. We trust in His divine operation to deal with our opinion, which is just the expression of the self.

Oh, brothers and sisters, this is critical, life-changing fellowship. We need to expose this horrible thing called opinion, because it is actually Satan sitting in the church. Opinion is what destroys the church. It disintegrates, damages, insulates, divides, and immobilizes us! How crucial it is that we all target this opinion — good opinion, right opinion, opinion about your husband or wife, or about the brothers and sisters. Just say, "Lord, crucify my opinion! Cut off its head! You are the Head. I am not the head. I do not like to hold any view. I just like to love You, to enjoy You, to be a person freed from opinion." We just want to be one spirit with the Lord and not hinder the Lord's movement among us in the church.

What Reasoning Is and Does

It prevents us from obeying God

Reasoning is another expression of the self. It is just the activity of our mind, the process of our logical thinking, with its solid proofs that support the way we think. If we want to discover how much we live in our self-life, we only need to see how much we reason. The fact that we reason away things in our lives tells us that we are constantly and deeply entrenched in the self. One of the tragic things about reasoning is that it prevents us from living a life of obeying God.

You cannot obey the Lord and be a reasoning person. This is because a reasoning mind will always find a reason why we should *not* obey the Lord. What if the Lord in your spirit one day told you to do something you had never done before. What if inwardly you were restrained by the Spirit from doing what you had always done? Wouldn't that cause your mind to reel? Wouldn't you begin to think and reason — "Why shouldn't I do this? What reason is there behind this? Why would the Lord be speaking to me this way?" But a person who knows the Lord would not question if the Spirit spoke in such a way. For example, when the Lord wanted to pour out His salvation upon the Gentiles, He spoke to Peter to do something he had never done before. He spoke to him to eat unclean foods (Acts 10:11-16). Later Peter testified that what he had done in going to the Gentiles was in obedience to the Spirit, without doubting or reasoning (Acts 11:12).

It is reasoning that prevents us from obeying. We have reasons why we do not obey, reasons why we do not deal with certain things. The Spirit has been speaking for years, but we have our reason, we have our proof, we have evidence, for why we do not obey. We can even support our disobedience with spiritual successes in other areas of our life in which we have touched the spirit and obeyed the Lord. We have all kinds of reasons for not obeying the Lord over the matter He has spoken about.

One of the most helpful spiritual writings on the matter of reasoning and obeying the Lord is the chapter entitled "Not Subjective" in Watchman Nee's *The Normal Christian Worker*. The following is a selection from his writing:

> God demands instant acceptance of His word. If He says, "Go," we should go at once. The trouble with subjective people [and you can also include reasoning

people, because it is the same principle] is that if God says, "Go," they are so set in their own ideas that it takes a long time before they can adjust to His command; and if eventually they go, they become so set in their going that they cannot instantly obey if God says, "Stop." They have to go through another difficult process of adjustment before they can do so. If God bids you go, can you drop everything and go at once? And when you have obeyed His command to go and are prepared to keep on going, can you stop instantly if God issues the order to stop?

Then Watchman Nee continues by giving Abraham as an example of an obedient person. God gave Isaac to Abraham. This was a great spiritual success on Abraham's part. He had believed the Lord when He said, "I will give you a son, the son of promise." So Isaac was God-given. Then one day God said to Abraham, "Go offer your son on the altar" (Gen. 22:2). A reasoning person would begin to think, "Didn't God give me this son? Why should I go offer him?" But Abraham obeyed the Lord. He took Isaac and went to the mountain. Yet just when he "stretched out his hand and took the knife to slay his son," the Angel of the LORD stopped him (Gen. 22:1-18). Abraham did not consider, "Why is the Lord now telling me to stop? He already told me to do it!" From this we see that Abraham was an example of instant obedience. Why? Because he did not reason.

I remember one of my first experiences of the Lord's dealing with me over my reasonings. Specifically, He was touching me about the sermons I had prepared. These messages were all typewritten. They were even used to bring people to the Lord. They were biblical and expository. Yet the Lord told me to burn them. I discovered that with obedience, there is no room for reasoning. If the Lord said it, that is good enough. There does not have to be a reason, especially when the Lord is breaking the stronghold of reasoning in our lives. In our mind, we want reasons. But when the Lord deals with us to overthrow strongholds, He does not give reasons.

We are disobedient because we reason things away. There are always "reasons" for not obeying the Lord. In 2 Corinthians 10:5-6 Paul describes the necessity of dealing with reasonings in order to obey the Lord: [5] "Casting down reasonings and every high thing that exalts itself against the knowledge of God, bringing every thought into captivity to the obedience of Christ, [6] and being ready to punish all disobedience when your obedience is fulfilled." This clearly shows that reasoning prevents us from obeying the Lord.

In Philippians 2:12 and 14 Paul again connects reasoning with disobeying. In verse 12 he says, "Therefore, my beloved, as you have always *obeyed,* not as in my presence only, but now much more in my absence, work out your own salvation with fear and trembling." Paul is exhorting the saints to obey. Then in verse 14 he describes how that obedience expresses itself: "Do all things without murmurings and reasonings." So here again we see an unmistakable relationship between reasoning and obeying or disobeying.

If we were all absolute in our experience, with no reasonings, and we went along with the anointing — with that feeling and consciousness of the Lord's life within us to apologize, to confess, to call upon the name of the Lord — immediately we would be ushered into a life of obedience, and out of a life of reasoning.

Reasoning is against the knowledge of God

Reasoning is an expression of living out of the self rather than living out of the source of the spirit. We live reasoning, and consequently we are disobedient. Again, 2 Corinthians 10:5 says, "Casting down reasonings and every high thing rising up against the knowledge of God." This knowledge of God is not only the objective truth, but the subjective, inward knowledge, the new covenant knowledge (Heb. 10:16). It is the knowledge of God that we have subjectively.

Paul says that we are to cast down "reasonings and every high thing rising up against the knowledge of God" because reasoning is against walking subjectively in the spirit. It is against knowing God subjectively. Reasonings rise up against that little step of obedience the Lord is requiring. Reasoning will come against it. So, brothers and sisters, we have to see how to deal with a reasoning mind.

How to Deal with Reasoning

Overthrow it

Let us look carefully at 2 Corinthians 10:4-5. Paul says, [4] "For the weapons of our warfare are not fleshly but powerful to God to the overthrow of strongholds, [5] overthrowing reasonings..." Notice that in these verses the word "overthrow" is mentioned twice, and reasoning is described as a stronghold. Paul speaks of overthrowing "strongholds" because our reasoning is like a high tower, a strong, fortified, built-up structure. This is the way Paul describes reasoning here. The only way to deal with this reasoning is to have it overthrown.

Overthrow the stronghold! That means destroy it. Destroy this thing that has kept you disobedient and has caused you not to follow the inward knowledge of God. You have to overthrow it in the realm of the spirit, not the flesh. The weapons of our warfare to overthrow reasonings are not fleshly, but powerful to God. To do anything through God, we must first access God in our spirit. Then we can overthrow the reasoning through the strength He supplies to us. This is a major step in our experience. It is not a small thing to overthrow these reasonings.

Take every thought captive

After you overthrow the reasonings, then you are in a position to begin to catch every single thought and take them captive "unto the obedience of Christ" (2 Cor. 10:5). In our experience, we will not be able to catch that many thoughts and take them captive unto the obedience of Christ until first the stronghold of reasoning is overthrown. In other words, we do not catch the individual thoughts that intrude into our thinking and take them captive because the stronghold of reasoning in us remains undealt with. So the first thing that is needed is to have the stronghold overthrown. Then our spirit with all our faculties will be sensitive to capture every thought.

One brother testified about the difference in his experience before and after overthrowing the stronghold of reasoning. He described it in this way: "It is like something that just cannot land anymore. The thoughts just cannot land. They have no landing place." That is the result of overthrowing the stronghold of a reasoning mind. The catching of disobedient thoughts comes by a deep touch with our spirit of sonship in which we cry, "Abba! Father!" It is this crying that brings us into the realm of the Spirit where we are led to put to death every disobedient thought (Rom. 8:13-16).

Let the Spirit prevail over our mind

The way to overthrow a stronghold is by not believing our reasoning, but instead letting our spirit prevail over our mind. In 2 Corinthians 2:12-13 Paul said, [12] "Furthermore, when I came to Troas for the gospel of Christ, and a door was opened to me in the Lord, [13] I had no relief in my spirit, because I did not find Titus my brother; but taking my leave of them, I departed for Macedonia." You may ask, "What does this have to do with the overthrow of a stronghold?" To answer this, let us consider the situation: Paul went to Troas, and there was an open door in the Lord to preach the gospel. But he said, "I had no relief in my spirit." In this situation, the mind can reason, "Here is an open door, an opportunity. There are good reasons to preach the gospel. Why not? The opportunity is here."

This reasoning could be likened to going shopping when you have a lot of money in your bank account. Instead of shopping by the spirit, you shop by "an open door" because you have a large bank account. You have an opportunity! You could buy anything! You have the money. In the same way, in Paul's experience the door was open to preach the gospel. But Paul said, "I had no relief in my spirit." This means he was not living by the source of himself, but by the Spirit. So at that moment, any potential reasoning in Paul's mind concerning the opportunity in Troas was overthrown because his spirit prevailed.

Undoubtedly, it is because Paul's spirit prevailed that he says in the next verse, "Now thanks be to God who always leads us in triumph in the Christ, and manifests through us the savor of the knowledge of Him in every place." Such a declaration, "Thanks be to God who leads us in triumph," comes from being led as a conquered foe. Paul was a defeated person there. He was defeated by the Lord. The opportunity of "an open door" and living according to reasoning was overthrown.

The same situation occurred in Acts 16 with Paul and those with him. Verse 6 says, "They were forbidden by the Holy Spirit to preach the word in Asia." And verse 7 says, "They tried to go into Bithynia, but the Spirit of Jesus did not permit them." They were attempting to preach the Word of God in Asia, but the Holy Spirit was forbidding them. They then attempted to go into Bithynia, but the Spirit of Jesus did not permit them to do so. This means that the Spirit prevailed over the reasoning mind. For example, they could have reasoned, "Shouldn't we go to Asia? Shouldn't we go to Bithynia? Isn't it right to go?" But the Spirit prevailed and forbade them. This simply means that to overthrow the stronghold of our reasoning, we must let the Spirit prevail.

When we follow the Spirit, when we go along with the Spirit, then our reasoning mind can be overthrown. Then we can be in a position to catch the thoughts. One by one, we take captive every thought that comes in — even a right thought. But in our experience, many times a right thought may come, and we surround that thought with reasons — more and more reasons. And then we just live by reasoning. Brothers and sisters, maybe you reason concerning your husband or wife. You have a view, you have an opinion, you have reasons why you speak to each other the way you do. When you speak, what you say may be right, but your self comes out. Your speaking does not taste like Christ, even though you are trying to help each other. It is because you are too enmeshed in your own thought, you are too mixed with your own view. So we have to let our spirit prevail to overthrow the reasonings in our mind.

Many times the Lord will ask us to do some simple little thing, something that does not seem so big. Yet we may reason about how insignificant it is and why we should not do it. But we have to realize that if our mind is a reasoning mind, if there is a stronghold there, the Lord may come in some unexpected way concerning an insignificant thing. For example, He may ask you to take back something you owe to your boss, or to do something that is so out of the ordinary that it causes your mind to begin to reel. You will find yourself reasoning and thinking about why you should not do it. What the Lord is trying to do is break the strength of your reasoning and overthrow the stronghold. He is saying, "I am the Lord. I said it. That is good enough. You do not need a reason."

Praise the Lord! We can overthrow strongholds by letting our spirit prevail. And then we can take captive every thought to the obedience of Christ. Oh, may the Lord grant us to see the expression of self in opinion and reasoning, and to be persons who exercise our spirit to get into another realm. May we let our spirit prevail and let the cross operate to put to death all the opinion and all the reasoning, that we could be a person who knows God, who is not against the knowledge of God. May we give the Lord a way in us to make us those who have an inward knowledge of God and obey Him all day long for His purpose of constituting us sons of God (Rom. 8:14).

5

THE SELF AND BEING SUBJECTIVE

Our new point of reference

The Lord's death and resurrection have made it possible for us to experience a wonderful transfer out of the self and into the Lord Jesus — to live *in* Him and *unto* Him. The apostle Paul speaks of this transfer in 2 Corinthians 5:15: "And He died for all, that those who live should *live no longer to themselves, but to Him* who died for them and rose again." This indicates that to be in the result of the Lord's death and resurrection — to be in "the good" of it — means that we are persons who are freed from the self and no longer live to ourselves. This means that our self is no longer our center and point of reference. Our self is no longer what we are oriented to or what we consult with. What a glorious release — *self* is no longer our center. We have been wonderfully rearranged. Hallelujah! This rearrangement means that now Christ in our spirit is our new center and point of reference.

This is the deep significance of the Lord's death — *we* are crucified. "It is no longer *I*," no longer *ego*, no longer *me,* "but Christ lives in me" (Gal. 2:20). We know that to become a regenerated person is not merely to receive eternal life as a future possession. It is to know that you are now a person who has been inwardly rearranged. There has been an organic, life change in your being so that you no longer need to refer to your mind, emotion, and will as your center, as your point of reference, as your base of operation. There is a new base of operation for your whole being. Now your spirit, joined to the Lord, is your new center. We no longer live to ourselves but to Him.

The goal of all the dealings with the self is to experientially effect a transfer so that we are living the identical life that the Lord Jesus lived on this earth. Of His life and living the Lord Jesus said, "I do nothing from Myself" (John 8:28). The Greek preposition *from* is very strong. It means "I do nothing *from the source of* Myself. I Myself am not the source." This is how the Lord lived. He lived a human life, one with the Father, not speaking from Himself. Indeed, He did nothing from Himself. He did everything in union and fellowship with the Father. The most striking thing about the Lord's human living is to see the source of His living. The source and base of His operation was His spirit joined to the Father. This in itself is revelation concerning the proper source of our human living.

What a glorious release — we no longer live to ourselves, but to the Lord. Of course, in our experience this depends on how much our self has been dealt with, how much we have practically dropped this self. For instance, how much have we dropped our opinion? How much have we not lived by our reasoning? Second Corinthians 5:15 says, "no longer live to themselves." This can be amplified to read, "no longer live to our opinion and no longer live to our reasoning, but to Him." This is what it means to be freed from the realm of the self-life.

After seeing opinion and reasoning as expressions of the

self in the previous two chapters, we need to look at the third primary aspect of self's expression, that is, being subjective. Opinion is one kind of expression of the self-life, reasoning is another, and being subjective is still another. Subjectivity is definitely the expression of living in the self. Let us consider this matter so that we could be transferred out of every degree and form of subjectivity.

WHAT BEING SUBJECTIVE IS

First, we need to understand the meaning of being subjective. The following three points will help us: (1) the definition of being subjective, or what being subjective is; (2) what being subjective does — how it operates, how it manifests itself, and what its characteristics are; and (3) how to deal with being subjective, which also means how to deal with the self.

Everything arising out of self and measured by self

Let us consider what being subjective means. For this we need to observe Philippians 2:3-4. In the first part of verse 3 Paul says, "Let nothing be done through selfish ambition or conceit." This means do not let the self be the source of your living. To do something by way of selfish ambition is to do something out of the self. Then the last part of verse 3 says, "but in lowliness of mind let each esteem others better than himself." And verse 4 says, "Let each of you *look out* not only for his own interests, but also for the interests of others." The Greek word for "look out" is *skopeo,* from which we get the word *scope*. Thus, the meaning of this word is "looking at, scoping, or focusing on an object." This indicates that the problem with some of the Philippians was that they were just looking at and focusing upon their own things. They were being subjective, fully in themselves.

Being subjective is the opposite of being objective. To be subjective means that there is no objective base in our experience. Everything arises out of ourselves, and we measure everything by ourselves and with ourselves. Our standard of measurement is how we feel, and it is based on our subjective states of mind and our subjective moods. We measure and relate to everything from ourselves. We relate to God and others subjectively, that is, according to our own moods and feelings. To us, "the final court of appeal" is how we feel. This is what it means to be subjective. It means to be literally sunk into ourselves. There is no objective standard in our experience.

There are four pillars that will pull us away from our subjectivity and bring us into a transfer of source. The first pillar is *Christ Himself:* "No longer I, but Christ." This Person, this lovely Person, loves us and died for us. He is now revealed in us. He lives in us and has become our glorious center. This Person will pull us out of ourselves. Holding the Head (Col. 2:19), that is, interacting exclusively with Christ, will pull us out of our subjective states and moods. The second pillar is *our spirit.* Hallelujah for our spirit! It is not only this Person, but this Person dwelling in our spirit. We hold and seize this Christ from our spirit by calling upon His name (Matt. 22:43; 1 Cor. 12:3). Calling upon the name of the Lord is how we let our spirit prevail. This pillar will make the transfer for us. If we stay in our spirit, our spirit will catapult us out of our subjective feelings. Hallelujah for Christ in our spirit! The third pillar is *the truth,* the pure Word, the revealed facts — all that the Bible reveals about us. The God-breathed Word will correct, instruct, rebuke, and realign us to the truth itself (2 Tim. 3:16). This will deliver us out of our subjectivity. The fourth pillar is *the Body*. Being in fellowship with the members of the Body will keep us in the light and out of our subjectivity (1 John 1:7).

To be a person who is not subjective and sunk into ourself is to be a person enjoying Christ, exercising our spirit, standing with the truth, and being in fellowship with the members of the Body. These pillars are the provisions for us to be delivered from our subjectivity, to no longer live to ourself but to Him.

Definitions of a subjective person

Let us read some of the dictionaries' definitions of being subjective. The first definition is "relating to the thinking subject; having its source in the mind." This is one dictionary's definition of a person who is subjective. That person's source is the mind. The second definition is "pertaining or peculiar to an individual subject or his mental operations; depending upon one's individuality or idiosyncrasy." You could add "peculiar ways of relating to ourselves and to others." In other words, it refers to the way we hear and perceive others. The third definition is "tending to lay stress on one's own feelings or opinions; given to brooding over one's mental states; excessively introspective or reflective." The fourth definition is "existing in the mind only, without anything real to correspond to it; illusory and fanciful." These are some of the definitions in *The Oxford English Dictionary* and *The Webster Dictionary* related to being subjective. By the Word of God and by these definitions, we realize that a person who is subjective is confined and bound up in himself, without objective reality.

The objective reality in this universe includes these four pillars: *Christ, our spirit, the truth, and the Body*. Apart from these four things we are left to ourselves, to measure ourselves by ourselves and compare ourselves among ourselves (2 Cor. 10:12). To measure others by our own subjective moods, feelings, and opinions is to be left in our self. Thus, we see that subjectivity is in this realm — just being shut up and confined to our own subjective states and moods, with no objective base.

Under this kind of definition, we all have to admit that there is some degree of subjectivity in us. And with some of us there is a great degree of subjectivity. Even though we know doctrinally about Christ, our spirit, the truth, and the Body, we are inwardly in disarray because we do not exercise ourselves in these four realms. We do not believe any of the objective facts. Experientially, we only believe *our* feeling. Our own feeling is the deciding factor. Our own feeling and thought-life looms larger than the truth itself. We are controlled by self because we live solely to our self. This makes it very difficult for Christ to be lived out and for us to have the proper organic relationships in the Body. May the Lord expose all subjectivity in us and give us a quick transfer into Himself.

WHAT BEING SUBJECTIVE DOES

If we are not clear about this definition of being subjective, if this is still too doctrinal, let us go to the second point to identify what subjectivity does to us, how it behaves, and what its characteristics are.

It makes us an opinionated and reasoning person

First, subjectivity makes us an opinionated and reasoning person. Opinions and reasoning are related to believing our own thoughts and remaining within the confines of our own reasoning. This is the way subjectivity acts. A subjective person is a person who believes his own opinion and feels his opinion is better and higher than others'. A subjective person will only believe his own mind and his own reasoning, making it very difficult to fellowship and receive the Lord's light.

Perhaps for our whole life some of us have never believed anyone. We only believe our reasoning mind. Our final court of appeal is our opinion, our view, and our judgment. This is why Paul in 2 Corinthians 10:4-5 calls reasoning a "stronghold" that needs to be overthrown. If we let our spirit prevail in prayer and open up to the fellowship in the Body, we can have this reasoning and opinionated mind overthrown and begin to experience a transfer into our spirit.

Being subjective leaves us ignorant of ourself

Subjectivity also leaves us ignorant of ourself so that we do not know ourself in God's light. This is what being subjective does. In 1 Corinthians 2:11 Paul says, "For what man knows the things of a man except the spirit of the man which is in him?" Who knows the things of man? Who knows the self? Who knows the rottenness of fallen man? Who knows that there is nothing good in himself? Who knows that this self is not to be trusted? Who knows that his opinion and reasoning is untrustworthy? Who knows himself? According to Paul's word, it is only the spirit of man that knows the things of man. This shows us that unless we are vitally joined to the most objective part of our being, our spirit, we are going to be ignorant concerning ourselves. The spirit of man is the factor in man that supplies to him his objectivity. In other words, to be objective — to be divided, to know yourself, even to condemn the self, and to not trust yourself, your opinion, or your view — is to be a person who is exercised in spirit — who uses the spirit, listens with the spirit, and is always conscious of the spirit's registrations (2 Cor. 2:12-13).

When you are in the realm of the spirit, you become wise concerning your real state. You discover that there is nothing good in you, and you can admit it, confess it, and humble yourself. You can repent without strain. You can admit your fallen state. You can say to your husband, "Dear, I'm stubborn, I'm rebellious, I'm jealous, I'm bitter." You can confess your state with ease, because when you are in your spirit you know that in your flesh dwells no good thing. You are not trying to defend or excuse yourself. Rather, you are objective about yourself. And that objectivity makes it easy for you to always agree with God's diagnosis of the flesh (Rom. 7:14, 18).

But when you do not exercise your spirit, you stay enmeshed with yourself. You remain a whole person, that is, an unbroken person. You are proud, you cannot admit, you cannot confess, you cannot apologize, because there is no objective base in you. You are caught up and immersed in the feelings of pride with its stiff neck and its inability to lose its face. This self is so intact and whole that it cannot be broken through, it cannot be penetrated, it cannot be reached, because it does not know itself. It does not know its folly. Apart from our spirit, we do not know ourself, and we are ignorant of ourself. But when we touch our spirit, oh, we loathe ourself. We recognize that there is nothing good in us; through and through we are altogether flesh. We are full of sin and the flesh with its reactions, bitterness, hatred, and lust. Indeed, every gross sin is a possibility with us.

The spirit of man is the key to knowing ourselves in God's light. This is revealed not only in 1 Corinthians 2:11, but also in Proverbs 20:27: "The human spirit is the lamp of the LORD, searching every inmost part" (NRSV). Furthermore, Ezekiel 36:31 tells us what happens at the time of receiving a new spirit (cf. verse 26): "*Then* you will remember your evil ways and your deeds that were not good; and you will loathe yourselves in your own sight, for your iniquities and your abominations." In other words, from our spirit (1) we know ourselves in God's light, (2) we are inwardly searched, and (3) we are able to loathe ourselves. Loathing ourselves has nothing to do with morbid introspection. It is actually a gift of grace imparting to us the ability to remain objective about our fallen state *by agreeing with God's judgment of it.*

When we remain in our self, or soul-life, we lose that God-given ability to know ourself the way God knows us. Paul states this in 1 Corinthians 2:14: "But the soulish man does not receive the things of the Spirit of God, for they are foolishness to him; nor can he know them, because they are spiritually discerned." The soulish man is the man that stays in himself. He remains locked up in his own thoughts and feelings. The things of the Spirit are foolishness to him; that is, the Spirit's judgment of the flesh as it is revealed at the cross is not grasped or understood. Instead of agreeing with God's judgment of the flesh, the soulish man seeks to protect, defend, and excuse what God condemned on the cross (Rom. 8:3).

To be subjective is to be left in a state of blindness and ignorance, in which we do not know ourselves according to God's estimate of things. When this is the case, whenever we come to fellowship with the saints, we basically trust our own view and opinion. We only see things with our own mind and feeling. We are not that flexible in fellowship, because when our opinion is rejected, we take it in a personal way and *we feel* rejected. Our opinion and self are so linked together that when things do not go our way, we get defensive and upset. Genuine fellowship is very difficult with a subjective person because he does not have a proper relationship with himself.

What is a proper relationship with ourselves in God's light? It is that we do not trust our mind and feelings that much. Yes, we fellowship about matters, but at the same time, we do not have that much confidence in our view. We are not like Peter who took the Lord aside and confidently said, "This shall not happen to You" (Matt. 16:22). Peter did not know himself. He was without any flexibility. He could never have said such a thing so confidently, with his opinion being expressed, if he had known himself. So the Lord had to expose him by allowing him to fail again and again until he experienced a transfer of source, as manifested in his two Epistles.

We have seen that being subjective means that we are ignorant of ourselves. So we need to seize our spirit, our objective base. When you are a person exercising your spirit, you become wiser and more discerning. That is, you are wiser and more discerning about *yourself*. You do not trust yourself anymore. You know yourself in God's light (Psa. 36:9). And because you know yourself, you know others. It is not a matter of a gift of discernment falling upon you. The more we know ourself — how fallen we are, how we cannot trust ourself, and how much we need to live moment by moment by the Lord Himself — the more we will know others' condition. This is surely a spiritual qualification for those who serve and take the lead in the church.

Those who have any responsibility in the church must know themselves. This knowing comes by exercising the spirit, being broken, and realizing our untrustworthiness. Without this, the Lord's testimony will be mixed and impure. It will be led by persons who do not know themselves, who trust their opinion and view, and who lead the church with an undealt-with self. May the Lord cause us to be in our spirit more and more so that we will discern everything with our spirit. When we get into the spirit we know the things of man. This includes all the basic things about man — man's creation, man's fall, man's fallen condition and state, man's redemption, man's regeneration, and man's state of simultaneously having both flesh and spirit (John 3:6). Being in the realm of the spirit is the secret of being delivered out of ignorance and into God's light.

Being subjective makes us prone to deception

Being subjective also makes us prone to deception. In 2 Corinthians 11:3 Paul says, "But I fear, lest somehow, as the serpent deceived Eve by his craftiness, so your thoughts may be corrupted from the singleness and the purity that is toward Christ." Here Paul says that the enemy deceived Eve by his craftiness. The way the enemy gained an entrance was through Eve's thought-life. When she was seduced and deceived by the enemy, she became utterly subjective. She did not touch the Lord Himself and His presence. She left her objective orientation to the Lord and stayed within the confines of her own thoughts and thinking. Because of this she was deceived and drawn out into sin. So we can see that when we stay in this realm, our own thoughts become our source and we are prone to deception.

This deception is especially related to the thoughts about ourself — high thoughts, elevated thoughts, proud thoughts, even thoughts based upon visions we have had (Col. 2:18), a calling we have had, who we think we are, the spiritual person that we think we are. This is what Paul warns against in

Romans 12:3: "For I say...to *everyone* who is among you, not to think of himself more highly than he ought to think." That means everyone is subject to this temptation. So if we are a person subjectively thinking about ourself, considering ourself, measuring ourself with ourself, we are prone to be deceived. The feeling within a subjective person who is deceived is that "I have the goods. I really know better." This is all subjectivity. And this is Satan's way of deceiving us from the simplicity and the purity which is toward Christ.

So we need to come back to the objective source of our spirit. From our spirit we deal with our high thoughts by praying, "Lord, my thoughts are untrustworthy. Lord, I need to pull down all this elevated thinking in my mind, this thinking of myself more highly than others." This attitude of distrust concerning ourself is also expressed in Philippians 2:3 where Paul admonished the saints to do things "in lowliness of mind." This means "Lord, we are nothing, and out of ourselves we can do nothing. We have no trust in our own thoughts. We are just persons trusting in You." This kind of exercise of our spirit will preserve us from being prone to deception.

Being subjective condemns us

Being subjective will always manifest itself in one's life by a stream of condemning thoughts. The real source of condemnation with many people is simply subjectivity. This is the kind of condemnation referred to in Romans 7 and 8 — subjective condemnation. A person lives with condemnation because he believes his own feelings and his own state of mind, both of which have their source in the flesh. Thus, he is set up for the accuser of the brethren.

If we do not stand with the four objective facts — Christ, the spirit, the truth, and the Body — we are left to the onslaught of condemnation from the enemy. This is because we are identifying with the sin in our flesh. It reacts, it moves, it has its tendencies, and it seeks to act itself out (Rom. 6:12). Paul's description of his subjective state in Romans 7 reveals that there was a fierce struggle going on within his being because he had no objective base to lay hold of. There was no truth, no spirit, no Christ, and no Body. So he ended up with a desperate cry, "O wretched man that I am!" (v. 24). His wretchedness was due to his being confined to his own thoughts and emotions. His subjectivity in handling himself resulted in subjective condemnation.

Then he bursts forth in Romans 7:25, "Thanks be to God through Jesus Christ our Lord!" (NASV). And again in Romans 8:1-2 he declares, [1] "There is therefore now no condemnation to them that are in Christ Jesus. [2] For the law of the Spirit of life in Christ Jesus made me free from the law of sin and of death" (ASV). These two facts uttered by Paul reveal the way he was delivered from subjective condemnation: "*through Jesus Christ*" coupled with "the law of the Spirit of life made me free." In these verses, Paul discloses *how* he was delivered. His deliverance did not come from an experience that he passed through. His deliverance came as a result of moving out of his subjective state into the objective reality of Christ, the spirit, and the truth.

Not only did Paul know himself *"in Christ,"* but he also saw that everything now was to be processed *"through Jesus Christ."* And the way he could process everything through Jesus Christ was by *"the law of the Spirit of life"* resident within him. In other words, his spirit mingled with the Holy Spirit became to him the great objective base for his deliverance out of subjective condemnation. In the spirit he could substantiate the reality of being "in Christ" and doing all things "through Jesus Christ." If we live condemned, if we live continuously accused, no doubt the reason is that we believe our own subjective feelings and state of mind rather than *Christ, the spirit, the truth, and the Body*. So we need to remain steadfast in these four pillars to be delivered from the subjective state of condemnation.

Being subjective makes us fearful

Subjectivity makes us fearful. That is, when we stay in ourselves considering our own feelings and thoughts, we are fearful and timid. Second Timothy 1:7 says, "For God has not given us a spirit of fear [cowardice or timidity], but of power and of love and of a sound mind." Then verse 8 says, "Therefore do not be ashamed of the testimony of our Lord." This testimony includes the meetings of the church. There may be some who have not testified in over six months or a year. Why would we not testify? Why would we not stand up to release the portion of Christ that we have enjoyed? It may be due to a subjective state and mood that comes over us during the meeting. We feel self-conscious. Our point of reference is our self. We are more occupied with what we are not, than with Christ. Being immersed in our personal failure, our own overall condition, and our present situation are symptoms of our subjectivity. When these things become our point of reference, we are fearful and feel ashamed. This is what subjectivity does to us. It binds us with a fearful self-consciousness and keeps us from functioning as a member of the Body.

But the Word declares that God has not given us a spirit of fearfulness or timidity, but of power, of love, and of a sound mind. With such a spirit, we can stand up and open our mouth with the testimony of our Lord. Some of us may need to spring up out of our seats calling upon the name of the Lord from our spirit, and overthrow our subjectivity. It is a paralyzing thing to be bound by your own thoughts about your condition. This is what subjectivity does — it makes us fearful to talk about Christ. We are more occupied with what others are thinking about us than with Christ. We are afraid of saying the wrong thing. We are caught up within the confines of our mind. So we need to exercise our spirit of power, love, and a sound mind to get out of ourself and be transferred out of our subjective state to enjoy Christ and flow Him out to others. When we exercise our spirit by calling upon the name of the Lord, we instantly usher our whole being into God Himself as our source. It is by this kind of action that all subjectivity is overthrown and Satan is defeated in our lives.

Being subjective damages
our relationship to the Body

In Romans 14:7-8 Paul says, [7] "For none of us lives to himself, and no one dies to himself. [8] For if we live, we live to the Lord; and if we die, we die to the Lord. Therefore, whether we live or die, we are the Lord's." These two verses are in the context of the Body life. Subjectivity in Romans 14 expresses itself by the saints despising and judging one another. In other words, being subjective means living by our own view and opinion. This damages our receiving of the members of the Body. When Paul fellowships his burden concerning the receiving of all the saints, he stresses the need for us to not live to ourselves. In Romans 15:3 he says, "For even Christ did not please Himself." Living to ourself and pleasing ourself are factors of subjectivity and damage the organic reality of the Body.

For the rich and full church life we need to be a person who is one spirit with the Lord and one with the members of the Body, not despising or judging the saints. Being distracted by our subjective views and opinions damages our relationships in the Body, making it impossible to have the Lord's expression of His one Body on this earth. This is why Paul says, "None of us lives to himself." With self out of the way, now we only need to care for "righteousness and peace and joy in the Holy Spirit," as Paul says in Romans 14:17. It is in this way that we will overthrow the divisive demon of subjectivity and allow "the God of peace" to crush Satan under our feet (Rom. 16:20).

Being subjective causes us to misunderstand and misinterpret

Subjectivity causes you to be a person that misunderstands and misinterprets things. This is surely a chief characteristic of subjectivity. When we are left to ourself we misunderstand and we misinterpret. That is, we do not hear right and we do not perceive right. How many times have you misunderstood your spouse? How many times have you misinterpreted the brothers and sisters? You judged them. You drew a conclusion about them, and later you discovered that you were far from the truth. Why? Because you believed your own thought. Whenever we leave Christ, our spirit, the truth, and the fellowship of the Body, we become prone to misinterpreting others. For example, we may misinterpret a person's countenance. We may look at his countenance and feel that he is thinking about us, condemning us, and judging us, when all the time such things only exist in our own mind.

This is what happened with the Corinthians. They misunderstood Paul. They misinterpreted him again and again. So in 2 Corinthians 1:12 Paul testifies that he was not relating to the believers by fleshly wisdom, but by the grace of God: "We conducted ourselves in the world in simplicity and sincerity of God, not with fleshly wisdom, but by the grace of God, and more abundantly toward you." So Paul was conducting himself in the spirit. But the saints in Corinth, the subjective selves that were not dealt with, misinterpreted his movements (cf. 2 Cor. 1:15-21).

When we are subjective and undealt with, we misinterpret and misunderstand those who are in the spirit. This shows us how prone we are to be deceived by our subjective mind. If we are not in the spirit, if we are not occupied with Christ, if we are not standing with the truth, and if we are not in the fellowship in the light with the Body, then we surely are open to misinterpret and misunderstand many things.

Being subjective makes us an outward person

Subjectivity also makes us a shallow, outward person. Paul exposes this aspect of subjectivity in 2 Corinthians 10:12: "For we dare not class ourselves or compare ourselves with certain of them who commend themselves. But they, measuring themselves by themselves, and comparing themselves among themselves, are without understanding." This shows that the Corinthians were just outward in their relationships, comparing outward things. This is a basic characteristic of subjectivity — we look at outward things. There is no depth, no inward reality, but just comparing ourselves among ourselves. We are superficial, measuring things in a mere outward way. There is no depth of spirit with us when we are subjective.

Being subjective closes our being to God and the Body

Another aspect of subjectivity is that you close your being to God and to the members. Subjectivity makes you a closed person. This was true of some of the believers in Corinth. In 2 Corinthians 6:12 Paul tried to open them up to fellowship by saying, "You are not restricted in us, but you are restricted in your own inward parts." This means they were narrow in their own inward parts. They were closed — closed to the Lord and closed to the Body. They were just living in themselves.

The reason the Corinthians were so closed was that they were not dealing with the Lord over their defiling associations. They were still compromising with darkness in their lives. That is why in verse 17 Paul says, "Come out from among them and be separate....Do not touch what is unclean." Sometimes when you come to a brother or sister, you just have the sense they are not open. There is no transparency, but rather there is an opaqueness due to their closing to the Lord.

When we are open to the Lord in our life, it is so easy to fellowship. But when things get confusing and we are very subjective, it is often because there is no genuine openness to the Lord. A lack of dealing with the Lord makes a person more subjective in his relationships with the members of the Body. Paul said to the Corinthians that they were closed and narrowed in their own inward parts. They were not open to the Lord or to Paul.

When Paul talked about being open and being enlarged, he immediately shifted the focus of his fellowship to an exhortation: "Do not be unequally yoked together with unbelievers" (v. 14). Then he went on to speak about not touching what is unclean. He knew that their subjectivity, which manifested itself by their being closed to him, was because there was still something defiling the release of their spirit. So Paul says in 2 Corinthians 7:1-2, [1] "Therefore, having these promises, beloved, let us cleanse ourselves from all defilement of the flesh and spirit, perfecting holiness in the fear of God. [2] Open your hearts to us. We have wronged no one, we have corrupted no one, we have defrauded no one." The way out of subjectivity is to keep our spirit cleansed from every kind of pollution and defilement.

Being subjective makes us suspicious

Subjectivity makes you a suspicious person. This is mentioned in 2 Corinthians 10:2, where Paul speaks of "some, who think of us as if we walked according to the flesh." There were "some" who were suspicious of Paul because they were living in their own subjectivity — in their reasoning and in their opinion. Subjective persons always bring in a suspicious atmosphere to the church.

Being subjective makes us distrustful and anxious

Subjectivity makes you distrustful and anxious. This is the pitiful end of a subjective person — you do not trust anyone. You only trust yourself. You only believe your feelings, and you do not trust anyone else. You are anxious about your condition. This is also due to believing your own feelings and your own thoughts. Oh, brothers and sisters, we all need to rise up and shout, "Lord, I reject my self! Oh, I love Christ! I love my spirit! I love the truth! I love the Body! Hallelujah! I am rearranged! I am in another source!" By declaring these facts we will get out of our subjectivity. Praise the Lord!

Being subjective makes us merge with demons

Subjectivity causes you to merge with demons. Believing your self is actually believing the demonic activity in your being. This is what it means to be subjective. James 3:14-15 makes it clear: [14] "If you have bitter envy and self-seeking in your hearts... [15] this wisdom does not descend from above, but is earthly, soulish, demonic." James puts these words together: earthly, soulish, demonic. *Soulish* means being subjective, being in your self. Then the next word he uses after *soulish* is *demonic*. So this literally means that a subjective person is a person who is subject to the activity of demons, which causes him to merge with their suggestions. For example, you think that those feelings in you are *your* feelings, but they are not really yours. They are the enemy's. He has found a nesting place in your subjectivity. If you refuse to turn to your spirit, if you do not take Christ, if you do not stand with the truth, and if you do not receive from the Body, then you are left to demonic activity. This is the pitiful end of subjectivity.

HOW TO DEAL WITH BEING SUBJECTIVE

Stop yourself

Now let us fellowship about how to deal with this fallen

state of subjectivity. First, stop yourself, and do not interpret anything concerning yourself or others. The way to be transferred out of yourself and into the spirit is to stop yourself. Do not try to interpret yourself. Do not trust your view, opinion, and reasoning. Just stop. Call a halt to this self that has controlled and lived out its life for so many years. In order to stop yourself you may need to spend some time with the Lord.

In 1 Corinthians chapter 4, Paul indicates that he did not trust subjective views or opinions. In verse 3 he says, "But with me it is a very small thing that I should be judged by you or by man's day." *Man's day* is a term in contrast to *the Lord's day*. Man's day means that man's opinion and man's judgment has the sway. Man's day means that it is man's turn to judge, view, and analyze. The Lord's day means the Lord comes in, as in Revelation 1:10: "I was in spirit on the Lord's Day." On the Lord's day the Lord came in to walk among the churches to judge them (Rev. 2—3). The Lord's day means that now it is the Lord's turn to judge. With this realization Paul continues in 1 Corinthians 4:3, "In fact, I do not even judge myself." Paul is saying that he is not trustworthy to examine himself, to introspect, or to analyze himself.

Then in verse 4 Paul says, "For *I know nothing against myself,* yet I am not justified by this; but He who judges me is the Lord." Just stop yourself. Do not interpret anything about yourself. Do not debate with yourself. Do not argue with yourself. Do not analyze yourself. Say, "Lord, I open to You with Jeremiah 17:9, 'The heart is deceitful above all things, and desperately wicked; who can know it?' " Who can know the heart? Who can know our real state? Verse 10 tells us: "I, the LORD, search the heart, I test the mind." The Lord is the One who is qualified to know you and change you. In the New Testament, there is a compound Greek word translated "heart-knower." The Lord is the Heart-knower. He is the One who really knows your heart accurately.

So the first way to deal with your subjective state is to stop yourself. Do not interpret yourself or others from your viewpoint. Just stop yourself. And the way to stop is just to be poor in spirit — to be emptied, to humble yourself and unload all your self-made schemes to save yourself. Say, "Lord, I just unload. Lord, transfer me into the spirit. Unload me from my subjective thinking and living. I just stop myself."

Do not sin by acting independently

The second way to deal with subjectivity is to not take any independent action and fall into sin. You ask, what do you mean? James 4:17 says, "Therefore, to him who knows to do good and does not do it, to him it is sin." Sin in the context of James 4 means independent action. This is what sin is — independent action. From the beginning, this has been the real source of all sin — man acting independent of God. In this chapter, James is talking about those who say, "Today or tomorrow we will go to such and such a city, spend a year there, buy and sell, and make a profit" (v. 13). To those James says, "Instead you ought to say, If the Lord wills, we shall live and do this or that" (v. 15). "If the Lord wills" is not merely a religious saying. It means we live dependent on God about everything.

In verse 16 James says, "But now you boast in your arrogance. All such boasting is evil." What is this boasting, this arrogance? It is being independent in our moves, in our daily life. Then he continues in verse 17, "Therefore, to him who knows to do good and does not do it, to him it is sin." What is the good here? The good here is dependence upon God. I am going to the store dependent upon God. I am going to fellowship with the saints dependent upon God. To live independently is to live presumptuously and sinfully. Brothers and sisters, perhaps we have never considered sin in this way. But this is the basic definition of sin — independence from God. Every sin is traced back to our independence.

So the way to have a transfer from our subjectivity is first to stop ourself, and second to not sin by acting independently. How can we do this? Such a life issues from spending time with the Lord to have thorough fellowship with Him. We need to nurture and cultivate our dependent relationship with the Lord.

Disassociate yourself from the devil

The third way to be delivered from subjectivity is to disassociate yourself from the devil. You have to disentangle this soul enmeshed with demons. The way to be delivered out of this old source that has controlled us is to disassociate ourself from the devil and from demons. This is exactly what the Lord did with Peter in Matthew 16:23. Peter had said to Him, "Far be it from You, Lord; this [the cross] shall not happen to You!" (v. 22). Here was a big temptation trying to penetrate into the Lord's soul. So the Lord looked at Peter and said, "Get behind Me, Satan!" (v. 23). The Lord saw Satan right there. The words in Greek for *"Get behind Me!"* can also be translated "Get out of My sight, be gone!" The Lord immediately disassociated Himself from the devil, who was trying to divert Him from the cross. Then the Lord said in verse 24, "If anyone desires to come after Me, let him deny himself." So this denying of the self and disassociating ourself from the devil go together. We need to disassociate ourself from the enemy.

How do you disassociate yourself from the devil? You do it by identifying his activity. Paul says it in this way in 2 Corinthians 2:11: "lest Satan should take advantage of us; for we are not ignorant of *his* thoughts." "*His* thoughts" refer to Satan's thoughts in our thoughts. They are Satan's thoughts in our subjective thinking. So Paul disassociates the thoughts from himself by identifying them as Satan's thoughts.

Brothers and sisters, in our experience the way to have this transfer out of subjectivity is to (1) stop yourself; (2) do not act independently and sin; and (3) disassociate yourself from the devil. Speak to the concealed devil. This means you are going to speak to your feelings. You are going to speak to your jealousy. You are going to speak to your doubt. You are going to speak to your envy. You are going to speak to your opinion.

You are going to speak to your reasoning. You are going to speak to what seems to be you! You have been enmeshed with demons, but now you have found out that an enemy has usurped your being. That is not Christ, that is not your spirit, that is not your real person, that is not really you. You discover that a hidden enemy has been occupying your thoughts and feelings.

When you start to disassociate yourself from the enemy with prayer, with the exercise of "the weapons of our warfare" that are mighty to God, you pull down the stronghold (2 Cor. 10:4). Not only does the stronghold of reasoning come down, but Satan is cast out. James 4:7 says, "Resist the devil and he will flee from you." And Revelation 12:10-11 says, [10] "The accuser of our brethren…has been cast down.…[11] And they overcame him because of the blood of the Lamb and because of the word of their testimony, and they did not love their soul-life to the death." That means they said, "Soul-life, I am not going to preserve you. You are the one that wants to preserve itself. You are the one that is holding back. Satan, you are the one hiding out in my soul. You are the one that is afraid. You are the one that hides from the light. You are the one crouching as sin in the flesh. You are the one that is independent. You are the culprit, soul-life. You are enmeshed with Satan." Declare the facts to the devil. Disassociate yourself from the enemy with a strong spirit, and demons will leave you and you will be free — free in a new source.

So stop yourself and open wholly to the Lord. You cannot do anything to change yourself, but you are connected to the source of power — to the Triune God, to the name of Jesus, to the Spirit of God who casts out demons. You are one with that Spirit. Stay one with Christ, hold Him as the Head, stay with your spirit, believe the truth, and stand with the Body.

This is how to have a transfer. It is by stopping ourself and opening to the Lord and contacting Him. We have been interpreting things, we have been doing the living, we have lived to ourself; and because of this we are a subjective mess — deceived and filled with demonic activity. Now we need to disassociate ourself from the enemy. And this enemy is not merely an objective enemy. This is a subjective enemy enmeshed with our soul, possessing us with our own state of mind and our own moods. We have to disassociate ourself from our mood and our own feeling. Oh, the enemy hates this word. Acting on this word will deliver us all.

The best kind of prayer to deliver us from this subjective state is to exercise our spirit and draw a line between us and Satan. Speak boldly to the enemy, and say, "You fallen angel, you devil, you demons, I have been enmeshed with you. I have thought your thoughts, I have believed your feelings. You have caused me to be shut up to myself. But this day, I am drawing a separating line between you and me. I declare war with the weapons of my warfare that are mighty to God. My real person is Christ. It is no longer I. I have been crucified with Christ. Now *Christ* lives in me. I am regenerated in my *spirit*. The *truth* is mine and I stand one with the members of *the Body*." Take these four pillars and you will overthrow the stronghold of self. You will drive out every subjective state that keeps you in bondage to self. The transfer will be there. Praise the Lord! Oh, may the Lord grant to us a full deliverance from the self and its subjectivity.

6

TRANSFERRED OUT OF THE HIDDEN SELF

THE TRANSFER OF SOURCE THROUGH THE WHOLE BIBLE

We must see that one of the most crucial things in our Christian life is to have a transfer of our source from self to God, from flesh to spirit. This transfer is not about improving our behavior by outward, cosmetic work. It is not about trying harder or doing more and better things. It is about coming to God Himself as the source of all things (Rom. 11:36). By this transfer we no longer take the self as our source, but we take God Himself from our spirit as our only source. This transfer of source is one of the great matters revealed in the Bible.

This was the way the Lord Jesus lived in His humanity. As the Son of Man in the Gospels, He lived a life of taking the Father as His source in all things. In John 5:19 He testifies, "The Son can do nothing from Himself." And again in John 8:28 He says, "I do nothing from Myself." Then He applies this same principle of living to us in John 15:5 when He says, "Without Me you can do nothing." These revealing words of testimony from the Lord's mouth show us how crucial it is to have a transfer of source out of one realm into another. Now we need to see the revelation of this transfer through the whole Bible.

The beginning and ending of the Bible

In the beginning of the Bible, God confronts man with two sources: the tree of life and the tree of the knowledge of good and evil. Then He commends man to eat of the tree of life. This shows us what God's thought was from the very beginning. He wanted man to take God Himself as his source. He wanted man to live by the tree of life, which represents God Himself as life. Man was to live by that tree, in contrast to the tree of the knowledge of good and evil, which is an entirely different source.

In Genesis 3:5 the serpent spoke to Eve about this other source: "God knows that in the day you eat of it your eyes will be opened, and you will be like gods, knowing good and evil." These words reveal that in living by that source — the tree of the knowledge of good and evil — man would become an entity in himself, living out of himself, knowing good and evil, independent from God. "You will be like gods" means that the self will be god, instead of God being God. The self becomes the point of reference. The self knows good and evil. The self knows how to make a decision. The self can figure it out. The self is god, rather than God being God. So we can see from the beginning that two sources are revealed.

Here we see the cause of man's fall: he took of that other source, the tree of the knowledge of good and evil. The real nature of sin was in man becoming independent from God, making his own choices, and living out of the source of himself. We see this at the beginning of the Bible.

Then at the end of the Bible we see God's purpose realized in the holy city (Rev. 21—22). Here God and man are fully mingled together. This city signifies all of God's redeemed children built up together as His habitation, representing and expressing Him. The tree of life is no longer outside of man, as it was in Genesis, but it is right in the middle of the city. This means that at the end of the Bible, in God's ultimate expression, He Himself is the very center, having become the source for all His redeemed children.

So at the end of the Bible we have the holy city as the full expression of God, with the tree of life and the river of water of life — the Triune God — inwardly being the source of the whole city. By this we can see that the crucial thing throughout the Bible is that God's children would be transferred out of living from the source of the self into living from the source of God Himself.

The Old Testament

Jeremiah 2:13 is a window in the Old Testament into God's diagnosis of the real situation of His people Israel: "For My people have committed two evils: they have forsaken Me, the fountain of living waters, and hewn themselves cisterns — broken cisterns that can hold no water." This was the whole problem throughout the Old Testament — God's people forsook Him, "the fountain of living waters." This verse shows that God's thought and desire was that He would be their source. It was as if He was saying, "Do not forsake Me. I am the fountain of living waters." Then in Psalm 36:9 God is mentioned again as a fountain. David says to the Lord, "For with You is the fountain of life." So we can see that in the Old Testament God desired to be our source.

The Gospels

In the Gospels the pinnacle of the revelation of man's dependence on God is found in John 14, 15, and 16. In these chapters the Lord opens up the process of His becoming the Spirit to enter into us so that we could live in Him. In John 15:4-5 He says, [4] "Abide in Me, and I in you. As the branch cannot bear fruit of itself, unless it abides in the vine, neither can you, unless you abide in Me. [5] I am the vine, you are the branches. He who abides in Me, and I in him, bears much fruit; for without Me you can do nothing." We can see the burden that the Lord opens up here. He is saying, "I am your source; you are just a branch. You are connected to Me. Just stay in Me, abide in Me. That is all I desire. Just live out of Me. Without Me you can do nothing. You cannot live, you cannot decide. Apart from Me nothing is of value; everything that proceeds out of yourself is a waste. Everything is empty that comes from the source of yourself. Apart from Me you can do nothing. Consult Me, open to Me, fellowship with Me, move with Me, obey Me, stay with Me. Do not do anything apart from Me. Whether it is good, whether it is right, is not the point. The point is Me — I am the Determiner. I am the Source." This is the Gospels.

The Book of Acts

In the book of Acts there is a struggle for a transfer — a transfer out of the Old Testament dispensation into the New Testament dispensation. This means a transfer out of the self, out of the flesh, out of being independent from God, into the realm of the spirit, into God as the source. The whole burden in the book of Acts was that all the saints be transferred into the New Testament dispensation, or economy — into the Spirit, where God is the source. This burden was carried out especially by the apostle Paul in his ministry. Yet many believers continued to hold on to the Old Testament economy. They were still clinging to the independent self doing something for God by the law (Acts 21:20-21), rather than having a full transfer into the Spirit. So the book of Acts is the beginning of the carrying out of this transfer into the Spirit.

Let us look at some specific situations in Acts to further appreciate how great a matter this transfer is. With Paul in the book of Acts we can see the testimony of a man who was in the good of the transfer. Acts 16:6 says, "They were forbidden by the Holy Spirit to preach the word in Asia." Then verse 7 says, "They tried to go into Bithynia, but the Spirit of Jesus did not permit them." This means that Paul and his co-workers were not living by the principle of right and wrong. Neither were they living independently — out from themselves. Rather, they were inwardly regulated and controlled by the source of the Spirit. Paul and those with him were following the Spirit with their movements. We see this in the fact that they were "forbidden" and "not permitted" to pursue their initial plans. This means they were paying attention to God as their source. Their burden was not merely to "do something for God" — to preach the gospel, to cover new territory — according to their own good idea. Their whole burden was simply to stay with the Spirit of Jesus. Whatever it meant, they sought to stay with the Spirit of Jesus. This shows that Paul was fully experiencing the transfer into the Spirit at that time. He was not thinking about what was good, what was right, or what he could do for the Lord. Rather, he was absolutely living in the source of the Spirit — restricted and shut up to the Spirit.

The Epistles and Revelation

Throughout the Epistles we see this transfer of source presented again and again. In 2 Corinthians 5:14-15 Paul speaks about the issue of the Lord's death: [14] "If One died for all, then all died; [15] and He died for all, that those who live should live no longer to themselves." This means that in our experience we would no longer live *to* the source of ourself, but *to* Him. Also, the book of Hebrews exhorts the believers to "come forward" out of the wilderness into the good land, out of the holy place into the holiest of all, out of the self into the spirit. So we can see that in the whole Bible, from the first two chapters to the last two chapters — through the Old Testament into the Gospels, into the book of Acts, through the Epistles, and ending with the book of Revelation — the burden is for man to have a transfer of source.

For the Lord to gain the church as a bride, believers must be transferred out of the self into the spirit. Practically, this means we must be transferred out of doing something *for* God and into the Spirit — doing things *in* God and *with* God as the source. There is no hope as long as the self is the source, as long as man is still making the decisions, controlling things, and using the Bible for his own ends and purposes. As long as man is still planning, organizing, controlling, and operating out of himself, there is no hope. The only hope is with a group of people who are rejecting the self as the source of their living and service, and being transferred into the realm of following the Lamb wherever He goes. This is the testimony of the 144,000, the overcomers, who are taken as firstfruits to God and to the Lamb (Rev. 14:4). Their unique testimony is that they follow the Lamb wherever He goes. He is their only source. This means they are absolutely one with the Spirit. So we see how crucial this matter of source is in relation to the Lord's testimony.

A summary of the transfer

Throughout the Bible there is a vision of God seeking to become man's source. Man's initial fall was a fall away from God as his source, into himself. He became independent, making his own decisions, becoming a god in himself, a self-determining entity. Then we see God seeking to recover man by coming in the person of His Son. The Son of God, in His incarnation, lived a totally dependent life. He lived out of the source of the Father, completely dependent, not taking Himself as His source, not judging people (John 8:15; 12:47), not analyzing (Matt. 11:25-26), not doing anything from Himself, but doing only what He heard, only what He received from the Father (John 5:30). He did not do anything apart from the Father. In this way His soul-life was processed in incarnation and human living. Then He was also processed in crucifixion, in resurrection, and in ascension. And finally He was installed into our spirit as the life-giving Spirit so that we could live out of the source of God Himself.

At the end of the Bible we see the ultimate consummation of all God's transferring work in His redeemed people. We see God's finished product — His building, His people fully transformed and conformed to His image, thoroughly mingled with Him. This all issues from the Triune God being the source, the center, as depicted by the tree of life and the river of life flowing out from the throne of God. This shows us that the vision of the transfer of source is throughout the whole Bible.

ASPECTS RELATED TO THE HIDDEN SELF

Dealing with the self touches the enemy

Having the self dealt with is a great matter in this universe. The dealing with the self as man's source of living touches the enemy, Satan, more than any other dealing. When the Lord declared in Matthew 16, "I will build My church," He meant, "I am the source. That means I do it, and I do it from within the saints. I am the Builder. I build." And Ephesians 2:22 tells us that this building is now *in spirit*. This means that the building work and the Builder, who is working, operating, and doing, is in our spirit. In saying, "I will build My church, and the gates of Hades shall not prevail against it," the Lord meant, "When I am the source of the building, then, and only then, the gates of Hades shall not prevail. But if *you* build it, if *you* are the source, then Satan will prevail just as he did with Peter."

In Matthew 16, Peter tried to work out God's economy by forbidding the Lord to go to the cross and by telling Him to pity Himself. That means Peter's mind suddenly became the source of some "good advice" for the Lord. And then the Lord turned to Peter and said, "Get behind Me, Satan! You are an offense to Me, for *you* are not setting your mind on the things of God, but on the things of men" (v. 23). Who is the "you" that the Lord is talking to — Satan or Peter? Peter was mingled with Satan. Peter's self, his opinion, was just the mingling of Satan with him.

Immediately after speaking that rebuking word to Peter, the Lord said to His disciples, "If anyone desires to come after Me, let him deny himself, and take up his cross, and follow Me" (v. 24). Here the Lord reveals that the practical way to deal with Satan's frustrating of God's purpose is by denying the self. From this we see that to touch the self is to touch Satan. The self is Satan's stronghold, his base of operation. It is the place from which he works to divide and insulate believers, to disintegrate and immobilize the Body. He comes from the source of the undealt-with self in man. So dealing with the self touches the devil and the principalities and powers, because it is through the undealt-with self that Satan finds an opening in man (John 14:30). Loving the self-life is also a factor that gives the enemy ground to accuse believers before God (Rev. 12:10-11). And when Satan's activity in the heavens is exposed in the book of Job, we see that it is related to the self-life of Job. In this entire universe, it is the self that is being targeted by Satan in the presence of God (Job 1:9; 2:4-5).

Dealing with the hidden self in Job

Dealing with the hidden self is fully revealed in the book of Job. Job 1:6-9 says, [6] "Now there was a day when the sons of God came to present themselves before the Lord, and Satan also came among them. [7] And the Lord said to Satan, 'From where do you come?' So Satan answered the Lord and said, 'From going to and fro on the earth, and from walking back and forth on it.' [8] Then the Lord said to Satan, 'Have you considered My servant Job, that there is none like him on the earth, a blameless and upright man, one who fears God and shuns evil?' [9] So Satan answered the Lord and said, 'Does Job fear God for nothing?' " Here Satan was questioning Job's motive in serving God. Was Job serving God purely for God Himself? Or was Job serving God for his own profit, to benefit himself? Was Job serving his own ends? Was he feeding his self and supporting his self-life? So Satan brought this accusation concerning Job's self before the Lord.

Then in verse 10 the Adversary, Satan, continues questioning God about Job's source: "Have You not made a hedge around him, around his household, and around all that he has on every side? You have blessed the work of his hands, and his possessions have increased in the land." In other words, who would not serve God as long as his self was fully satisfied, blessed, and had everything? So Job's inner, hidden life is brought into question by Satan in the presence of the Lord.

Then verses 11-12 say, [11] "But now, stretch out Your hand and touch all that he has, and he will surely curse You to Your face! [12] So the LORD said to Satan, 'Behold, all that he has is in your power; only do not lay a hand on his person.' Then Satan went out from the presence of the LORD." So the Lord allowed Satan to touch all of Job's possessions, his family, and all the blessing that he and his family had experienced. And we know what happened — calamity upon calamity, one thing after another, rapidly befell Job. From the conversation between Satan and the Lord in the first chapter of Job, we know that all this happened to Job in order that he would have a full dealing with his hidden self, that he would be tested and tried and his hidden self exposed.

Knowing God and knowing the self

At the end of the book of Job in chapter 42:5-6, Job tells the Lord, [5] "I have heard of You by the hearing of the ear, but now my eye sees You. [6] Therefore I abhor myself, and repent in dust and ashes." Here we can see that the issue of a man's dealing with the self is that he abhors himself — "I despise myself, I abhor myself" — and he repents in dust and ashes. The Hebrew word translated "repent" is not the same word that is used in the book of Hebrews for the repentance of sins. Here in Job it is another kind of repentance, that is, a repudiating of the self. It includes a self-abhorrence, a depreciation of the self, and is the result of a process that was taking place through the whole book of Job.

The ultimate issue, or "the end of the Lord" (James 5:11, KJV), that is, the end of the Lord's dealing with Job, is that he meets God. He no longer has a secondhand experience and relationship with God. But from firsthand experience he can say, "I have heard of You by the hearing of the ear, but now my eye sees You." This means, "Now, with this hidden self exposed and dealt with, I meet You, Lord. I know You, and I know myself. And I repent in dust and ashes." Then the Lord "turned the captivity of Job" (Job 42:10, ASV), and he became greatly blessed. So what we especially see in this book is the dealing with the hidden self and the transfer of a person out of the hidden self.

After seeing the self and its expression in our opinion, in our reasoning, and in being subjective, we need to see more concerning the hidden self and how to be transferred out of the hidden self. In dealing with opinion, reasoning, and being subjective, the expression of the self is more obvious than it is in dealing with the hidden self. Yet there is some overlapping of the characteristics. So we need to see how to deal with this self that is so hidden and so enmeshed with the enemy. Being transferred out of the hidden self could also be defined as being transferred out of the hidden Satan or out of the hidden demons, because the self and the enemy are so enmeshed together.

The meaning of the word "deny"

Wherever the self has sway, Satan has sway. This principle is clearly revealed in Matthew 16. If the self is there, then demons are operating. This is why when the Lord dealt with the enemy, He dealt with the self, saying "deny" the self (Matt. 16:23-24). Here in this passage in Matthew, the Lord uses the most intensive word in Greek for *deny*. It means to utterly reject, to disassociate yourself from something, to have no connection with it. Thus, we need to utterly reject and disassociate ourselves from this self that is so enmeshed with Satan. This intense form of the word *deny* is also used by the Lord in Matthew 26:34 and 75 to describe Peter's denial of Him. The Lord foretold the events, saying, "Before the rooster crows, you will deny Me three times." So Peter utterly denied the Lord. He disassociated himself from the Lord Jesus, swearing that he had no connection with the Lord. In the same way, we must utterly deny our self.

Deny by drawing the line

To deny the self means to disassociate ourself from it, to have no connection with it, to draw the line, declaring, "That is not me anymore. That is no longer my source. Hallelujah, that has been crucified! That old man has been crucified. I stand crucified with Christ." In this way, objectively draw the line and deny the self. Utterly repudiate it. Have no connection with it. Do not identify with it. With the same intensity that Peter would not identify with the Lord, do not identify with your self, and do not identify with its reactions of jealousy and envy. Do not identify with its thoughts. Draw the line, disassociate yourself from it, and deny it. Do not let it live. Do not even let it suffer. Do not let it whine. Do not let it pity itself. Do not give it one moment of life. Just deny it. The Lord said, "If anyone desires to come after Me, let him deny himself, and take up his cross." Terminate the self. The cross means termination. It does not mean a kind of suffering in which the self is still alive. No, we can be rid of the self, done with the self, by terminating it in the realm of the spirit.

It is crucial that we experience this dealing with the self because it really touches the enemy. In the book of Job, the enemy is accusing, "Does Job fear God for nothing?" In other words, "Is Job pure? Is he serving the Lord from a pure heart? Or is he serving for what the self can gain from it, for what benefits the self?" Then all the dealings came in Job's life. And out of the dealings the enemy was dealt with and the Lord's testimony came forth.

In Revelation 12:10-11 again the accuser is there: [10] "The accuser of our brethren, who accused them before our God day and night, has been cast down. [11] And they overcame him…" These overcomers, called the man-child (v. 5), are the stronger part of the woman, brought forth in Revelation 12. Verse 11 says, "And they [the man-child] overcame him because of the blood of the Lamb and because of the word of their testimony, and they did not love their soul-life to the death." This means they did not preserve their soul-life, they did not keep it.

By not loving the soul-life, or the self, even to the death, the overcomers give the archangel Michael the ground in the heavens to throw the devil out of the heavens to the earth (Rev. 12:7-9), and they also give the Lord a way to consummate everything into the kingdom: "Now salvation, and strength, and the kingdom of our God, and the authority of His Christ have come" (12:10). Why? Because there is a group of overcomers on the earth who have not only enjoyed the blood and given the word of their testimony, but they have dealt with the self to the uttermost. They did not love their soul-life. They did not preserve the self. Brothers and sisters, this is why dealing with the self deals with the enemy — because it touches his base of operation.

The blindness of the hidden self

After exposing and dealing with opinion, reasoning, and being subjective, we come to a further dealing — the dealing with our hidden self. The hidden self is a unique kind of self because it is hidden from us, just as the self of Job was hidden from him. He did not know himself. He did not know his vindicating, justifying, hidden self. Why? Because he was blinded to it by his goodness, by his spirituality, by all that was upright in him. Job 1:1 says, "There was a man in the land of Uz, whose name was Job; and that man was blameless and upright, and one who feared God and shunned evil." This verse shows that concerning the hidden self, there was no conscious fault with Job. He was "blameless and upright." Other translations use the word "perfect" to describe Job. This means that with this person there was no conscious problem, no conscious fault.

When we are talking about the hidden self, we are not talking about something that is so obvious to us. We may be a person that is just like Job, perfect and upright. And that is part of our problem — we are blinded to this hidden self because we are occupied with the fact that there cannot be found in our living a conscious fault. And if we do become conscious of a fault in our living, we take care of it. We repent or we deal with it.

In spiritual experience, there is a shallow dealing and a deeper dealing. A person who deals in a shallow way deals only on the level of the feeling of his conscience. For example, if your conscience testifies that you are wrong about something, you make it right so that you have nothing on your conscience. Of course, this is proper and right (Acts 24:16). But it is possible that we could be a person taking care of the feeling in our conscience, eliminating every conscious fault in our living, and *still* be buried and enmeshed in the hidden self. This hidden self then becomes a base for Satan and for his accusation.

We have seen that with Job there was no conscious fault. This is one of the characteristics of the hidden self. Job 1:1 says that Job was "one who feared God and shunned evil." He turned from evil. This means that he not only had no conscious fault, but he was exercised to turn away from evil and to turn to the Lord. Can you imagine a person with this kind of condition still being enwrapped in his self?

Factors that cover the hidden self

With Job there was no conscious fault, and he was also exercised to fear the Lord and to turn away from evil. Yet we have seen that these things can be blinders to the hidden self. Being blessed by God can also be a blinder to the hidden self. Job was obviously blessed by God. Job 1:3 says, "Also, his possessions were seven thousand sheep, three thousand camels, five hundred yoke of oxen, five hundred female donkeys, and a very large household." That means he was fully blessed. Yet again, having the Lord's blessing resting in a kind of outward way can be a blinder to the hidden self. This was the case with Job.

The prosperity gospel is perpetrated today in so many places — through radio and television. What you hear predominately is "To be blessed is to be rich." Some preach that God's blessing is to have numerous expensive automobiles. They say this is what it means to have the blessing of God. How blinding is this kind of religion.

Of course, we may not be wealthy, but we may have a little answer to prayer, we may have some success in preaching the gospel, or we may be materially blessed by the Lord sending us a better-paying job. We may feel like the Lord's blessing is really with us. Yet all the time this is blinding us from the hidden self. So these are some of the factors that cover the hidden self.

Job also had a good reputation. Job 1:3 says, "This man was the greatest of all the people of the East." Our reputation has to do with how people feel about us, what they think about us. They may praise and compliment us. Some of these compliments may even come to our own ears. For example, someone may say to you, "Your testimony in the church meeting really helped me," or "Oh, your prayer just released the meeting," or "Brother, your sharing of the Word was so anointed." All these things said about us can be a big factor to blind us from seeing our hidden self with its secret pride. A good reputation can also feed and support our self-vindication, making us less entreatable, less open to God's light on ourselves.

In addition to all of Job's personal attributes, he also had an exceptional family. We may take pride in our family, in our stock or lineage. Perhaps we are proud of our children and find ourselves often speaking of their achievements. So even the estimate we have of our family can have a blinding effect on us, keeping us from seeing our hidden self.

When God comes in to touch this hidden self, He may touch our family or He may touch our reputation. He touches whatever outward blessings occupy our heart. He comes in to deal with something deeper in us, something enmeshed in us, something built up and fortified by all these outward things. God came into Job's life with these definite dealings.

The inward activity of the hidden self

Job chapter 29 reveals the inward activity of Job's hidden self. In this chapter alone, he speaks of *me, I, my,* and *myself* nearly 50 times. If you read chapters 29—31 you will discover that these personal pronouns are used by Job over 150 times. This shows us that in Job's thought, everything centered around him. He did not see his hidden self. At this time he was not yet abhorring himself; rather, he was *in* himself.

In Job 29 we have a detailed description of the inward activity of the hidden self, that is, how it behaves. In verses 2-5 Job says, [2] "Oh, that I were as in months past, as in the days when God watched over me; [3] when His lamp shone upon my head, and when by His light I walked through darkness; [4] just as I was in the days of my prime, when the friendly counsel of God was over my tent; [5] when the Almighty was yet with me." Here Job is fantasizing about all of his past spiritual experiences. This is the activity of the hidden self. We fantasize, creating images in our mind about all our spiritual experiences. This is what Job was doing in these first few verses when he said, "His lamp shone upon my head," "by His light I walked through darkness," "the friendly counsel of God was over my tent," and "the Almighty was yet with me."

In our own past, we may have received the baptism of the Holy Spirit, or we may have experienced other manifestations of the gifts of the Spirit. Now we may fantasize about the events, saying, "God was with me here," and "God was with me there." A person who fantasizes about his spiritual experiences is living in a hidden self that is a base for Satan. This is what Job was doing in chapters 29—31.

To fantasize is to create images in our mind, imaginations in our mind, even using the raw material of our past spiritual experiences. Brothers and sisters, the reason that a blameless, faultless saint can open his mouth and say something that has the taste of death and the taste of self is that something is wrong inwardly, something is not quite right. This is often due to a self that is hidden and that fantasizes about spiritual experiences. Outwardly there is nothing wrong — he is a good brother or she is a good sister, having no fault, exercised, turning, even blessed. But inwardly the self is hidden there, indulging in a mental replay of past spiritual experiences.

Job 29:5 says, "when my children were around me." This is Job fantasizing about his family. The hidden self in us likes to think pridefully about our children, about our family, about those closest to us. For example, we may think, "How wonderful my children are in comparison to others." The self fantasizes over these things in a hidden way.

Then Job was reflecting about how others respected him. In verses 7-11 he says, [7] "When I went out to the gate by the city, when I took my seat in the open square, [8] the young men saw me and hid, and the aged arose and stood; [9] the princes refrained from talking, and put their hand on their mouth; [10] the voice of nobles was hushed, and their tongue stuck to the roof of their mouth. [11] When the ear heard, then it blessed me, and when the eye saw, then it approved me." In other words, Job was saying, "I'm respected. Others look up to me. Others defer to me." To live in this feeling of being respected by others is to live in the hidden self.

Job also muses upon his service. In verses 12-13 he says, [12] "Because I delivered the poor who cried out, and the fatherless and he who had no helper. [13] The blessing of a perishing man came upon me, and I caused the widow's heart to sing for joy." Then he continues his fantasy in verses 15-17: [15] "I was eyes to the blind, and I was feet to the lame. [16] I was a father to the poor, and I searched out the case that I did not know. [17] I broke the fangs of the wicked, and plucked the victim from his teeth." So Job defended the poor and did all these other things in service to the Lord. This sounds just like 1 Corinthians 13:3: "And though I bestow all my goods to feed the poor, and though I give my body to be burned, but have not love, it profits me nothing." Here the reason there is no profit in doing these things is that the source is the self.

So Job's hidden self was being fed through serving, through others' respect, through his family, and through his spiritual experiences. Then he waxes eloquent in Job 29:20-25: [20] "My glory was fresh within me, and my bow was renewed in my hand. [21] Men listened to me and waited, and kept silence for my counsel. [22] After my words they did not speak again, and my speech settled on them as dew. [23] They waited for me as for the rain, and they opened their mouth wide as for the spring rain. [24] I smiled on them when they had no confidence, and the light of my countenance they did not cast down. [25] I chose the way for them, and sat as chief; so I dwelt as a king in the army, as one who comforts mourners." This all means that in his hidden self, Job was coddling feelings of "I am important" and "I impress others." In his thought, others were awestruck by his person and all that he had done. But then God's hand touched Job. God's hand came to deal with that hidden self, to take away everything that supported the inward hidden activity of the self.

After passing through calamity upon calamity, in chapter 30 Job was wallowing in self-pity. Then in chapter 31 Job continues to justify himself, recounting how good his behavior has been in all kinds of situations. For example, he says in verses 5-6, [5] "If I have walked with falsehood, or if my foot has

hastened to deceit, ⁶ let me be weighed in a just balance, that
God may know my integrity." Here Job is coming out to
justify the self, asserting that if in anything he had acted
unrighteously, he would have properly dealt with the Lord. In
verses 9-10 he seeks to justify himself in relation to his moral
standards: ⁹ "If my heart has been enticed by a woman, or if
I have lurked at my neighbor's door, ¹⁰ then let my wife grind
for another." Then in verses 13-14 he vindicates himself in
relation to his ethical standards: ¹³ "If I have despised the cause
of my manservant or my maidservant when they complained
against me, ¹⁴ what then shall I do when God rises up?" Next,
in verses 16 and following, Job parades his philanthropy: ¹⁶ "If
I have kept the poor from their desire, or caused the eyes of the
widow to fail, ¹⁷ or eaten my morsel by myself, so that the
fatherless may not eat of it…¹⁹ If I have seen anyone perish for
lack of clothing, or any poor man without covering…" Thus,
throughout Job 31 we read, "If I have" done this or that. Then
Job follows each hypothetical case with his own view of a just
retribution.

Job's words expose that the hidden self projects all these
things in the mind. Rather than openly acknowledging, "I am
nothing; I am no good," the self is continually coming out to
defend itself. So Job speaks all these defenses and vindications in chapter 31. Then this chapter closes with "The words
of Job are ended" (v. 40).

God's dealings over a justifying self

Job 32:1 summarizes all the preceding chapters by saying

that Job was "righteous in his own eyes." Then verse 2 says, "Then the wrath of Elihu, the son of Barachel the Buzite, of the family of Ram, was aroused against Job; his wrath was aroused because he justified himself rather than God." So the problem with Job was that he justified himself, vindicated himself, rather than God. This he did until God came to him toward the end of the book of Job in chapter 38. At that point God spoke to him out of a whirlwind. Thus, at the beginning of the book of Job, God came in a calamity; and at the end of the book, He came in a whirlwind.

Brothers and sisters, there is no way to deal with this hidden self apart from calamities and whirlwinds. So this is how God deals with it. He comes in with calamities — calamities in your family, in your job, in your relationships. And He comes in with whirlwinds — things you cannot understand, things that suddenly appear in your life with no explanation. These things have the effect of whirling you around. This is the kind of dealing God measures out to these pompous, hidden selves that are nourishing themselves on their own spiritual experiences, on their service for the Lord, and on all their fantasies and self-justification.

The self is so neatly nestled and settled down in us like a stronghold that it seems we cannot know ourself. Yet we need to know ourself. We need to know that we are rotten to the core, that we are nothing, so that we could deny the self and trust in God, living from Him alone as our source. But this does not happen apart from the Lord's coming in with severity and allowing Satan to touch us. This is exactly what the Lord allowed with Paul in 2 Corinthians 12:7. Paul says, "And lest

I should be exalted above measure by the abundance of the revelations, a thorn in the flesh was given to me, a messenger of Satan to buffet me, lest I be exalted above measure." The Lord allowed a messenger of Satan to come in with a whirlwind, with a calamity. Why? Because of Paul's hidden self, his pride. Yes, the Lord did give the revelations, and Paul had "the abundance" of them. But there was a tendency in Paul to rest in that, to settle in that. So the Lord had to allow what Paul called "a thorn in the flesh." No one knows what the thorn was, which is sovereign. Though some have speculated about what it was, the point is, it had its effect; its purpose was fulfilled in Paul (2 Cor. 12:8-10).

In the book of Job the Lord came in a whirlwind to the hidden self, to the proud self that was hidden there. The only way to deal with the secretly proud person is calamity, whirlwind, and thorns. Praise the Lord that He does not hold back what is needed. He does not leave us to ourselves. He comes in our environment in the most unusual way to draw out our reasoning to the uttermost, to draw out our analytical mind. He comes in a way that causes us to want to vindicate and explain ourselves.

DEALING WITH THE HIDDEN SELF

Being absolute about God's sovereignty in our environments

If we want the Lord to deal with the most hidden self, we have to be absolute in our acceptance of our environment from Him. This is crucial. In Matthew 11:25 the Lord Jesus absolutely accepted the environment the Father had allowed: "At that time Jesus answered and said, I thank You, Father, Lord of heaven and earth." The words "at that time" have a specific meaning. The time here, when Jesus was responding and answering with thanks to the Father and confessing that He was the "Lord of heaven and earth," was a time when Jesus was defamed and His ministry was rejected.

In the previous verses in Matthew 11, people were saying that John "has a demon" (v. 18), and they were calling the Lord "a gluttonous man and a winebibber" (v. 19). Then in verse 20 the Lord began to "upbraid" the cities because they had rejected His word and had not repented. Humanly speaking, the environment of the Lord Jesus at that moment was miserable. We would think it was the exact opposite of anything that would evoke a confession of thanks to the Father. Yet verse 25 says, "At that time Jesus answered and said, I thank You, Father, Lord of heaven and earth."

Answering our environment

Our environment demands an answer, a response. If you have to answer your environment, how do you answer it? How do you respond to it? When everything was against the Lord Jesus, He addressed the Father as "Lord of heaven and earth." This means the Lord categorically accepted all the defaming, all the rejection — all the events taking place around Him — as being one hundred percent from the sovereignty of the Father's hand. By calling the Father "Lord of heaven and earth," Jesus is acknowledging that nothing has "gone wrong" on the earth, but instead everything is as it should be. He is not hoping for a better day, not escaping the environment; but He is giving an absolute response to the Father about the environment that is against Him. He is thanking the Father for it, praising Him for it.

Then in verse 25 the Lord Jesus further acknowledges and submits to the Father's sovereignty and His will: "because You have hidden these things from the wise and intelligent and have revealed them to babes." In other words, "Father, You have not made a mistake. You allowed all these things — the rejecting, the defaming. This is from You. There are no mistakes here. This is under Your control."

Brothers and sisters, the hidden self will never be exposed and dealt with until we take our environment absolutely — until we take our husband or wife absolutely, until we take the brothers and sisters absolutely. There cannot be even one inch of reservation in us — of thinking that others are wrong or that we are not being treated fairly. As long as there is just one little bit of blame toward someone or any self-vindication, Satan is still there lurking in our being in this hidden self.

The Lord Jesus dealt with His environment by taking it by the horns, so to speak. At the very time when He was rejected, called "a winebibber" and "a gluttonous man," insulted to the uttermost, He answered and said, "I thank You, Father, Lord of heaven and earth." That means, "Father, You are sovereign over the insult. You are sovereign over this environment." Then Jesus continues, "because You have hidden these things from the wise and intelligent and have revealed them to babes. Yes, Father, for so it seemed good in Your sight." That means,

"Father, I am saying 'Yes' to Your will. This is Your pleasure to insult Me. It is Your pleasure that I am rejected. It is Your pleasure that these cities have rejected My speaking. You have done it. You have hidden these things from them. Yes, Father, for so it seemed good in Your sight." This means the Lord Jesus unreservedly accepted the will of God in His environment.

Then in Matthew 11:27 the Lord says, "All things have been delivered to Me by My Father, and no one knows the Son except the Father. Nor does anyone know the Father except the Son, and he to whom the Son wills to reveal Him." That is to say, "The Father is doing this revealing. He reveals these things to whomever He chooses." These verses show us that the Lord was living before the Father, out of the source of the Father, and not out of Himself. Because He was living from the Father, there was no place for any vindication of Himself, for any blaming of others. Unlike Job, the Lord Jesus was a person under the hand of the Father, whose attitude and response to His environment was one of absolute acceptance. Nothing was refused or looked on as a mistake. Nothing was despised. All was accepted as from the Father's unerring hand.

Taking His yoke and learning from Him

If our hidden self is to be dealt with when the calamities come, when the whirlwinds come, when the thorns come, when the bizarre things come — and they do come many times in our daily life — our response, our answer, to that environment is critical. It is critical whether or not we will take the yoke. In Matthew 11:28-29, the Lord shows us the result of taking the yoke: ²⁸ "Come to Me, all you who labor and are heavy laden, and I will give you rest. ²⁹ Take My yoke upon you and learn from Me, for I am meek and lowly in heart, and you will find rest for your souls."

A yoke is what is laid upon two oxen. How those oxen respond to that yoke makes all the difference. They can resist the yoke, rubbing against it, trying to break away from it. Then the yoke is harsh. It is bitter. It hurts. But if the oxen simply submit to the yoke, all is well. What is the "yoke" the Lord is speaking of here in Matthew? The yoke is what God has put on you. He has put your husband or your wife on you. He has put your children on you. He has put your finances on you. The yoke is the will of God in our experience.

How we respond to the yoke that God puts on us will make all the difference in how much our self gets dealt with. Whether or not we take up the yoke — the calamities, the whirlwinds, the unexpected things that the Lord sends — determines whether our self gets touched or remains intact. To take up this yoke means to willingly accept the environment. This is crucial. In Psalm 40:8 the Lord says through David in spirit, "I delight to do Your will, O my God." This means that we do not hold any reservation toward God and what He has allowed. We do not hold the view that there is something better that could be measured out to us, or that God could work in a different way. No! No! No! A thousand times, No! Your dear wife is the best that God could send you. And your husband is the best that you could have. And the brothers you serve with are the best. Everything is the best that it could be.

The Lord says, "Take My yoke." It is what He has laid "upon you." Take it upon you. And after you have taken it, He says, "Learn from Me." It is as if He is saying, "Stay under it and start consulting with Me now. You are under the yoke. Do not resist it. Do not try to get out of it. Take it. Accept it absolutely, just as I took the yoke. I said, 'Thank You, Father, for the rejection. Praise You for the insults. Praise You for the lack of response. Praise You for everything against Me, Father. You are Lord of heaven and earth. Thank You. It was well-pleasing to You.' " This was the Lord taking the yoke. He just took it and He praised and thanked the Father for it. So now we take the yoke upon us and begin learning from Him.

The meaning of taking the yoke

To take the Lord's yoke means to inwardly stay with Him in spirit and consult with Him. Do not consult with your mind. Do not use your mind to consider or deliberate about your environment. You have to learn from the Lord. He says, "Learn from Me." So you begin asking, "Lord, what is in this calamity for me? Lord, what is in me that You are trying to touch by allowing this whirlwind to come?" Now stay under the yoke. Do not resist it. The Lord is saying, "Inwardly learn from Me. Inwardly touch Me. Inwardly consult with Me." Do not resort to your mind and say, "This should not have happened." Do not hope for a better day. Do not blame. Instead, begin learning. Begin touching Him. Go inward to the Spirit.

"Learn from Me," He says, "for I am meek and lowly in heart." To be meek means not to resist any opposition. So the Lord is saying, "I am a Person who does not resist. If you touch Me and learn from Me, if you stay in the Spirit when you are under the yoke, then you will not resist. You will just stay there. You will lie there. You will simply say 'Amen.' You will say, 'Yes, Father. It seemed good to You. It seemed pleasing to You.' This means you will learn from Me by touching Me. If you touch Me, you will find that I am not resisting. I am not fighting. Also I am lowly. That means I am not proud. I am not asserting Myself. I am not vindicating or defending Myself. I am not trying to hold the self up. I am the One who is not resisting and who is lowly in heart." This is the Lord Jesus in Matthew 11:25-29.

In our experience of the Lord, the self is dealt with when we do not resist the environment He sends. We simply stay snuggled under the yoke, not resisting it, but learning from Him. We learn His meekness, His resignation, His absolute surrender. We learn His lowliness — that there is no place for the self or pride or vindication.

Then Matthew 11:29-30 says, [29] "and you will find rest for your souls. [30] For My yoke is easy and My burden is light." This means that when we are in the Spirit, His yoke is pleasant, it is gentle, it is wonderful. Regardless of what yoke is laid upon us by the hand of God, when we learn from the Lord and stay with Him, we have an altogether different response. But the moment we step out of that realm of "take My yoke" and "learn from Me," everything is harsh, bitter, and cruel. You cannot understand why things are happening the way they are.

You have no answers. That is the realm of the mind. So to have this self dealt with, we need to come to the Lord, stay with Him, and rest in Him.

Inwardly keeping the Sabbath

The Lord gives rest to our soul. In our experience this means we inwardly keep the Sabbath. In the next chapter of Matthew, the Lord purposely broke the outward Sabbath (12:1-8) because He had ushered in the keeping of the inward Sabbath, the inward rest (11:25-27). This means that if we accept His yoke, if we take it up and do not resist our environment, the Lord can expose this hidden, law-keeping self and deal with it. So we stay with the Lord, learn from Him, and keep the inward Sabbath. This means we do not work (Exo. 20:8-11), we do not gather sticks (Num. 15:32-36), we do not bear any burdens (Jer. 17:21-22), we do not pick up anything (John 5:9-10). We inwardly open ourselves to rest in the Lord. Tell Him, "Lord, You are doing it. You are operating. You are changing. You are transferring. And You do it as I keep the inward Sabbath."

Though the Lord broke the outward Sabbath in Matthew 12, He was keeping the inward Sabbath. What He did first of all was to have a feast (v. 1). When we keep the inward Sabbath, we feast. While keeping the inward Sabbath, the Lord also healed a withered hand (vv. 10, 13), and cast out demons (v. 22). So when we stay with the Lord, learn from Him, and rest in Him, we enjoy a feast, we get healed, and we get rid of demons. This all happens by our keeping the inward

Sabbath. To learn what the inward Sabbath is you have to know about the outward Sabbath. On the outward Sabbath you do not do any work (Exo. 31:14). You cannot bear a burden, you cannot carry anything. A number of years ago when we visited Israel, we observed that in Jerusalem on the Sabbath everything stops. All the businesses close. The streets are empty. No one does anything. No one bears anything. That is the outward Sabbath.

Today as believers we enjoy the inward Sabbath. We simply keep ourselves resting in the Lord: "Lord, I cannot change myself, I cannot even transfer myself. I am just here under the yoke. I am learning from You. Lord, You are meek. You are not resisting. Lord, You are lowly. You are not vindicating Yourself. You are not exalting Yourself." And then He gives rest to the soul.

The way for this transfer to take place is by absolutely accepting our environment and taking up the yoke with "Yes, Father," and "Praise the Lord!" and "This is Your sovereignty." Do not resist. And then while you are under the yoke, stay open to the Lord and learn from Him. Let His disposition be wrought into your being, and just inwardly rest and trust Him. Feast with Him, and in that feasting and enjoyment there is the healing and the casting out of demons. This all happens when we stay with the Lord in the Spirit.

May the Lord deal not only with our opinion, our reasoning, and our being subjective, but also with our hidden self in every dimension, in every manifestation. This hidden self is there in our being, manifesting itself in secret pride, fantasies, imaginations, and self-importance. It is also buried or cloaked in our religious practices. In Luke 18:11-12, the hidden self is manifested in the Pharisee who "stood and prayed thus with himself, 'God, I thank You that I am not like other men — extortioners, unjust, adulterers, or even as this tax collector. I fast twice a week; I give tithes of all that I possess.' " This shows that the hidden self is buried in religious practices. It can be buried in Bible reading, in praying, in preaching the gospel — buried in all kinds of religious activities — and we are blinded to it.

This blinded hidden self is also depicted in Luke 15 with the prodigal son's older brother, who was staying at home and musing upon his good record. The hidden self likes to think about its good history over the years — how spiritual it has been, how consistent, how few faults it has had, how few outward problems. So while the younger son was out in the pig's pen, his older brother was home priding himself on how commendable his record was and how wonderful he was. Eventually he became the biggest problem because his hidden self with its anger, self-righteousness, blame, self-pity, and envy was undealt with and just grew and grew (vv. 28-30).

May the Lord deal thoroughly with the hidden self so that there will be no more ground for the enemy, Satan. By this dealing, the enemy will be uprooted and the Lord will transfer us completely into Himself as our source. May this transfer be effected in each of us.

7

THE CROSS AND THE HIDDEN SELF

God's intention in our regeneration

God's intention in regenerating us is that we would have a transfer of the source of our living out of our self *into* Christ — so that we would live *to* Him. For this transfer to take place there must be the dealing with our self. We need to observe all the verses in the Gospels where the Lord says that in order to come after Him, we must deny ourself, take up our cross, and follow Him. He repeats this many times. And often in the same context He says that if a man desires to save his soul-life, he will lose it; but if a man will lose his soul-life for the Lord's sake, he will find it (Matt. 10:38-39; 16:24-25; Mark 8:34-35; Luke 9:23-24; 14:26-27; 17:33; John 12:25).

In these kinds of verses the Lord shows us that our experience of Him involves a transfer of source — from living in our own soul-life to finding the proper function of our soul-life. This happens not by saving or preserving the self-life of our soul, but by losing it. To have a transfer out of the soul into the spirit, we must experientially lose something. We must lose our soul-life. This includes losing our way of doing things, our way of choosing and determining things, and our way of proceeding. By losing the soul-life in these ways, we will then find it.

How We Preserve the Self

Preserving the self by keeping a false peace

Matthew 10:38-39 is one of the passages in the Gospels in which the Lord talks about our taking the cross and following Him, and losing our soul-life in order to find it. In the context of these verses, the Lord also gives us real-life situations for the practical working out of the cross and the losing of our soul-life. For example, in Matthew 10:34-39 the Lord says, [34] "Do not think that I came to bring peace on earth. I did not come to bring peace but a sword. [35] For I have come to set a man against his father, a daughter against her mother, and a daughter-in-law against her mother-in-law. [36] And a man's foes will be those of his own household. [37] He who loves father or mother more than Me is not worthy of Me. And he who loves son or daughter more than Me is not worthy of Me." And then the Lord says, [38] "And he who does not take his cross and follow after Me is not worthy of Me. [39] He who finds his soul-life will lose it, and he who loses his soul-life for My sake will find it."

In these verses the Lord makes the losing of our soul-life very practical. He shows us how to effect the transfer from our soul to our spirit. The way is to not preserve our soul by keeping a false peace with others, particularly our closest relatives. The reason a person is not faithful to follow the Lord's life and repudiate the self is that he is trying in himself to keep things calm and peaceful and not cause any discord in relationships. However, by keeping *this* kind of peace you deny the Lord and do not lose your soul-life.

The Lord's word here is very strong. He did not come to bring peace on the earth, but a sword. What He means is that in order for us to be transferred out of our self into the spirit, we must be willing in the most intimate relationships — husband and wife, father and mother — not to live pretentiously or falsely. Rather than keep a false peace and deny the Lord, we can be faithful to follow the Lord and not preserve our soul-life with our relatives, including our spouse, our children, and our in-laws. All these relationships are closely related to the natural life. If we live according to the natural life and preserve a false peace, we will never be transferred into the realm of the Spirit.

In some situations, for a brother or a sister to be faithful to their spirit requires speaking the truth in love to their spouse. So they follow the Lord rather than disobeying Him and preserving the soul for the sake of keeping an outward peace. To be persons living by the Lord's life will at times mean a sword. It may mean being rejected. It may mean that some get offended because they do not want Christ and the experience of His life. This does not mean that we are to purposely offend people. But it means that in our experience offenses come when we follow the Lord as He transfers us out of our self into the spirit. Of course, in our relationships there is the genuine peace that we experience by letting Christ arbitrate, or rule, in our hearts (Col. 3:15). But in Matthew chapter 10 the Lord is speaking of keeping a false peace with others in order to preserve our self, our soul-life.

It is so precious when saints are faithful to the Lord, even when it means a sword in the relationships that are closest to the natural life. Oh, brothers and sisters, we need to be faithful to the Lord's life — faithful to His life in our relationships with one another — so that the Lord has a way on this earth.

Preserving the self by the natural thought

In the context of the Lord's speaking about losing the soul-life in Matthew 16:24-25, He says to Peter, "You are not setting your mind on the things of God, but on the things of men" (v. 23). This means that we preserve our self, our soul-life, by living in our natural thought. A lot of self is preserved by natural thinking. So in these verses we see how the self is preserved by our setting our mind not on the things of God, but on the things of men.

Preserving the self by resting on a few experiences

In Luke 9:23 the Lord says, "If anyone desires to come after Me, let him deny himself, and take up his cross *daily,* and follow Me." This verse reveals that the self is preserved when we isolate the experience of the cross to only a few things, rather than taking up our cross daily. We preserve the self by applying the cross merely in an intermittent way, only occasionally. When the Lord says, "Take up your cross daily," He is telling us that the cross is a daily matter. It is a way of life. The self must be terminated daily. The cross is the way we live as we follow the Lord.

Preserving the self by clinging to material things

In Luke 17:33 when the Lord speaks about preserving the soul-life, it is in the context of reminding us about Lot's wife, whose heart was attached to material things (vv. 31-32). Brothers and sisters, the way we often preserve our self is by our entanglement with material things — with our possessions. In Genesis 19:26 Lot's wife looked back toward Sodom when she was supposed to be fleeing that city. When she looked back, she became a pillar of salt — a symbol of shame. Why? Because her soul-life was strongly attached to something material, some goods in the house. This is why when the Lord begins to deal with our self as our source, He often touches a material thing that we are attached to. From this we can see that another way the self is preserved is by holding on to material things.

Preserving the self by seeking man's popularity

In John 12:24 the Lord says, "Unless a grain of wheat falls into the ground and dies, it abides alone; but if it dies, it produces much fruit." Then He continues in verse 25 by saying, "He who loves his soul-life will lose it, and he who hates his soul-life in this world will keep it unto eternal life." The context of these verses was a time of great popularity for the Lord. Both the Jews and the Greeks were seeking Him (vv. 12-22). Everyone wanted to see Him. But rather than preserve His soul-life by seeking man's praise and popularity, the Lord said, "Unless a grain of wheat falls into the ground and dies, it abides alone." This means He was choosing death, not popularity, not man's praise. He did not love His soul-life or preserve it by living on popularity and man's praise. Instead, He hated His soul-life in this world and did not preserve it. This shows us that our soul-life is preserved by living on man's praise, living for popularity, living to be well-thought-of, even to be sought after. The soul is preserved in these kinds of ways.

Soul = natural life worldly life

How to deal with a preserving self

From all these verses in the Gospels, we can see that apart from the cross and denying the self, the soul-life will be preserved. The way for the source of the self to be terminated is by denying our self and taking up the cross. To deny the self is to disregard it as your source. Do not interact with it. Do not consult with it. We are not qualified to handle the self with the self. Indeed, in Christ we are no longer obligated to it (Rom. 8:12). Instead, touch the source of the Spirit. It is the Spirit that supplies self-denying power (Gal. 5:24-25).

To take up the cross is first to discover the willingness for the cross in your spirit by crying, "Abba! Father!" (Mark 14:36, 38; Phil. 2:13). Second, it is to learn how to merge with the inclinations of the cross that are intrinsic to the leading of the Spirit (Rom. 8:13-14). Third, taking up the cross is to obey the supplied impulse of life to interrupt the activity of the self. Do not wait for the self to be agreeable to die. Let the cross operate on it in the midst of its struggle to live. The experience of the cross is not a long, drawn-out process. No, the cross in the Spirit today is already an accomplished fact and reality. It only needs to be executed by our touching the Spirit. This is why Paul speaks in the imperative mood in Colossians 3:5 when he says, "Therefore put to death your members which are on the earth." This is execution. The "therefore" in this verse is based upon the crucifying activity that is integral to the "Christ who is our life" in verse 4. That is, the nature of the "life" in verse 4 is *crucifying* life in verse 5. In other words, life supplies death — death to the self.

To "take up the cross" under the new covenant economy is to take up what is supplied to us in the Spirit and to obey the impulses of the crucifying life that are written on our heart and on our mind (Heb. 8:10). Because the law is written on our heart, the nature of our experience of the cross is an inward fellowship with the Lord. Obeying the Lord to take up the cross is not a lonely step on a solitary spiritual journey. Yet this may be the impression left in our mind by some of the mystics of the past. But under the new covenant, to obey the Lord in the way of the cross means fellowship and intimacy with Him (Rom. 8:28). It is "the *fellowship* of *His* sufferings" (Phil. 3:10). It is a paradoxical and simultaneous experience of being "killed all day long," while nothing is "able to separate us from the love of God which is in Christ Jesus our Lord" (Rom. 8:36-39).

In Philippians 2:8 Paul describes the Lord's experience of absolute obedience related to the cross: "And being found in appearance as a man, He humbled Himself and became obedient to the point of death, even the death of the cross." Then in verses 12-14 Paul continues with the believers' experience of the cross: [12] "Therefore, my beloved, as you have always obeyed, not as in my presence only, but now much more in my absence, work out your own salvation with fear and trembling; [13] for it is God who works in you both to will and to do for His good pleasure. [14] Do all things without murmurings and reasonings." Murmurings and reasonings are two expressions of the undealt-with self. They are exactly the opposite of taking up the cross. So by this process of working out our own salvation, we will be experientially transferred out of the self into the spirit. This transfer takes place by obedience to God's supplied life operating within us to deny the source of our self.

The Hidden Self in the Book of Job

We have seen that the book of Job is about dealing with the hidden self. Indeed, this book in the Bible unveils the hidden self in a detailed way. It describes a man who was upright, blameless, and apparently very good in every respect. But within him there was the hidden self with its self-righteousness, self-confidence, and self-vindication. So Job represents a person who is not on the level of dealing with sin and the flesh in its outward, gross forms. Here is a man who is not practicing anything outwardly sinful or fleshly. Yet his self is still there, hidden from him. He is blinded to his self because he is righteous in his own eyes. Thus, the book of Job gives us the full picture of self in its hidden form.

Self-reflection as the main activity of the hidden self

In Job chapter 29 we find the main activity of the hidden self — self-reflection. Self-reflection means looking at yourself, considering yourself. The hidden self with this kind of activity is the very embodiment of Satan, because the very nature and essence of Satan is self-reflection. A synonym for Satan is pride. Pride can be defined as being lifted up and reflecting upon oneself. In chapter 29 this is what was exposed in Job.

Reflection upon the past

Job was filled with self-reflection by looking upon his past. Such activity is related to the devil within our being. When we reflect upon ourself — when this hidden self finds its pleasure in fantasies and thoughts and imaginations about itself — we are merging with the devil. We are becoming one with the devil.

The devil was not always the devil. He was once a beautiful archangel, who is described in Ezekiel 28. Verse 12 says, "Son of man, raise a lamentation over the king of Tyre, and say to him, Thus says the Lord GOD…" In this verse, "the king of Tyre" represents and typifies Satan. Then verses 12-15 continue to describe him: [12] "You were the signet of perfection, full of wisdom and perfect in beauty. [13] You were in Eden, the garden of God; every precious stone was your covering, carnelian, topaz, and jasper, chrysolite, beryl, and onyx, sapphire, carbuncle, and emerald; and wrought in gold were your settings and your engravings. On the day that you were created they were prepared. [14] With an anointed guardian cherub I placed you; you were on the holy mountain of God; in the midst of the stones of fire you walked. [15] You were blameless in your ways from the day you were created, till iniquity was found in you" (RSV). Then verse 17 says, "Your heart was proud because of your beauty." That means this archangel, called Lucifer, began to engage in reflection upon himself.

Isaiah 14:13-14 reveals that the result of Lucifer's self-reflection was rebellion: [13] "For you have said in your heart: I will ascend into heaven, I will exalt my throne above the stars of God; I will also sit on the mount of the congregation on the farthest sides of the north; [14] I will ascend above the heights of the clouds, I will be like the Most High." So Lucifer's rebellion against God and against his God-ordained position in the universe came out of reflecting upon his beauty.

Lucifer became the devil by self-reflection — by fantasizing about the self, looking at the self, enjoying the self, reflecting upon the self. The main activity of the hidden self is our self-awareness with its self-reflection. To indulge in this is to give the devil a place in our being. The stronghold of the devil is self-reflection. You may indulge in self-reflection by standing in front of the mirror looking at yourself, enjoying this look at yourself. Today in the world there is so much emphasis on physical appearance that sometimes women will stand in front of a mirror for hours to beautify their face and to fix their hair. People spend hours just looking, just reflecting. Of course, this does not mean that we should be careless or sloppy in our appearance. But consider how much self-reflection there is related to physical appearance. The activity of the hidden self is expressed in this kind of self-reflection.

Job 29:1-2 says, [1]"Job further continued his discourse, and said: [2] Oh, that I were as in months past, as in the days when God watched over me." At this point Job began to reflect upon all his past experiences. Particularly in verses 1-6 he reflects upon his spiritual experiences of the past — the protection he had from the Lord, God's light, the fellowship he had with the Lord, the Lord's blessing to him with his children, and the rich supply that he enjoyed. In verse 6 he describes this rich supply: "My steps were bathed with cream, and the rock poured out rivers of oil for me!" So in this section of the Word, Job is reflecting upon the past, particularly his spiritual experiences. He engaged in this kind of reflection upon past experiences rather than taking up the cross in the present. Instead of facing his present situation and experiencing the cross to terminate his self, he began to fantasize and to reflect upon his spiritual experiences.

Reflection upon our reputation

In Job 29:7-11 Job begins to reflect on his reputation and the respect that he once had. He says, [7] "When I went out to the gate by the city, when I took my seat in the open square, [8] the young men saw me and hid, and the aged arose and stood;

[9] the princes refrained from talking, and put their hand on their mouth; [10] the voice of nobles was hushed, and their tongue stuck to the roof of their mouth. [11] When the ear heard, then it blessed me, and when the eye saw, then it approved me."

This reflecting upon his reputation and upon the respect that he once had is the activity of the hidden self. It includes reflecting upon our image and what people think of us. It is being occupied with the self, reflecting upon the self, instead of enjoying God. Often in our experience, we are reflecting upon the self rather than living in the enjoyment of the Triune God, rather than beholding the Lord and no longer living to ourselves. To be living in constant self-reflection is to be subjective, to live in our self, in our own thoughts.

Reflection upon our successes

In Job 29:12-17 Job reflects upon all his successes, all the work that he accomplished. Verses 12-13 say, [12] "I delivered the poor who cried out, and the fatherless and he who had no helper. [13] The blessing of a perishing man came upon me, and I caused the widow's heart to sing for joy." Here Job is reflecting upon his service, upon his work. This is another activity of the hidden self — to reflect upon the self and how it has served the Lord, how much it has worked for the Lord, how many souls it has won to the Lord, how much life it has supplied to others.

To inordinately reflect upon what we have done for the Lord and how successful we have been is to be on dangerous ground. This reflecting is dangerous because it is Satan's disposition and his nature to reflect. He is proud. He is filled with pride. To be proud is to be lifted up by reflecting on how wonderful you are, how successful you are, how many good spiritual experiences you have had. So reflecting upon the self is merging with the disposition of the enemy within your being.

Reflection upon our future prospects

In Job 29:18-20 Job is reflecting upon the possibilities for himself in the future. This kind of self-reflection involves thinking thoughts about how you are going to gain a new position for success in the future. In verse 18 Job says, "I shall die in my nest, and multiply my days as the sand." Here the Greek word for *sand* in the Septuagint can also be translated *phoenix.* The phoenix is a bird that symbolizes revival, renewal, and a new beginning.

Verses 19-20 also express the thought of a fresh, new beginning: [19] "My root is spread out to the waters, and the dew lies all night on my branch. [20] My glory is fresh within me, and my bow is renewed in my hand." This is a kind of self-reflection in which you begin to think about yourself in the future. You may make plans for the future, plans to be somebody — to be an elder, an apostle, a "spiritual" sister. These are thoughts about our self in the future, thoughts about new prospects and obtaining new positions. All this kind of mental activity just feeds and builds up the self. It is nothing but the self and pride.

This same thinking is exposed in Satan's heart in Isaiah 14:13-14. He said, [13] "I will also sit on the mount of the congregation on the farthest sides of the north. [14] I will ascend above the heights of the clouds…" These words reveal that Satan was looking all the way into the millennial kingdom. He thought of himself there in the future as reigning and being "like the Most High."

It is true that we need to have a new beginning every day. But this new beginning is in resurrection life, not in the hidden self that builds itself up. Job in his hidden self was saying, "I shall…multiply my days as the sand." He was thinking about himself from the source of himself. His thoughts were of the future and gaining a new position for the self to be supported once again. All these thoughts about future prospects — what the future holds for us — are a kind of self-reflection.

These kinds of thoughts about the future build up our self all the more because they keep us from experiencing Christ today in the details of our living and terminating the self. Rather than living in this imaginary realm of the future with dreams about the self having some position, we need to think soberly: "Lord, today I need to know You and deal with You and be dealt with by You." We will have a transfer out of the source of the self and soul-life into the spirit by accepting the Lord's environments and experiencing Christ today, rather than living in self-reflection about the future.

Reflection upon the effect our life has on others

In Job 29:21 Job begins to reflect upon the influence, or effect, his life has had on others. This too is self-reflection. He says in verses 21-24, [21] "Men listened to me and waited, and kept silence for my counsel. [22] After my words they did not speak again, and my speech settled on them as dew. [23] They waited for me as for the rain, and they opened their mouth wide as for the spring rain. [24] I smiled on them when they had no confidence, and the light of my countenance they did not cast down." Just consider the effect Job had when he moved among others.

Then he says in verse 25, "I chose the way for them, and sat as chief; so I dwelt as a king in the army, as one who comforts mourners." Here again Job is reflecting upon the effect he has had on others. Oh, brothers and sisters, this is dangerous. This is just the hidden self. To reflect upon your testimony, to reflect upon how you have brought someone to the Lord, to reflect upon the impact your words have had — to reflect upon any influence you may have had on others — gives the devil ground in you. This kind of self-reflection is what made the devil the devil. He reflected on his beauty, and then he rebelled against God. So here Job, with his hidden self, was really one with the devil, one with the enemy.

Dealing with self-reflection by the cross

In the midst of all this self-reflection, we need to experience the cross. When we deal with dreaming about ourselves and reflecting on ourselves in any dimension, we can actually be brought out of ourselves into another source. The way that you know you are out of yourself is by your enjoyment of the Triune God. You are simply enjoying God. You just get transferred out of yourself by the enjoyment of Christ. In

2 Corinthians 3:18 Paul tells us that by beholding the glory of the Lord, we are "being transformed." It is not by beholding ourselves, but beholding the Lord.

Self-reflection is what Paul counted loss in Philippians 3. In verses 4-6 he says, [4] "though I also might have confidence in the flesh. If anyone else thinks he may have confidence in the flesh, I more so: [5] Circumcised the eighth day, of the stock of Israel, of the tribe of Benjamin, a Hebrew of the Hebrews; concerning the law, a Pharisee; [6] concerning zeal, persecuting the church; concerning the righteousness which is in the law, blameless." This is all Paul's past — just like Job's past. But in verse 7 see how Paul relates to his past: "But what things were gain to me, these I have counted loss on account of Christ." And Paul not only counted all things loss, but in verse 8 he says, "I have suffered the loss of all things, and count them as rubbish, that I may gain Christ."

Then in verse 13 Paul says, "Brethren, I do not count myself to have apprehended; but one thing I do, forgetting those things which are behind and stretching forward to those things which are ahead…" So Paul is saying, "If there is anything I do, it is this one thing — I do not engage in any inward activity of self-reflection about my past." This is how Paul experienced the cross — he did not reflect upon himself. His testimony was "What things were gain to me, these I have counted loss on account of Christ."

Let me give a personal testimony. In my own early years of ministering the Word, I would go home after a meeting and do nothing but reflect upon myself, upon how I had shared the message. This kind of self-reflection would sometimes cause me to go into darkness for a whole week. I would be depressed just because of the self wanting to be good, the self-image wanting to be kept, the reputation wanting to be preserved, not wanting any bit of failure. This was all reflecting upon the self. This is where depression often comes from — from reflecting upon the self. This is the hidden self. It manifests itself in these ways.

The answer for this self-reflection is the cross — counting everything loss that we may gain Christ experientially. And like Paul, this one thing we do: forget those things which are behind. This means no self-reflection. When there is no self-reflection, there is no way for the enemy. That is why Peter says, "God resists the proud, but gives grace to the humble. Therefore humble yourselves under the mighty hand of God" (1 Pet. 5:5-6). God gives more grace when we humble ourselves and do not build up or exalt ourselves in any way.

So Job's looking back on his past and looking into the future could all be summarized as reflecting upon himself. In every aspect it was just self-reflection. This is the activity of the self.

self-justification → self-aggrandizement.

HOW THE CROSS TOUCHES US

To be transferred out of the source of our hidden self with its self-reflection, the cross must touch us. In Job chapters 1 and 2, the cross came into Job's experience. The cross was the environmental dealings allowed by God. Even though Satan was involved, God allowed it. God allowed Satan to come into Job's environment and touch him. This was Job's opportunity to experience termination of the self by applying the cross to his hidden self. So when the cross comes, it comes to touch us.

Touching our self-importance

In Job chapter 30, we begin to see what the cross touches in relationship to the self. After all Job's self-reflection, after all the activity of his hidden self, he says in verse 1, "But now they mock at me, men younger than I, whose fathers I disdained to put with the dogs of my flock." This means that after reflecting upon his past and dreaming about his future, Job is now facing the present situation and what has happened to him. The cross has come to touch him. And specifically what the cross touches here is Job's self-importance. The cross always touches our self-importance.

Let us see how the Lord touched this aspect of Job's hidden self. In the past the nobles and the princes waited for his words. These were the people in Job's life that were important to him, that fed his self. When he walked down the street, they were there waiting for the words to drop out of his mouth. They were hanging on every word. This was important to Job. But now those who were the least important people in his eyes were the ones mocking and laughing at him, holding him in derision. They were making sport of him, making him a laughing-stock. Job says, "Now they mock at me, men younger than I, whose fathers I disdained." These mockers were even younger than Job, and their fathers were those whom he had despised. Here a blow was dealt to Job's self-importance. Persons he did not esteem as important were actually mocking him and making fun of him. In verse 9 he even says, "And now I am their taunt-song; yes, I am their byword." This is how the cross touches us when we have a self that feels so important. The Lord allows someone to come into our experience to make fun of us, to laugh at us, even to bring us into derision, to make light of us, to insult us — to do something to make this self-important self feel pained and die.

This is how the cross works. This is how the cross worked with Job. He felt very important, so the Lord came in to touch that self-importance by allowing the most base kind of people to mock him and even cause him to be a byword. God allowed these things so that Job's self-importance would shrivel up and die — *if* he would take the environment as from God. This is often the way the cross comes, yet many times we do not see the cross in this way in our daily life. For example, we feel so important, but then we get neglected! We are neglected in some way by our husband or wife, or we are not included in a fellowship, or we are not consulted about a matter. All this is the cross! Let us say it loudly and clearly. This is the cross! Do not miss it! This is what it means for the Lord to touch your self-importance — you have just been neglected, you have just been forgotten, you were not consulted, a decision was made without you. This is how the Lord touches our self. There is no other way. This was His way with Job and this is His way with us. God uses the cross to touch us in our self-importance.

Brothers and sisters, let us not miss these opportunities, but rather let us open to the Lord to deal with Him and to be dealt with by Him. Simply say, "Lord, thank You that I was forgotten. Thank You that I was insulted. I need to be insulted. I need to be offended. Thank You, Lord, that You can transfer me out of the self." Do not suffer through your environment. The cross is not a suffering. Do not grit your teeth and try to make it through. And do not try to suppress your reactions. Rather, deal with the Lord in the spirit. Deal with that offended feeling, because it is your self-importance that was offended. Deal with God directly from your spirit. Tell that old man that he was crucified — "This offended feeling was crucified." Lay hold of the objective truth. And then subjectively, in spirit, speak it out: "Hurt feelings, feelings of being left out, I am not one with you. You are not my life. You are terminated." This is what it means to deny the self. You disregard it. This is taking up the cross and following the Lord. And this is how we deal with the Lord when He touches us by the cross.

Touching our acceptance-seeking self

Job 30:10-14 shows us that the cross also touches our acceptance-seeking self. Verse 10 says, "They abhor me, they keep far from me." This was the cross coming to touch Job's self that was seeking acceptance. We have a self that seeks acceptance. We may contact others to seek acceptance, all the while feeding the self. We are not caring for Christ or living according to the Spirit. We are just doing things and making contacts because our self is seeking acceptance.

How does the cross touch this kind of self? In this way — God causes those people that we deem important to stand aloof from us. This is the cross. Because this self so much wants to be accepted, many times the Lord will come with His cross in our environment. Someone will be aloof from us, will not fellowship with us, will not reach out to us. Now, either we experience the Lord and deny this self with its hurt or forsaken feelings, or we live in this self and indulge it all the more. Today, if there is not much Christ in us, it may be because we have been living on the level of seeking acceptance rather than gaining Christ.

9-15-08

Touching our attention-getting self

There is also the attention-getting self, the self that wants to get attention. In verse 15 of chapter 30 Job says, "Terrors are turned upon me; they pursue my honor as the wind, and my prosperity has passed like a cloud." Of course, the characteristics of the acceptance-seeking self and the attention-getting self overlap in verses 10-15. But we can see that the cross comes specifically to the attention-getting self by touching our honor. The Lord deals with us in this way because our seeking to get attention and living in our honor go hand in hand. So our self-importance, our acceptance-seeking self, and our attention-getting self are all ways the self expresses itself. And the Lord by His cross comes to touch each of these ways.

Touching our self-centered relationship with God

Job uses the personal pronouns *I, my,* and *me* over 150 times in chapters 29—31, showing us that the hidden self is there even in our relationship with God. In Job 30:16-23 the cross comes to touch our self-centered relationship with God. In verse 16 Job says, "And now my soul is poured out because of my plight; the days of affliction take hold of me." And he says in verse 19, "He has cast me into the mire, and I have become like dust and ashes." Then verses 20-21 say, [20] "I cry out to You, but You do not answer me; I stand up, and You regard me not. [21] But You have become cruel to me; with the strength of Your hand You oppose me." This exposes a self-centered relationship with God. It exposes a person who feels that somehow he is special to God. Maybe you have felt this way from childhood — that you are special. This feeling of being "a favorite" leads to delusion, even to deception. Job had this kind of feeling about himself. And then the cross came. When the cross came Job said to God, "You have become cruel to me." It seemed to Job that the Lord did not answer his prayer, that he was not heard. It seemed like God was against him.

Have you ever felt that the Lord was cruel? Often in the experience of the cross we pass through a period where we feel like God is against us. And yes, He is against us — He is against the self. He is not coddling the self. Job had the opportunity to experience the cross in this way when his environment turned the way it did and caused his inward state to be what it was. Part of the cross was even in feeling that his prayer was not answered, and that God had become cruel. The reason that Job misunderstood and misinterpreted God, as well as his environment, was that the whole foundation of his relationship with God was off-center. He was coming from the hidden self. So he had to pass through an experience of feeling that God was against him.

God is against us! He is against this self — this self-centered, stubborn, deceived self. So, often we may go through dry periods, or periods where we feel like the heavens are brass and that God is cruel. This is the experience of the cross. And this is what the Lord Jesus passed through on the cross: "My God, My God, why have You forsaken Me?" (Matt. 27:46). He had to go through that period of feeling forsaken. He had to pass through that experience for us. He was terminated for us. He was the Substitute. He took that cross for our sake, so that we might take up our cross and terminate this self-centered relationship with God, and no longer live to ourselves but to God.

Touching our self-pity

Another aspect of the hidden self that the cross touches is our self-pity. We see this in Job's experience in Job 30:25-31. In verses 25-26 he says, [25] "Have I not wept for him who was in trouble? Has not my soul grieved for the poor? [26] But when I looked for good, evil came to me; and when I waited for light, then came darkness." Here Job is saying that because he did so many wonderful things, he is expecting now to be rewarded. But God did not meet those self-centered expectations. So what we see in these verses is the expression of the self that pities itself.

Like Job, we may say, "Look how much I have done in the church. Look how much I have served." Then we do not get congratulated. We do not get rewarded. We do not get what we expected. Oh, brothers and sisters, this is just our self. If there is anything within us that feels that we are not getting our due in the church — our due attention, even our due help — this is just the activity of the self that wants to be rewarded and that pities itself. And this is the activity of the self that was exposed in Job's life.

Touching our self-composure

The cross also comes to touch our composure. Composure means the poise our self-life is able to maintain. In Job 30:27 Job says, "My heart is in turmoil and cannot rest." This verse is also translated, "My heart is made to boil and is never still." Job is seething inside. That means he is not able to keep his composure. He continues in verse 27, "Days of affliction confront me." And in verse 29 he says, "I am a brother of jackals, and a companion of ostriches." These are two animals that screech and make strange sounds. Job likens himself to these creatures. So this was Job — boiling and making unusual sounds. This was the cross in his experience. And then in verse 31 he says, "My harp is turned to mourning, and my flute to the voice of those who weep." This further tells us that Job had lost his composure. So in this chapter we see all Job's environments in which the cross came to touch the many different aspects of his self.

We have to see that in our experience the cross is operating. Even now the cross is operating, touching our self-importance, our acceptance-seeking self, our attention-getting self, our self-centered relationship with the Lord, our self-pity, and our self-composure. The cross in our experience is touching us in all these areas. We need to allow the cross to work and operate so that we can be transferred out of our self. The more we live in attention-getting, acceptance-seeking, and self-pity, the more the cross does not terminate us, the bigger our self gets over the years, and the less useful we are to the Lord for His economy and purpose. We have a thousand opportunities every day to experience death to our self. God continually allows the cross to touch us — to touch this self and all its activity. But we may be escaping the cross through many devious ways.

THE WAYS WE ESCAPE THE CROSS

Escaping the cross by justifying our self

Job 31 is a chapter on the experience of escaping the cross. It describes how you escape the cross by clinging to the self in many different ways. After this whole chapter about Job escaping the cross, we read in verse 1 of chapter 32, "So these three men ceased answering Job, because he was righteous in his own eyes." This means that Job silenced these three men, Bildad, Zophar, and Eliphaz, who had previously conversed with him at length. Job was able to argue his way out of everyone's case against him. He was able to so defend himself, vindicate himself, and maintain his righteousness in his own eyes, that he stopped these men from talking. This is what we often do. We escape the cross. We win the argument and stop the mouth of others by escaping the cross.

Then verse 2 says that Job justified himself: Elihu "was aroused against Job; his wrath was aroused because he justified himself rather than God." So from these two verses in chapter 32, we can see the final analysis of Job's talk and vindication — he was righteous in his own eyes, and he justified himself rather than God. This means he did not experience the cross to the hidden self. He was still very much alive.

Escaping the cross by clinging to our past dealings with our self

What are the ways that we escape the cross? One way is by clinging to the past dealings we have had with our self, even our dealings concerning personal purity. When the Lord comes to touch the inward activity of the hidden self in one area — our self-reflecting, our image, our importance — we may escape the cross by beginning to cling to thoughts that we are not that bad. We reason, "After all, I have had dealings with the Lord." We may even have dealt thoroughly with the Lord concerning the flesh. Job began to reason in this way. Instead of being laid bare for God to deal with his hidden, self-righteous self, he began to think about some of the dealings that he had already had. In Job 31:1 he says, "I have made a covenant with my eyes; why then should I look upon a young woman?" This means "I have dealt with the flesh — the lust of the flesh and the lust of the eyes." And verses 1-12 of this chapter describe how Job was so upright and had a proper testimony concerning his dealings over personal purity. Even his personal purity was without reproach. Yet that was an escape from the real issue. Many times we begin to cling to dealings that we have had with God in certain areas, rather than face the present issue. By doing this, we escape the cross over the present dealings.

Escaping the cross by clinging
to our dealings with others

Job was not only clinging to his dealing with himself (Job 31:1-12), but he was also clinging to his dealings regarding others (vv. 13-23). In verses 13-14 he says, [13] "If I have despised the cause of my manservant or my maidservant when they complained against me, [14] what then shall I do when God rises up? When He punishes, how shall I answer Him?" Basically, verses 13-23 are about Job's dealings with others, and how, if there were a complaint brought against him, he would deal justly with it. This was yet another way Job escaped the dealing of the cross related to his hidden self — by dwelling on how he had dealt with others.

Escaping the cross by clinging
to our dealings with money matters

Job clings to yet another dealing as an escape from the cross in Job 31:24-28. This was his dealing over money: [24] "If I have made gold my hope, or said to fine gold, You are my confidence; [25] if I have rejoiced because my wealth was great, and because my hand had gained much…" He continues to talk about this dealing through verse 28. If you analyze all these verses, you can see how Job escapes the present issue and the present cross by dwelling on his past dealings about money matters, about his self, about his flesh, and also about his relationship to others.

Escaping the cross by trusting our attitude

Then in verse 29 Job says, "If I have rejoiced at the destruction of him who hated me, or lifted myself up when evil found him…" This verse begins to touch Job's attitude. He believes his attitude is quite good. In verse 30 he says, "Indeed I have not allowed my mouth to sin by asking for a curse on his soul." In other words, he begins to think about how good his attitude is toward others. Even this is an escape. Thinking about our attitude in contrast and in comparison to others' is an escape and a substitute for the cross.

Escaping the cross by boasting in our frankness

Then in Job 31:33-34 Job escapes the cross by boasting in his frankness. He says, [33] "If I have covered my transgressions as Adam, by hiding my iniquity in my bosom, [34] because I feared the great multitude, and dreaded the contempt of families, so that I kept silence and did not go out of the door…" These verses expose that Job was actually boasting and justifying himself in his frankness, rather than allowing the cross to touch his hidden self. This was also an escape.

-22

The ultimate confidence of the hidden self

Finally in Job 31:35 Job says, "Oh, that I had one to hear me! (Here is my signature! let the Almighty answer me!) Oh, that I had the indictment written by my adversary!" (RSV). By the end of this chapter Job is so bold. He is so confident. He has justified himself. He has escaped the cross in such an effective way that he can sign his signature on everything he said — all his vindications, all his justifications. He even calls the Almighty to come and answer him — "Look at me. I have dealt with myself, I have dealt with others, I have dealt with money matters. My attitude is the best." He is so confident and bold because he is filled with self-righteousness, self-justification, and self-vindication. This is all Job's hidden self.

This shows us one thing, brothers and sisters: clinging to our self-righteousness in all these ways is an escape from the cross. Day by day the Lord is touching us to overthrow the self, to topple it, and to make a transfer out of that source. The cross comes in all kinds of ways, especially to touch our self-importance, our self-reflecting, our self-respect, our reputation, our acceptance-seeking, and our attention-getting. The Lord comes in many ways in our environments, so we have to allow the cross to work.

The hidden self dealt with by seeing God

Later in Job's experience, God came in to speak through Elihu (Job 32—37). And then God Himself spoke to Job (Job

38—41). At the end of all God's speaking, Job made the confession, "I have heard of You by the hearing of the ear, but now my eye sees You. Therefore I abhor myself, and repent in dust and ashes" (42:5-6). Finally this person, who had been so righteous in his own eyes, saw God. When he saw God he saw himself and abhorred himself, and then he repented.

Then Job 42:10 says, "And the LORD restored Job's losses when he prayed for his friends. Indeed, the Lord gave Job twice as much as he had before." This shows us that when this transfer of source takes place in our experience, we will become useful to the church, fruitful, and life-supplying. And our usefulness will increase as we deal with the hidden self, because we will no longer be reflecting upon ourself, but we will see God. Instead of self-reflection, like Job we will say to God, "Now my eye sees You." This means we have turned away from the self. We see God because the self is terminated. And we abhor ourself because we have seen that there is nothing good in ourself. The language that issues from this seeing is, "I no longer have any trust in myself. I count everything loss." This is the apostle Paul's testimony in Philippians chapter 3. So our boast, our confidence, is no longer in ourself, but in Christ Himself.

Take the cross

From Job's experience we see the hidden self, with its activity of self-reflection. Then we see the cross coming in to touch this self. When the cross comes in to touch our self, we have the option of escaping the cross or taking the cross. We escape it by vindicating ourself or by rearranging our thoughts to think of other dealings we have had — how we have dealt with our flesh, with other people, with money. We say to ourself, "I have experienced the Lord." The more we talk this way, the more our self is going to live.

Even now the Lord has come to you to touch you, to deal with you, to expose you. But as long as you are thinking about how you have known the Lord, how you have prayed and your prayers have been answered, and how you have experienced Christ, your self will just keep on living. This is because all our resting on past experiences is self-righteousness. It is self-reflection.

So, brothers and sisters, this one thing we do — we forget the things that are behind. Today we let the cross touch us, and we deny the self and take up our cross and follow Him. We get terminated today. We interrupt our self today. We are persons no longer allowing this self to live. Oh, may the Lord take us the way of the cross to deal with our hidden self.

8

Experiences of the Cross

The objective and subjective cross

Our subjective experience of the cross is always based upon the objective facts of the cross. Romans 6:6 is the objective cross — "Our old man was crucified with Him." And Romans 8:13 is the subjective cross — "By the Spirit you put to death the practices of the body." Based upon the objective fact of the cross, we can by the Spirit apply the subjective working out of the cross daily and hourly. Thus, the objective side of the cross and the subjective side are interrelated in our experience.

The objective and subjective aspects of the cross are seen in many passages of the Word. Second Corinthians 5:14 says, "If One died for all, then all died." This is the objective cross — all died. The fact that Christ died on the cross means that we also died. We all died in Him. This is because we are the mystical Body of Christ and are part of Him in an organic way. We may wonder how we could have been crucified with Christ if we had not yet been born. To us this is a problem, but according to God's viewpoint everything is "one eternal present." Even before the foundation of the world, we were chosen in Him (Eph. 1:4). In eternity past He foreknew us and also predestined us to be conformed to the image of His Son

(Rom. 8:29). When God put us in Christ our history was forever bound up with His history. Thus, when He died for all, all died. This is the objective cross.

Second Corinthians 5:15 says, "And He died for all, that those who live should live no longer to themselves." This is the subjective working out of the cross. Now we no longer live to ourselves. On one hand, the self is terminated on the cross; on the other hand, we are no longer to live to the self. Now practically, experientially, we are putting to death all the risings of the self and all the reactions of the flesh. Experientially we are no longer living according to that source. Based upon the objective cross — the fact that we all died in Him — we are putting to death all that activity.

Our minds must be renewed with the revelation of the objective cross in order that we might experience the subjective working of the cross. These two aspects are put together very clearly in Colossians 3:3 and 5. In verse 3 the objective aspect is given: "For you died, and your life is hidden with Christ in God." That is the fact, and nothing can change it. Our feeling cannot change it. The atmosphere cannot change it. It is a fact. Whether we believe it or do not believe it, it still remains a fact. Disbelief cannot eradicate it. The fact is the fact. We died. Hallelujah! This is the objective cross.

Then in verse 5 we see the subjective side: "Therefore put to death your members which are on the earth." This is the subjective working out of the cross. So the two sides of the cross are revealed in Colossians 3: "You died" in verse 3, and "put to death" in verse 5. In other words, we put to death our members which are on the earth *because we died*. The truth is that objectively we were crucified with Christ. But now subjectively we need to apply this truth and experience it.

So whenever we talk about the subjective cross, it is based upon the objective fact of the cross. We are not subjectively putting to death something in order to get crucified objectively. We are not trying to make our crucifixion with Christ happen in that sense. But we are subjectively putting to death because *we are* in fact crucified with Him. Our having been crucified is a fact. It is the truth. We believe it and enter into it. If we believe anything else, we are living in a lie. We are not relating to ourselves according to the truth. So we have to see what is what and who is who. We need to know what happened to us in the death of Christ. We need to be clear about it so that we can respond properly to every rising of the self.

By knowing the truth, you know exactly how to relate to yourself. You know how to relate to your reactions. For example, you know how to relate to that ugly thing rising up in you. You are not intimidated by it, anxious about it, or hoping that it will somehow disappear. You are not in that false kind of realm, wishing for a change. Once you have seen the fact that your old man was crucified, that you died, then when that reaction rises up in you — when you feel it, when you sense it — you know your position with it. You know exactly how to relate to it. You say, "That is not me anymore. That thing died and right now I am going to put it to death." This is faith. This is the exercise of our spirit. This is being clear and knowing what is the truth. So we can see how crucial it is for us to know the facts of this revelation from the Word

— that our old man was crucified. Oh, it is good to declare it. It is so good to announce it and then to apply the subjective working of the cross by the Spirit.

The three aspects of the cross

There are three aspects to our subjective experience of the cross in daily life. First, there is the outward aspect of the cross. This has to do with our environment — God sending the cross to us in our environment. Hebrews 12:2 describes this aspect of the cross in the Lord's life: He "endured the cross, despising the shame." This refers to the outward aspect of the cross. God arranged a certain environment for the Lord Jesus — an environment in which He was treated shamefully, despicably. He was rejected. He was despised. He was scourged. He was betrayed. He encountered all kinds of outward opposition. His whole environment was against Him. It was this shameful environment that was part of the cross He endured.

The Lord's experience reveals that the outward aspect of the cross is related to environment. Our outward environment includes every new situation, not only *outside* of us, but even *inside* of us — what we encounter in our soul, including our own reactions, our own inward being. This is the outward aspect of the cross.

Second, there is the inward aspect of the cross. This aspect of the cross is related to how we meet the outward environment. In other words, the outward cross (our environment) must be met by the inward cross (in the Spirit) for the cross to operate in us (2 Cor. 4:10-12). This aspect of the cross is an exercise of our spirit. By exercising our spirit, we draw the cross afresh out of the realm of the Spirit. By this we let the inward cross meet every outward cross — every new situation, every rising of our self, and everything that is against us in our environment. This aspect of the cross is an inward exercise in spirit to interact with the Lord.

When we talk about the cross, we have to understand these aspects — the outward aspect of the cross in our environment and the inward aspect of the cross working and operating in our spirit. How does the cross work from within us? It works as we by our spirit join ourselves to the Spirit of Jesus. This is because in the Spirit of Jesus are all the elements of what He is and what He has passed through. He passed through incarnation, human living, crucifixion, resurrection, and ascension. All that the Lord Jesus experienced is now in the Spirit. This is why we say the Spirit of Jesus is all-inclusive. Nothing of Himself and His experience has been lost. It is not that we look back at His life and history 2,000 years ago and try to imitate it and hope we could be "like Jesus." That is not how to live the Christian life. Although His life was an example, a pattern, and a model for us, the glorious thing is that this Model Life is now flowing in the Spirit. His all-inclusive life is now available to us. Because He as the Spirit is installed in our spirit, the riches of His crucifixion — the power of it, the effectiveness of it — are now in our spirit.

Today I can touch the Spirit, and when I touch the Spirit I am touching the crucified life. This Person who lived a crucified life is now in me as the Spirit. Now inwardly I can draw out of the Spirit this crucifying element, this killing element, that is in me. Day by day this inward aspect of the cross needs to be drawn out and brought to the surface of my being. In God's economy this inward aspect of the cross is coordinated with the outward aspect. Thus, when we are talking about the subjective experience of the cross, we are talking about these two aspects of the cross: the outward and the inward. The cross comes outwardly in our environment and inwardly in the realm of the Spirit.

Then there is the third aspect of the cross, which is the operating aspect of the cross. This aspect of the cross has to do with our own inability to change ourself and reproduce Christ in our being. So in this aspect there is the matter of trusting and not doing anything out of ourself. We simply trust the Lord and allow His operation to work in us and to reproduce in us His very life (2 Cor. 13:4).

The Outward Aspect of the Cross and Answering Our Environment

The outward aspect of the cross has to do with our environment, and the inward aspect of the cross has to do with how we respond to and answer our environment. For us to experience the transfer out of our self into the spirit depends very much on how we respond to what God sends us in our environment. By our response we will either escape the cross or experience the cross.

We have seen the Lord's response to His environment in Matthew 11:25-26. It says, [25] "At that time Jesus answered and said, I thank You, Father, Lord of heaven and earth, because You have hidden these things from the wise and prudent and have revealed them to babes. [26] Yes, Father, for so it was well-pleasing in Your sight." When you read the first part of this verse — "At that time Jesus answered and said" — the logical question is, Who was He answering? Who had spoken to Him? Who had evoked an answer from Him? *Environment* just spoke! And what was environment? Environment was His being rejected. Environment was His being insulted, being called a gluttonous man and a winebibber.

Jesus' forerunner, John the Baptist, had been insulted by being identified as one who had a demon (Matt. 11:18). And then the cities rejected Jesus Himself (Matt. 11:20). So the environment the Father allowed in the Lord's ministry was altogether negative. Then verse 25 says, "At that time Jesus answered." The reason the Spirit mentions this phrase is to point out to us that Jesus did not passively endure His environment. He answered His environment. He responded to His environment.

When the cross comes in our environment, it demands an answer. We have to answer our environment. We cannot neglect it. We cannot pass over it or it will be wasted. We may go for years without the experience of the cross unless we answer our environment. So to respond to our environment is crucial. It is not a matter of waiting for it to be over, or hoping it will go away and something different will come to take its place. We have to solidly answer our environment.

Jesus answered His environment and said, "I thank You, Father, Lord of heaven and earth...it was well-pleasing in

Your sight." So the Lord responded to what came to Him, not as something accidental, but as something that was under the sovereign hand of God. We also need to answer to the outward aspect of the cross. We have to respond. And the proper kind of response is the response of absolute acceptance of the sovereignty of the Lord's hand over us.

Our personalized cross

In our experience the cross must become very personal. It must become a personalized cross. But what is a personalized cross? Matthew 10:38 indicates that if a man is going to follow the Lord, he has to deny himself and take up *his* cross and follow the Lord. He must take up *his* cross daily. It is always referred to as *his* cross — a personalized cross.

The Lord Jesus had His own cross. He had the Pharisees and the Sadducees — the religious people 2,000 years ago. He had His Judas. He had His environment that was against Him, that was ordered before the foundation of the world (Acts 2:23). He had His particular circumstances with particular persons such as Pilate, Caiaphas, and Judas. Everything that happened to Him was His own personal experience of the cross. And in Isaiah 50:6 He says, "I gave My back to those who struck Me, and My cheeks to those who plucked out the beard." The Lord Jesus was not rebellious when Judas betrayed Him. He was not rebellious with Caiaphas or with Pilate when they were trying to make Him answer their questions in a way to vindicate Himself. He was not rebellious.

The Lord accepted His own trials sent by God. He took everything — one hundred percent. Watch Him when He was under the testing of fire, under His environment. And now the Lord tells us to follow Him. Each of us has to take up *his own* cross. It must become personalized. We must see our environment in the same way the Lord saw His environment.

For God's New Testament economy to be worked out in us requires death and resurrection. We have to have *our* cross and know it in a personal way. "Let *him* deny *himself,* and take up *his* cross" (Mark 8:34). This means in each of our lives the Lord has allowed certain situations. He has allowed certain troubles and insults. He has allowed a certain kind of husband, wife, or children. Each of these is a certain kind of environment. And for each, we have to take up the cross in a personal way. Let a man take up *his* personalized cross.

Embracing the cross

To take up our cross means to embrace it. It means to embrace our environment as the outward cross the Lord has sent to us. To take up our cross is to embrace what God allows in our lives by relating to Him in it. Brothers and sisters, we have to see that the cross must become this personal. But have we really personalized it? For example, you may complain about your husband, or you may have an issue with your wife. You are hoping that the other person will change — he or she is too hard on you and it is too difficult. When you have a blaming attitude or want to change the situation, it just tells you that you are a person who has not embraced your cross.

The Lord says to such a person, "Let him *take up* his cross, and follow Me."

Concerning His cross, the Lord said that He set His face "like a flint" (Isa. 50:7). He was on the pathway of the cross. And in our experience, this is the same disposition that must be in us (1 Pet. 4:1). In daily life, God has allotted to us many dealings — giving us the exact Judas, the exact Caiaphas, the exact Pilate, that we need. He gives us the exact husband, the exact wife, that we need. He gives us someone who insults us, even someone who betrays us. Can we say that we have taken up our cross? Have we embraced our cross? How personal this is.

Paul's personalized cross

For us to genuinely experience the cross it must become personalized. In other words, our present environment is no mistake. It is what God has given us to transfer us out of the self-life into the spirit. But we skirt the cross in our environment. We refuse it. We sidestep it. We do not want it. We run away from it. We blame it. But in order to be transferred from our soul to the spirit, we have to take up our cross — take up what has been given to us. This is the essence of 2 Corinthians 12:7, where Paul says, "And lest I should be exalted above measure by the abundance of the revelations, a thorn in the flesh *was given to me,* a messenger of Satan."

In God's governmental dealings with us, He utilizes the devil, allowing him to be an instrument in His arrangement of the outward cross in our lives. Satan entered into Judas, and yet that was allowed under God's sovereignty. Job was touched by Satan, yet that was allowed. Paul was attacked by a messenger of Satan, yet that was allowed. In each case, that was the cross. That was the cross coming to the Lord Jesus. That was the cross coming to Job, and that was the cross coming to Paul. And in each case, Satan was involved. So in the outward things we have to see that God even uses Satan to effect His purpose, to give us a transfer into the spirit.

Concerning Paul's thorn in the flesh in 2 Corinthians 12:7-10, he says that it was given for a purpose: "to buffet me, lest I be exalted above measure" (v. 7). When Paul entreated the Lord to remove the thorn, He answered him with, "My grace is sufficient for you, for My strength is made perfect in weakness" (v. 9). Then notice Paul's attitude: [9] "Therefore most gladly I will rather boast in my infirmities, that the power of Christ may rest upon me. [10] Therefore I take pleasure in infirmities, in reproaches, in needs, in persecutions, in distresses, for Christ's sake. For when I am weak, then I am strong."

In these verses we can see that Paul took up his cross. He accepted his environment, his thorn. But he did not accept it in a passive or light way. Rather, he seems to almost boast: "A thorn in the flesh was *given* to me...I take *pleasure*." That means he really embraced this cross for his termination, for the self to be terminated. This embracing shows us that the outward cross must become wholly personal. This is how we should view it — as something personalized by God. God has taken such an interest in you. He has not left you to yourself. He is so concerned to transfer you into Christ as the source of your living that He has allowed the devil to stir up things in your environment, producing in you a sense of weakness and reactions. He even allows insults and necessities — things that are against you. All these things cause you to open to Him in a deeper way. A fresh faith arises in you to let the cross terminate you.

The cross in daily life

When you see how the cross is a personalized matter, you see how crucial it is to embrace the very disposition of your husband or wife. You can thank God that it has been well-pleasing on His part to give you such a person with such reactions and such a disposition. Or perhaps He has allowed you to be misunderstood. Misunderstanding is often a big problem in the family life. So today in the Christian world, there is a great deal of focus on marriage, with many books on "how to have a happy marriage." Many times the emphasis in these writings has nothing to do with God's thought of allowing the cross to operate in our life. Rather, the goal is to improve your marriage so that you could have a happy life and everything would be wonderful according to your natural thought. In other words, your expectation is a "happy marriage," not Christ. If this is all we are expecting and hoping for, we have missed the heart of God's economy.

We have to see that God's economy in our marriage is to terminate us. So sometimes your husband may be a Judas, betraying you. And sometimes others are like the passersby when the Lord was on the cross. They passed by and wagged their heads — mocking Him, insulting Him. These situations in our lives are the Lord's sovereignty in order to terminate the self-life. And yet we chafe under them. We complain, not recognizing that God has gone to all the trouble, even using the devil, to allow something to happen over us to work out His economy.

Consider all that happens in our life at home. What if some pictures were taken of us in our homes? What if some recordings were made of our conversations with our husband or wife? Or what if we could view our reasoning mind on a screen? Just consider it. If we are light and shallow, without much life supply, it is because of the way we have treated the working of the cross which God has measured out to terminate us. The Lord says that to be His disciple you must take up your cross. *What* is your cross right now? *Who* is your cross today? Can you name your cross? Can you say, "This is *my* cross"? Can you take pleasure in it, as Paul did his? He said that there was "given" to him a thorn in the flesh. Oh, brothers and sisters, there is no full transfer out of the self until we have reached this stage. This is when the cross operates — when we set our face like a flint. There is no question about it. It is not that *maybe* I am on the pathway of the cross. There is only one pathway. There is only one life, and that is this crucified life with many cycles of death and resurrection.

We must respond to this outward aspect of the cross. It demands a response. And the response we need is simply the Lord Jesus' response to His environment: "I thank You, Father, Lord of heaven and earth." That means, "Father, You are not only controlling heaven, but You are controlling the earth. You controlled that whole group of cities that rejected

Me. All those cities that would not repent — You controlled it. And now You are hiding these things from the intelligent, because it is well-pleasing to You" (Matt. 11:25-26). This was the mentality of the Lord Jesus. And this same disposition and mind which was in Christ Jesus is to be in us (Phil. 2:5). This kind of word exposes how unrenewed we are, how removed we are from God's thought, and how much we miss the mark of God's economy.

Being forced to deal with God

The cross is a matter of responding to what the Lord has given us. The kind of environment God gives us forces us to deal directly with Him. This was what happened with the Lord Jesus in His agony in Gethsemane when the actual hour came for Him to go to the cross (John 12:27). The Father came in the Lord's environment, and it meant the cross for Him and forced Him to deal with the Father's will. The Lord was dealing with the Father in Gethsemane (Heb. 5:7). With His spirit repeatedly crying "Abba" and with persistent prayer, He prayed through (Mark 14:36). He had to pray three times due to the intensity of the environment. He had to get through all the pangs of His soul-life (Mark 14:33-34). Finally, He came to the point of saying to the Father, "Not as I will, but as You will" (Matt. 26:39). So we can see that the Lord dealt three times in prayer concerning the environmental "cup" that was given to Him to drink (John 18:11). The outward cross forced Him to deal with the Father all the way into the willingness of His spirit (Matt. 26:41).

Dealing to have nothing outside of God

The apostle Paul's thorn in the flesh forced him to deal with God. He prayed three times that the thorn would be removed, but the Lord did not remove it. Yet out of the dealing, Paul's whole attitude changed. He accepted the thorn. He embraced it. He took it gladly. This kind of dealing of the cross in our experience means that we do not want anything outside of God. Do you want something outside of God? Do you want your husband or wife to pamper you, to dote over you, to treat you like a king? Do you want that outside of God? In other words, what do we want? To deal with the Lord thoroughly is to deal to the point that we do not want anything outside of God.

Draw a circle around yourself

In His dealings, the Lord Jesus only wanted the Father's will. Paul also only wanted what God had for him. But so many times we ourselves want something else. We want something other than what God is giving us. Because of this, I think the best fellowship that can be given is — draw a circle around yourself. Do not touch anything outside of that circle. Just deal with yourself and want God alone. Just take God. Just pursue God Himself. This is what it means to follow the pathway of the cross. Brothers and sisters, if we do not come to this point in our experience, then we will have to settle for another level of Christian life — a life in which you want a little bit of God, but you want a lot of other things. So you eventually become shallow, empty, without any spiritual weight, because you have settled for another kind of Christian life. You want something else besides God.

Taking the pathway of the cross and dealing with the Lord by the cross means that we do not want anything outside of God. I do not want a marriage outside of God. I do not want a happy family outside of God. I do not want finances outside of God. I do not want a good job outside of God. I do not want to be successful for the Lord outside of God. I do not want to do anything outside of God. I just want God! This was Paul's attitude in prison in Rome. There he was — bound. If he had wanted something other than God, he could have never testified, "For to me, to live is Christ" (Phil. 1:21). So also in our own experience in relation to the outward aspect of the cross, it is crucial that we want nothing outside of God.

Dealing to recognize God's sovereignty

Dealing with God in this way also causes us to recognize God's absolute sovereignty in our experience. God can do what He wants to do. He can act the way He wants to act. He can allow what He wants to allow. And we bow. Without any deliverance and without any answer, we just bow and acknowledge, "You are God! I don't need to know the reason for this environment, and I don't need an answer. Neither do I need some kind of deliverance outside of You. I just need to worship You and praise You. You are God and You do what You want to do with me."

Recognizing God's sovereignty is the whole lesson that Job ultimately learned in the dealings he had. When the cross came to him in Job chapters 1—2, outwardly he lost everything. He was even afflicted with painful boils over his whole body. This environment precipitated a lot of empty talk. Everyone was trying to find an answer for why he had all these problems. Job's three friends and Job himself were all trying to analyze the situation, seeking an answer. Ultimately, Job's mouth was shut: "The words of Job are ended" (31:40). Praise the Lord! Our mouth needs to be shut. Our words need to be ended. No more words means no more striving, no more trying to get an answer. This indicates that Job had been dealt with to the point of recognizing God's sovereignty.

God comes in

When Job's words were ended, God came in. He came in first through a young man named Elihu. Job 32:2-3 says, 2 "Then the wrath of Elihu...was aroused against Job; his wrath was aroused because he justified himself rather than God. 3 Also against his three friends his wrath was aroused, because they had found no answer, and yet had condemned Job." So here Elihu comes into the situation after listening to Job and his three friends. Elihu was there during all their conversation from chapters 3—31. He was standing by, just holding himself in, boiling, burning in his spirit, wanting to release his spirit to bring God into Job's overwhelming environment.

Many times we are just like Job's comforters — we talk a lot but *never bring God in*. In chapter 32 Elihu brought God in, because he brought the human spirit in. In verse 8 Elihu says, "But there is a spirit in man, and the breath of the Almighty gives him understanding." It is the breath of the Almighty that gives us an understanding of what is going on in our environment. It is the spirit of man that brings God in. Oh, how precious it is when all of a sudden, in the middle of empty talk, analysis, reasons, and all kinds of conversation, someone opens up his spirit and God comes in. And when God comes in He does not give you any answer. He does not deliver you. He does not give you reasons. He just comes in to speak and say that He can do whatever He wants to do. And He is going to do what He wants to do whether we approve of it or not.

Your environment is under God's mighty hand, and if He determines in His counsel to allot certain situations to you, that is up to Him. You cannot do a thing about it. He is God. And this is what Elihu began to speak to Job and his friends in Job 32:21-22. There is no flattery here. Elihu says to them, [21] "Let me not, I pray, show partiality to anyone; nor let me flatter any man. [22] For I do not know how to flatter, else my Maker would soon take me away." Elihu was not going to speak what they would like to hear. He was just going to speak the truth, that is, that God can do what He chooses to do.

Because Elihu released his spirit in his speaking, his words in chapters 32—37 became an introduction into the Lord's own speaking. Job 38:1-3 begins, [1] "Then the Lord answered Job out of the whirlwind, and said: [2] Who is this who darkens counsel by words without knowledge? [3] Now prepare yourself like a man; I will question you, and you shall answer Me." When God comes in and begins to speak concerning Job's situation, He does not answer Job's questions. He does not give him any answer, because Job is contending with Him. Job has a controversy with God. In trying to find the answer, Job is justifying himself and condemning God. This is how proud his self was, how self-righteous he was — he was vindicating himself and virtually blaming God. Eventually this was all exposed.

When God comes in, He doesn't get on Job's level. Instead, He begins to speak in this way — *"Where were you?"* In verses 4-5 He asks Job, ⁴ "Where were you when I laid the foundations of the earth? Tell Me, if you have understanding. ⁵ Who determined its measurements? Surely you know! Or who stretched the line upon it?" God is bringing in some humor here: "Surely, Job, you know about these things!" Then the Lord makes known more of His wondrous works in creation by telling Job about the sea: ⁸ "Or who shut in the sea with doors, when it burst forth and issued from the womb… ¹⁰ When I fixed My limit for it, and set bars and doors; ¹¹ when I said, This far you may come, but no farther, and here your proud waves must stop!" (vv. 8, 10-11). At this point, God begins to expose Job's problem — his pride. And all through His speaking to Job, God uses the word *pride*.

It was pride and self-righteousness in Job's hidden self that the Lord was coming to deal with. But Job was blind to all this. He just wanted to know why he had all these problems — why he lost his children, why he lost his possessions, why he was afflicted with boils. Why was all this going on? He was trying to figure it out. Yet all the while, God was dealing with this man according to his deepest need — the breaking of his pride.

God's way of talking

God uses all kinds of illustrations in nature to expose the pride in Job's hidden self. In Job 38:17-18, the Lord says to Job, [17] "Have the gates of death been revealed to you? Or have you seen the doors of the shadow of death? [18] Have you comprehended the breadth of the earth? Tell Me, if you know all this." In other words, the Lord is saying, "Job, can you comprehend what I have been doing?" Then the Lord questions Job about his knowledge of light and darkness (vv. 19-21), snow and hail (vv. 22-23), the wind (v. 24), the rain (vv. 25-28), the constellations (vv. 31-33), and the clouds (vv. 34-38). God tells Job to observe all these things, while all the time presenting this penetrating question, "Where were you?" It was as if He was asking, "Did I consult you, Job? I am God! I do what I want to do." In this way God was breaking down Job's pride.

In the same way, God comes to us, asking, "Why are you complaining about your husband?" or "Why are you finding fault with your wife? Do you think I made a mistake with you? Why are you questioning Me? What answer are you looking for? I am God. I do with you what I want to do with you. I have not made one mistake with you. There has not been one insult, one neglect, one thing done to you, that I have not known about. Not one sparrow falls to the ground apart from My knowing it, and the hairs of your head are all numbered (Matt. 10:29-30). I am God. I do what I want to do with you. I send the outward cross in the form that I choose to send it."

In Job 38:39 the Lord asks Job, "Can you hunt the prey for

the lion?" And in verse 41 He asks him who provides food for the raven. Then in Job 39:1 the Lord questions Job about the mountain goats: "Do you know the time when the wild mountain goats bear young?" Here the Lord is telling Job to study all the creatures He had made — the wild donkey (vv. 5-8), the wild ox (vv. 9-12), the ostrich (vv. 13-18), the horse (vv. 19-25), the hawk (v. 26), and the eagle (vv. 27-30). The Lord's purpose in bringing all these creatures before Job is to cause him to realize that he does not know anything. And then in Job 40:2 the Lord further answers Job, "Shall the one who contends with the Almighty correct Him?" Job was finding fault with God. Now God challenges Job — "Are you going to contend with the Almighty?" Job had a controversy with God. This is just like us.

Dealing until there is no more controversy

Look at the whole universe. Look at the animal life. Look at what God wanted to do and did. Job, do you think God made a mistake with your boils? Did He make a mistake in taking your children away? Are you going to contend? Do you have a controversy with the Almighty? He who argues with God, let him answer God's kind of questioning and he will be subdued. Job 40:3-4 says, [3] "Then Job answered the LORD and said: [4] Behold, I am vile." Here Job is beginning to break down. Then he adds, "What shall I answer You? I lay my hand over my mouth. Once I have spoken, but I will not answer; yes, twice, but I will proceed no further" (vv. 4-5). Job's mouth was stopped.

It is the same with us. One day we see God! God has done what He wanted to do. So there is no complaint, no argument, no questions. Our mouth is stopped. That is when God becomes real to us. That is why Job could say, "I have heard of You by the hearing of the ear, *but now my eye sees You*" (42:5). Because Job saw that God did what He wanted to do, the way He wanted to do it, he made no further inquiries. Once God revealed Himself to Job, he did not need any more answers for his understanding.

Then finally, in Job chapters 40—41 the Lord specifically pinpoints the mainspring of Job's hidden self. Job's problem was his hidden, proud self. In Job 40:8 the Lord says to Job, "Would you indeed annul My judgment? Would you condemn Me that you may be justified?" That is how far Job had gone in his pride and self-justification — to the point of actually condemning God. Then in verses 11-12 the Lord says to Job, [11] "Disperse the rage of your wrath; look on everyone who is proud, and humble him. [12] Look on everyone who is proud, and bring him low." This is God speaking. He is the One who brings the proud down. It is God who deals with the proud to make him humble (Dan. 4:28-37).

Then the Lord says in Job 40:15, "Look now at the behemoth, which I made along with you." Here the Lord's sense of humor comes out again. The "behemoth" is the hippopotamus. So the Lord is saying, "Job, behold the hippopotamus. I made him like I made you." Then the Lord describes the hippopotamus. In verses 15-18 He says, [15] "He eats grass like an ox. [16] See now, his strength is in his hips, and his power is in his stomach muscles. [17] He moves his tail like a cedar; the sinews of his thighs are tightly knit. [18] His bones are like beams of bronze, his ribs like bars of iron." And in verses 23-24 the Lord says, [23] "Indeed the river may rage, yet he is not disturbed; he is confident, though the Jordan gushes into his mouth, [24] though he takes it in his eyes, or one pierces his nose with a snare [trap]." Look at this huge hippopotamus — how strong he is. Who can handle him? Who can tame him? Who can trap him? How fierce he is! He is not afraid of anything. He is so confident. Do you think he could be caught with a fishhook? Do you think that a fishhook could catch a hippopotamus?

God knows how to deal with a proud self

God knows how to deal with a hippopotamus. He knows how to catch it. The hippopotamus symbolizes a proud self — strong and confident. You cannot catch it with a hook. You have to catch it with boils. You have to catch it with the whole family being taken. You have to catch it with the wealth disappearing. You have to catch it with insults. The only way to deal with this proud self that is so strong, like a hippopotamus, is the way God did it. You deal with it the way *God chose* to do it.

Then in Job 41:1-34 the Lord uses another illustration to depict the self. In verse 1 He says to Job, "Can you draw out Leviathan with a hook?" Leviathan is the crocodile. Now the Lord spends a whole chapter describing the crocodile. In verses 1-2 He says, [1] "Can you...snare his tongue with a line which you lower? [2] Can you put a reed through his nose, or pierce his jaw with a hook?" In other words, you are talking about impossibilities when you talk about dealing with a crocodile. The Lord continues in verse 3, "Will he make many supplications to you?" That is, will the crocodile pray to you? Will he submit to you? Verse 3 ends with, "Will he speak softly to you?" Do you expect that out of a crocodile? Do you expect that out of your strong self? How can you deal with this thing?

Then the Lord continues to question Job about the crocodile in verses 4-10: ⁴ "Will he make a covenant with you? Will you take him as a servant forever? ⁵ Will you play with him as with a bird? Or will you leash him for your maidens? ⁶ Will your companions make a banquet of him? Will they apportion him among the merchants? ⁷ Can you fill his skin with harpoons, or his head with fishing spears? ⁸ Lay your hand on him; remember the battle — never do it again! ⁹ Indeed, any hope of overcoming him is vain; shall one not be overwhelmed at the sight of him? ¹⁰ No one is so fierce that he would dare stir him up. Who then is able to stand against Me?" And then the Lord says, ¹³ "Who can remove his outer coat? Who can approach him with a double bridle?" In other words, who can penetrate this crocodile? ¹⁴ "Who can open the doors of his face, with his terrible teeth all around?" Who can open the doors of the face of the crocodile? ¹⁵ "His rows of scales are his pride, shut up tightly as with a seal; ¹⁶ one is so near another that no air can come between them." How tight, how whole, and how strong is the crocodile! This describes the self. It is just a crocodile! No one can deal with this crocodile. Verse 24 says, "His heart is as hard as stone." And then verse

29 tells us, "He laughs at the threat of javelins." Nothing can penetrate. Then verses 33-34 say, [33] "On earth there is nothing like him, which is made without fear. [34] He beholds every high thing; he is king over all the children of pride."

Seeing God's way

The Lord describes the self as being proud and impenetrable, just like the hippopotamus and the crocodile. This is how He talked to Job. He showed him that there is no human way to handle these untamed animals. But God has a way to touch the proud. Which way is it? It is just God's way. It is whatever He does. It is whatever He has for you in your environment. And it was with this dawning realization produced through his environment that Job answered the Lord, "I know that You can do everything, and that no purpose of Yours can be withheld from You" (42:2). In other words, Job saw that God can do all things. No purpose, no design, and no plan of His can be thwarted.

In all this speaking, God was brought in and Job's mouth was shut. He saw that his environment was altogether under the sovereignty of God. In verse 3 he says to the Lord, "You asked, 'Who is this who hides counsel without knowledge?' Therefore I have uttered what I did not understand." Here Job is acknowledging that he darkened the whole situation. He complained. He tried to get an answer. He tried to solve the problem. But he did not understand anything. He had no knowledge. These were "things too wonderful" for him, which he did not know.

Then in verses 5-6 Job says to the Lord, [5] "I have heard of You by the hearing of the ear, but now my eye sees You. [6] Therefore I abhor myself, and repent in dust and ashes." Job's words reveal that he has seen his hidden self in God's light and renounced it. This is God's way. He just comes in our environment and does what He needs to do because He knows He is dealing with a proud self — a hippopotamus and a crocodile. And you cannot catch this self with a fishhook. It has to be in God's way. And when we see it this way, we know God. We see God. How do we see Him? We see Him in the way He has measured out the exact persons, matters, things — the exact environments — to transfer us out of our self into Christ, to cause us to abhor the self and terminate it.

The outward cross effecting a transfer of source

In 2 Corinthians 1:8 we see again that the outward cross is sent by the Lord to produce a certain effect in us. Paul says, "For we do not want you to be ignorant, brethren, of our trouble which came to us in Asia: that we were burdened beyond measure, above strength, so that we despaired even of life." This is just like Job's environment. Paul and those with him were in a situation that was causing them to despair even of living. What was this for? God allowed this. In verse 9 Paul adds, "Yes, we had the sentence of death in ourselves." In other words, the sentence of death was hanging over them. They were like men on death row. There was no alternative in sight. When they looked at their environment, when they looked at their situation, they were faced with nothing but death.

What then was the effect of this environment? Paul tells us: "That we should not trust in ourselves but in God who raises the dead" (v. 9). This shows that the Lord allows the outward cross in our environment to be so beyond our natural ability that we have no answer in ourselves. Many times environments happen in which there is no way out. What is this for? It is so that we would have no more confidence in ourselves, that we would be transferred out of the self into the spirit.

The effectiveness of the outward cross, however, depends upon our responding. And our response is simply to bow down and say, "Lord, I worship You that You have acted the way You want to act. You know that You cannot catch me with a fishhook. You need something else to catch me in order to deal with my pride and my self, so that I would have no more confidence in my self." This is what God would like to accomplish in sending the outward cross to us.

THE INWARD ASPECT OF THE CROSS

The inward aspect of the cross has to do with applying our spirit in order to merge with the cross that is available there. The effectiveness of the cross is always flowing in the realm of the Spirit. This means that in our experience we can apply the cross to meet every situation. For example, we can apply the cross when we are listening to others, when we speak, when we look, when we think, when we decide, and when we react. The subjective cross is ready to be applied by simply walking according to spirit (Gal. 5:24-25).

Applying the cross while we listen

We need to experience the cross subjectively in order to be transferred from the self to the spirit when we are listening. Listening is quite a phenomenon from the viewpoint of our experience of the Lord. If we are in our self while we are listening to someone, what we hear comes in and "sets off" this self. So while they are talking, we may feel threatened, angry, or condemned. We react in some kind of way while we are listening.

Have you ever considered why you sometimes feel threatened while you are listening to someone? It is because your self is still alive. So whatever you hear triggers a reaction in the self. And the reaction of the self is to feel threatened by what is being said. So while we are listening, we need to apply the cross. We need to experience the cross by drawing the cross out of our spirit while we are feeling threatened, while we are feeling condemned, while we are feeling a demand.

When the Word of God is being ministered, some saints listen and say "Hallelujah!" regardless of how strong the word is. Other saints who are listening to the same word feel it is a demand. This is because some are listening from the spirit, and others are listening from the self. For example, when you listen from your spirit to a message about the cross, it is sweet, it is freeing, it feeds, it supplies. It is what you want to hear. You spontaneously say "Amen!" You want more of this word when you listen from the spirit. But when you listen from the self, the word is a big demand because you still see yourself as the one doing it.

So while you are listening, that is the time to apply the cross. When you feel there is a demand on you, that is the time to say, "Amen, Lord. Thank You that this self is terminated. This self that takes things as a demand, that thinks it has to work it out, that tries to crucify itself by its own energy — this whole mind-set is crucified." We can apply the cross in this way while we are listening.

In Matthew 16, Peter was listening to the Lord as He told the disciples He would be rejected and suffer many things and be killed. While the Lord was talking about the cross, Peter's self was right there listening. So he countered the Lord, saying, "Far be it from You, Lord; this shall not happen to You!" (Matt. 16:22). This is because Peter had listened from the self. And right away the Lord said to His disciples, "If anyone desires to come after Me, let him deny himself, and take up his cross" (v. 24). So we, like Peter, need to take up the cross while we are listening to the message about the cross.

Brothers and sisters, we can experience a lot of crucifixion in our listening and hearing. Not hearing properly was the problem in the parable of the sower (Matt. 13:3-23). The Lord says, "Hearing you will hear and shall not understand, and seeing you will see and not perceive" (v. 14). Throughout the Gospels the Lord says to take heed how you hear (Mark 4:24; Luke 8:18). And the way we hear depends upon what is in our heart. If you have a wayside heart, a worldly heart, then you hear according to that. Or if you have some rocks beneath the surface, then you hear according to that. If the word that is being spoken touches your rock — what you are holding on to — you get defensive. And then you do not open up completely. You are listening according to your own subjective self with its undealt-with rock. Or you may hear according to the thorns — the cares of this world and the deceitfulness of riches. In other words, we hear according to our heart. The way we hear reveals the condition of our heart and the source from which we come. So if we are threatened, if we are deflated, if we are discouraged, it simply reveals where we are and what our heart is like.

With others of us, when we hear things, all it does is feed our pride. It supports us all the more. For example, if someone says to you, "Praise the Lord, I sure enjoyed your testimony," how do you hear that? If you hear with your spirit, there is a genuine praise to the Lord — "Thank You, Lord, for the supply to that saint." But you can hear the same appreciative word for your self. And consequently it builds up your self and feeds your self. So compliments and praise heard from the source of our self do nothing but support and build up the self all the more. Thus, we need to apply the cross when we are listening to what others say about us or to us.

The inward experience of the cross is an exercise of applying our spirit to bring the cross out to face the situation. If we are threatened and deflated, or if we are supported and built up, feeling so good because everyone is talking about how wonderful we are, then at that time we need to draw the cross out of the realm of the Spirit and terminate the self. Do not suffer through it and let the self live; but terminate it, saying, "Lord, I am one with You."

Applying the cross while we speak and look

When we speak, we need to apply the cross. Philippians 2:14 says, "Do all things without murmurings and reasonings." That is how you experience the cross — while you are speaking, stop your murmuring. While you are deciding, while you are considering, apply the cross. We also need to apply the cross when we look. In Matthew 5:28 the Lord says, "Whoever looks at a woman to lust for her has already committed adultery with her in his heart." Then immediately He adds, "And if your right eye causes you to sin, pluck it out and cast it from you....And if your right hand causes you to sin, cut it off and cast it from you" (vv. 29-30). What does this mean? Apply the cross. Apply the cross when you are looking, and apply the cross when you are speaking.

Applying the cross daily to face new situations

We need to experience the cross inwardly by drawing the cross out of our spirit to face every new situation. That is why the Lord tells us to take up our cross "daily." Daily we face the self, because the self does not change. This is one of the basic principles of the subjective experience of the cross. That is, the flesh, with the self as its source, does not change. It will not change (John 3:6). So we need to draw out of our spirit the crucifying life to deny, disregard, and terminate this self — the flesh — that will not change. We cannot change the self with ourselves. We do not handle it. We do not try to change it. We just deal with it by this cross flowing in the Spirit. Thus, we need to exercise ourselves in spirit to draw out the cross to inwardly meet every new situation. This is what it means to respond in an absolute way to the outward cross.

ALLOWING THE CROSS TO OPERATE

We need to allow the cross to operate to completely terminate this self and to germinate resurrection life. In this way, the life that is manifested in us is life out of death (2 Cor. 4:10-11). Life out of death! For this we need to let the cross operate. And how do we let the cross operate? Philippians 2 gives us the way — we empty ourselves, not grasping anything, just as the Lord Jesus emptied Himself (v. 7). And then verse 8 says, "He humbled Himself and became obedient unto death, even the death of the cross." So the Lord emptied Himself and humbled Himself, and in that emptying and humbling, God was operating. This is the context of Philippians 2: "It is God who operates in you" (v. 13).

Let God operate. You simply empty. You cannot do anything. Just empty. Empty out your energy, empty out your striving, empty out your self in its religious workings. This is the meaning of Paul's word, "I have been crucified with Christ; it is no longer I" (Gal. 2:20). Terminate and end that self. Just empty it out. And then humble yourself. The humbling is uniquely related to obedience. Though you cannot change yourself and you cannot reproduce resurrection life, you can let God operate by emptying out your own energy and self and then obeying. Just go along with whatever He is saying, whatever He is doing. In your emptying and in your obeying, God is operating. The cross is operating. Death is operating to change us, to transfer us out of our self into the spirit, and to reproduce and form Christ in our being until we are completely conformed to His image. This is God's New Testament economy (Rom. 8:29).

May the Lord grant to us such a clear vision of the experience of the cross — in its outward aspect, in its inward aspect, and in its operating aspect. The outward aspect is related to our environment. The inward aspect is a matter of exercising our spirit to draw out the cross to face every new situation. And the operating aspect is a matter of trusting, believing, emptying, and then obeying the impulse of life. Just be like a little child, not knowing anything but to obey.

You do not have to understand. God does what He wants to do, and He sends out the impulses of His life when He wants to. When God sends out those impulses, He is infusing us about the matters He wants us to follow, because God is just God. He is dealing with a hippopotamus, and He is dealing with a crocodile. And you do not catch this self with a fishhook! It has to be God's way — how He wants to do it. He knows how to topple the self, to bring down this pride, and to give us a transfer into the Spirit. Amen!

Oh, may God's New Testament economy have its way in our being — to give us such a transfer by the experience of the cross. By this word we have a clear way to go on with our environment, with our spirit, and by resting, trusting, and obeying the impulses of His supplied life.

9

How Death Operates in Us

In our experience of the Lord, it is crucial that we have right thoughts about the cross and the working of the cross. Oftentimes due to an improper presentation of how the cross operates, we may have taken in the wrong thought, resulting in a wrong expectation, and thus frustrating a proper experience of the Lord. May His grace unfold the word of the cross to usher us into His life in a simple way. The proper word of the cross does not threaten, intimidate, or move us in the wrong direction. Our experience of the Lord in this dimension of the cross has far-reaching effects for the church life.

The way death operates in us

The bountiful supply of the Spirit of Jesus Christ operating in our being makes us, as members, a rich supply to the Body. Being a rich supply is always according to this operation in each member (Eph. 4:16). And the operation is always an operation of death and resurrection. Once the Lord's life comes into us, we are joined to the cycle of His life. And that life-cycle is death and resurrection (Rom. 6:5). This is foundational to understand the way the Lord will work in our lives. We need to have a proper realization from the Word of God concerning the operation of the cross in our experience.

The crucial verses that show us the operation of death and resurrection life are 2 Corinthians 4:10-12. Here we see Paul's testimony of the operation of death in the midst of all the experiences he was passing through. Verse 10 says, "Always bearing about in the body the putting to death of Jesus." This verse in itself may not be so easily understood by us, but it is there. "The putting to death of Jesus" is also translated as "the dying of Jesus." Others have expanded on it to mean "the death process of Jesus." Thus it would read, "Always bearing about in the body the process of His dying." Then the last part of verse 10 reveals the purpose of this experience: "that the life of Jesus also may be manifested in our body." This shows us that death and life always go together. The death is working and then the life is manifested.

Paul continues in verse 11, "For we who are alive are always being delivered." The phrase "we who are alive" is not speaking simply of human beings who are existing. It does not merely imply human existence. Rather, it means "we who are living in the divine life, we who are regenerated and joined to His life, we who have His life in us." We are "alive" in that sense. We are not just existing. We who are living in the Lord, we who are Christians, "are always being delivered unto death for Jesus' sake." Then the purpose of this experience is seen in the last part of verse 11: "that the life of Jesus also may be manifested in our mortal flesh." So here again death and life go together.

One aspect of the death is that we bear it about in our body. That is inward. The other aspect of the death is that we are *delivered over* to it. The Greek verb means "handed over."

That is outward. We are bearing the death inwardly and handed over outwardly to the realm of death. Bearing the death in our body is *the inward cross.* And handed over to death is *the outward cross.* This refers to environment. In the Lord's experience it was the betrayal, the denial, the beating and the mocking, the thorns on His brow. That kind of outward environment was all part of the cross.

The Lord had experienced the inward aspect of the cross in Gethsemane, where in His spirit He was crying "Abba! Abba!" He cried "Abba, Father!" and touched His willing spirit. Thus, what God handed Him over to outwardly was matched inwardly by His exercised spirit crying in child-like dependency. He felt the effect of the outward cross upon His soul to the extent that the only way He could make it through Gethsemane was to keep pressing through the troubling in His soul until He found the willingness for the cross in His spirit. His own testimony of this experience was, "The spirit indeed is willing, but the flesh is weak" (Mark 14:38). So the Lord matched the outward cross with the inward cross to say, "Yet not what I will, but what You will" (v. 36). We can see death operating in the Lord inwardly and outwardly. He was both inwardly bearing the cross and outwardly handed over to it.

Then Paul concludes in 2 Corinthians 4:12, "So then death operates in us, but life in you." Notice the words "So then." These words are the direct result of verses 10 and 11. "So then death operates in us." How does death operate? (1) by always bearing the cross inwardly and (2) by always being handed over to the cross outwardly. It is in these two ways that death operates. So we see the two-fold aspect of the operation of death — inward and outward. And when this death is operating, it results in "life in you." Death and life — they always go together. This kind of life is not a shallow kind of life. It is life out of death. It is resurrection life. That is the kind of life that is imparted into the Body whenever the operation of death is going on.

In these few verses we can see the operation of death. Of course, some may not be able to fully understand this word of the cross. Others will have a deeper understanding. And still others will have a panting spirit for what is said about the cross (cf. 1 Cor. 1:18; 2:14). This kind of ministry is according to our capacity. But God will give us all something of His thought for where we are. And what we hear today and do not understand today, we will understand next week, or we will understand next month, or we will understand two years from now. We will discover what Paul unveils about the operation of death in us and life in others.

THE GOAL OF THE OPERATION

There is an operation going on — death *is* operating. Yet, to be supplied for the operation of death, we need to be focused to see the goal of this operation. Without seeing the goal of the operation, oftentimes when the cross is spoken of, we will hear it in the context of our little subjective circle of *me, myself,* and *I.* We will merely be concerned with — How am *I* doing in *my* experience of the cross? So it is critical that we see that the goal of the operation is that we would become a rich supply in the Body. As a member, as a gift to the Body, we all have a measure with a rich supply according to the operation in us.

Being a rich supply

In Ephesians 4:15-16 Paul says, [15] "But holding to truth in love, we may grow up into Him in all things, who is the Head, Christ, [16] out from whom all the Body, being joined together and being knit together through every joint of the rich supply…" These verses show us that the way the Body happens on this earth — the way it is joined and knit together — is through the joints of the rich supply. Then verse 16 continues, "according to the *operation* in the measure of each one part, causes the growth of the Body unto the building up of itself in love."

So the goal of this operation of death is that we would become a rich supply in the Body. The church cannot exist without supply. If there is no operation happening in the members — in a portion of the members, in a remnant of the members, in two or three of the members — there will be no life. If there are not some in the Body having an operation of death and resurrection, the church in that place will not have the rich supply. May there always be those who are bearing about in their body the process of the dying of Jesus so that there is always an inward cross matching what God allows of the outward cross.

When I am handed over to these environments — when I have been betrayed, when I have been misunderstood, when my self has been affected — and I match those environments with "Abba," with my spirit engaged and contacting God, then death operates and life is manifested. There is life supply, there is an invisible current flowing beneath the surface. This supply of life coming out of death causes life to be generated in others — including rebellious ones, sinners, ones who are inert and seemingly cannot make a move toward God. Life is supplied. Oh, Lord, make us ones who afford rich supplies to the church. This is the goal of the operation of death.

The growth of God and the growth of the Body

In Ephesians 4:16 Paul says, "*the growth of the Body* unto the building up of itself in love." But in Colossians 2:19 Paul speaks of this growth a little differently. He adds more riches by saying, "And not holding the Head, out from whom all the Body, being richly supplied and knit together by means of the joints and sinews, *grows with the growth of God*." In Ephesians it is the growth of the Body, but in Colossians it is the growth of God. This shows us that the genuine, proper growth in our life results in our becoming a supplying member in the Body, causing the growth of the Body. This is the growth of God. In other words, the growth of God is relational — the Lord's life is manifested *corporately* in the church. The growth of God is the growth of the Body, and the growth of the Body is the growth of God. And this growth comes by holding the Head. So we can see that this is the goal of God's operation in us — that we could be a rich supply for the church and a vital factor to cause the growth and the building up of the Body.

To be a rich supply is to be a person who sees that

everything in his life is for the building up of the Body. Nothing happens in my experience that does not add to or subtract from the church, because I am an organic member with all the other members. Therefore it is vital that we experience this inner operation so that we might be a rich supply.

The Supply for the Operation

There is a supply for this operation of death and resurrection. Do not think that the cross inwardly or outwardly is left to us to work out from our own resources. This is often where the wrong thoughts come in concerning the cross. Even the songs that we sing about the cross can be understood in the wrong way. Some of the lyrics may lead us to believe that the cross is something to work out in ourselves. But we must understand that the Spirit is *the source* and *the supply* of the cross for death to operate in us. It is the Spirit that operates this death. When the cross is put into the realm of the Spirit, and we see it in that realm, we are turned in the right direction, to the right source. Our expectation changes.

For many years we may have sung songs about the cross such as, "Olives that have known no pressure, no oil can bestow; if the grapes escape the winepress, cheering wine can never flow. Each blow I suffer is true gain to me. In the place of what Thou takest, Thou dost give Thyself to me." Yet when we sang these songs, we may have been singing from the wrong source. Our expectation for the working out of the cross may have been ourself. But thank God for the revelation that the Spirit is in our spirit supplying us with the life whose nature is constituted with the cross. This rich supply of the life-giving Spirit is the Spirit of Jesus Christ coming into our spirit, causing and producing in us an inner operation of death. This operation is the cross working inwardly to match what God hands us over to outwardly. Praise the Lord!

The all-inclusive Spirit of the glorified Jesus

In John 7:37-39 we see the accumulated, all-inclusive Spirit of the glorified Jesus: [37] "On the last day, that great day of the feast, Jesus stood and cried out, saying, If anyone thirsts, let him come to Me and drink. [38] He who believes into Me, as the Scripture has said, out of his innermost being will flow rivers of living water. [39] But this He spoke concerning the Spirit, whom those believing in Him would receive; for the Spirit was not yet, because Jesus was not yet glorified." In verse 37 the Lord says, "If anyone thirsts, let him come to Me and drink." Drinking is the refreshing way for thirsty ones to participate in all that Jesus is. He is saying, "Come to Me and drink. Come to Me and be supplied."

Then verse 38 begins, "He who believes *into* Me." The word "into" shows us that this is a participation in Christ, a partaking of Him. Verse 38 continues, "as the Scripture has said, out of his innermost being will flow rivers of living water." Here we see the Spirit described as rivers of living water coming from our innermost being. So we drink and we flow.

Now let us look at the operation in the flow of these rivers. Look at what these rivers are doing. They are defined in verse

39 as the Spirit of the glorified Jesus. That is, the Spirit here is depicted as rivers streaming forth from the glorified Christ. These rivers are operations of the indwelling Spirit of Christ flowing from our spirit. There is a river of death operating in us. There is a river of resurrection, giving life to our mortal body. Indeed, the entire process of the Lord Jesus Christ, from His incarnation to His ascension, is now flowing in the Spirit as operations of His glorified life.

In this passage from John 7, the Lord reveals Himself as the Spirit to drink. This Spirit includes everything that He is and everything that He has passed through. All that He is now flows in the Spirit as rivers of living water, supplying to us His Person, His life, His experience of the cross, the death that He died. The crucifying power and ability flows in this all-inclusive Spirit. So when we drink the Spirit, we are drinking a putting-to-death life. It is a putting to death of all the negative things that are not of God, that are outside of God. So the source and the supply for the death to operate is the all-inclusive Spirit of Jesus, which embodies His glorified God-man life.

The Lord Jesus was glorified as the God-man, with His entire history embodied in His Person. As the Spirit, He is alive forevermore, putting forth resurrection power into all those joined to Him. This shows us that the source of death operating in us is the Spirit. It is the Spirit of the glorified Jesus.

The Spirit supplies death to what is not of God

In Romans chapter 8 we see the cross's relationship with

the Spirit. We see how the Spirit supplies death in us to what is not of God. In verse 9 Paul says, "But you are not in the flesh, but in the spirit, if indeed the Spirit of God dwells in you. Yet if anyone does not have the Spirit of Christ, he is not of Him." Here we have the Spirit of God and the Spirit of Christ. This is because in this wonderful Spirit is the entire Triune God. All that They are in Themselves and to us is flowing as rivers of living water, supplying Their life to us.

Then Paul says in verse 11, "And if the Spirit of the One who raised Jesus from the dead dwells in you, He who raised Christ Jesus from the dead will also give life to your mortal bodies through His Spirit who indwells you." From these verses we see that Paul was totally saturated with the Spirit — the Spirit of God, the Spirit of Christ, the Spirit of the One who raised Him from the dead. Paul was in these rivers of living water.

But now look at what the Spirit supplies in verses 12 and 13: [12] "So then, brothers, we are debtors not to the flesh to live according to the flesh; [13] for if you live according to the flesh, you must die, but if by the Spirit you put to death the practices of the body, you will live." Verse 13 reveals the key point about the cross in a believer's experience. To have right thoughts about the cross, it is imperative to understand this verse — "If *by the Spirit* you put to death the practices of the body, you will live."

Sometimes because we have not seen the Spirit when relating to the cross, we have thought of verse 13 in this way: "If *I* put to death the practices of my body, if *I* take the cross, if *I* bear the death." Yet when we try to take the cross by our own energy and self, we find there is no supply and ability to apply the cross. Oh, brothers and sisters, putting to death the practices of the body *by the Spirit* is an awesome endowment. It is a privileged gift to participate in. It is not an ascetic effort on our part. It is not my self-life coming up with something. Putting to death is a gift of God. Putting to death is part of those rivers of living water that are torrents in my being dealing with everything that is not God. *I* can't deal with what is not God in me. *You* can't deal with what is not God in you. Only *God* can deal with what is not God. So it is by the Spirit we put to death.

The Spirit is the starting point for crucifixion

God begins not with ourself, but with Himself. The starting point is not me. The starting point is Him. When I see myself in my uncrucified state, my starting point in that state is not me. My starting point is the Spirit of God who dwells in me. It is the Spirit who is in my spirit, where I am crying "Abba, Father!" And His Spirit witnesses with my spirit that I am a child of God (Rom. 8:15-16). I belong to a death-operating life — "By the Spirit I put to death the practices of my body." The result of that action of the Spirit over a practice of the body is "you will live."

We need to be renewed in our mind by the Word of God about the cross, and get it out of the wrong realm, the realm where it has been misunderstood. Even when the presentation of the cross has been proper, it may have gone into the wrong slot in our perception. That is why we must start with *the source* and *the supply* of the operation of death working in us — the all-inclusive life-giving Spirit. "Come to Me and drink!" This is where we start. We learn to drink God and allow the divine life to operate to the extent that there is an inward cross in us that always matches the cross in our environment.

The effect of the cross on the soul

The cross may be so terrific in my environment that the force of it stuns me and often cripples and weakens me. Due to this weakening, I may not react quickly to throw off its force over my soul. This is also what happened to the Lord. His soul was shocked, stunned, awed, when the hour came for His outward cross. He was awestruck. His soul was sorrowful, deeply distressed (Mark 14:33).

When the cross comes, our soul is sorrowful. This is what happens when death operates. You pass through a period where sorrow seizes your emotion. And it may be prolonged. But simultaneously, with that operation of death weakening the outer man and decaying the ability of the outer man, there is an inner man that is deeper than that sorrow and that can only be touched by going back to pray the first time and the second time and the third time, crying "Abba, Father!" This is what the Lord did until the willing spirit came forth and He could say, "Not My will, Father, but Yours be done" (see Mark 14:32-41).

At these times when our soul is deeply affected by the

outward cross, there is a supply for the experience of the cross inwardly to match what happens outwardly. It is the Spirit who supplies — "If by the Spirit we put to death."

In our experience we may be condemning ourself over the lack of the cross in our life. We see the symptoms and evidences of this lack in our disposition — there is no cross on my mouth, no cross on my thoughts, no cross on my actions, no death in me. If we become aware of this and our orientation for change is our self, then all we can do is play religious games in our mind, going around in circles until we are on the floor again. But if our orientation is the Spirit as our source, we will begin to drink God and allow the divine life to operate, to put to death all the crossless things in our being.

We must ever see that the working of death in us is the grace of God over us. It is the gift of God imparted into our being. The greatest privilege is to cooperate with this God-given operation. It is an operation in which death subtracts everything that is not of God and is outside of God in our being. This is awesome. It is the working of death, and it is the way the church has life.

—THE ANATOMY OF THE OPERATION —

The anatomy of the operation of death has to do with two primary factors: the factor of the outer man and the factor of the inner man. The operation and working of death is specifically related to the disabling of the outer man and the renewing of the inner man. These are the two factors.

The outer man and the inner man

In 2 Corinthians 4:7 Paul says, "But we have this treasure in earthen vessels." We know that the treasure is Christ in our inner man, our human spirit. But this inner man is surrounded by an outer man — our body and our soul. Our outer man is constituted with that which has been independently developed through the years. We have this treasure, Christ, contained in the earthen vessel of our outer man.

The operation of death is related to the outer man, the earthen vessel, being disabled and weakened by the cross so that the treasure in the inner man will shine forth. We see the anatomy of the operation of death in 2 Corinthians 4:16: "Therefore, we do not lose heart; but though our outer man is decaying, yet our inner man is being renewed day by day." The outer man is falling apart. The outer man is weakening. The outer man is crumbling. The outer man is decaying. But the inner man is being renewed. Both of these processes are going on at the same time within us. According to this verse, death operates in a way in which environments so affect the outer man that it cannot avoid going through depression, discouragement, defeat, wretchedness, rebellion, sorrow, and wanting to give up. You cannot help but go through this with your outer man. This is because it takes a *real* defeat to make us a person dependent on God. It is not mere doctrinal or theoretical defeat we are talking about — it is real defeat.

So an aspect of experiencing death operating in us is to have a soul that is totally troubled. This is death operating over our outer man. God sends the cross and we are handed over to death, and that death environment reacts in us as, "I can't handle this! I'm so troubled!" That kind of reaction is death operating to deal with the outer man in the form of a troubled soul.

11-24-06

The operation of death in the Lord's experience

To understand how death operates in us, we need to study how it operated in the Lord's life as a man. Watch how death operated in His own experience. Consider what happened to the Lord's soul when He faced the cross. Death was operating in Him at every juncture. In John 12:23-24 the Lord says, [23] "The hour has come for the Son of Man to be glorified. [24] Truly, truly, I say to you, Unless the grain of wheat falls into the ground and dies, it abides alone; but if it dies, it bears much fruit." This is the Lord speaking as the Son of Man without sin. In other words, we are talking about humanity in a generic sense, apart from sin.

These words concerning the death of the grain of wheat reveal the principle that, even without sin, death will always be the way to life. When we remove sin out of the picture, we still have the natural soul-life. The faculties of our soul, which are given to us by God, must all go down into death so that man's life would be processed with God's life by the governing principle of death and resurrection. That is, God's original intention for man, before sin entered the picture, was that man would live by the divine life by voluntarily laying down the soul-life in death.

Consider the Lord Jesus as the grain of wheat that fell into the ground and died. His natural, human life was laid down and given up to the will of the Father in a death that would produce many grains. The principle of death and resurrection works in the realm of nature itself, as seen in the grain of wheat. The grain of wheat that dies bears much fruit by losing its life.

This illustration of the grain of wheat reveals how the soul-life of man is to be treated. To let the grain of wheat die is to treat our soul-life in a way of not loving it, but hating it (John 12:25). The Lord says, "He who loves his soul-life loses it." The Greek word used here for "love" is *phileo*. It means to be friendly with, affectionate with, to pity yourself or pamper yourself. By loving your soul-life in this way, you will lose it. But "He who hates his soul-life in this world shall keep it unto eternal life." Then verse 26 continues this thought: "If anyone serves Me, let him follow Me; and where I am, there also My servant will be. If anyone serves Me, the Father will honor him." Together these verses in John 12 show that the Lord intended to identify us with Himself in the same process of death and resurrection.

Now we see death operating in the Lord's soul. We observe the process of how He "hated" His soul when it gave Him trouble. In verse 27 the Lord says, "Now is My soul troubled; and what shall I say? Father, save Me out of this hour?" A troubled soul is a soul feeling the pressure of the trial, and wanting to say, "Lord, get me out of this. Just take the pressure off." In other words, we may go through some kind of inward cogitations where we are considering, "And what shall I say? Father, save me from this hour?" This demonstrates that when death operates in us, all kinds of thoughts and proposals may surface in our mind.

Sometimes when death is operating on our soul, there are lingering things, things passing through us — "Why is this happening? Why do I get treated this way? Why am I misunderstood? Why do I always lose my job? Why is this? What should I say? Father, save me from this hour?" As the Lord was contemplating, as His soul was troubled, He was not like a bird flying above it all, singing praises in the midst of the church. He was not in that state yet. He was troubled. Death was operating. He was considering, "What shall I say? Father, save Me from this hour? But for this cause I came unto this hour."

Then in verse 28 the Lord says, "Father, glorify Your name. Then a voice came out of heaven: I have both glorified it and will glorify it again." So the Lord immediately opened His whole being to the Father and experienced the release of His inner man and the dying of the outer man. By this example, we see that when the outer man dies, he dies with feelings. He dies sometimes with tears. He dies with heaviness and sorrowful emotions. When you feel that way, it is not a cause for condemnation. Rather, it is an occasion to look your soul straight in the face and say, "Soul, this is all that can be expected of you!"

Death operates in a way to totally convince you that your soul will never be capable of submitting to God. It is weak to the uttermost. As you and I feel this weakness, two things are happening: the outer man is decaying, and the inner man is being renewed progressively, day by day. There is a growing sense that I can't trust myself. I lose trust in myself. But at the same time there is a release of the spirit with a greater sense of dependency upon God.

Death operates from the transforming Spirit

There is more and more realization of becoming dependent upon the sufficiency of God when death operates. That is how dependency happens in us. It happens by death operating. Second Corinthians 4:12 says, "So then death operates in us, but life in you." To see the full context of this verse, we need to consider the previous verses in chapter 3. Second Corinthians 3:16-18 says, [16] "Whenever their heart turns to the Lord, the veil is taken away. [17] And the Lord is the Spirit; and where the Spirit of the Lord is, there is freedom. [18] But we all with unveiled face, beholding and reflecting like a mirror the glory of the Lord, are being transformed into the same image from glory to glory, even as from the Lord Spirit."

Now I have turned and I am beholding. And with that turning and beholding, I am getting transformed by the Lord, the Spirit. I am being changed spontaneously into the same image. Then 2 Corinthians 4:1 says, "Therefore having this ministry…" These two passages show us that beholding and reflecting the Lord *is* our ministry. To be in His presence and reflect Him is ministry. Thus, the ministry is simply to enjoy the Lord by beholding Him and getting saturated with all that He is into your spiritual constitution, and then reflect Him. Let Him shine in your heart and give light to others.

Then Paul continues in verses 1-2, [1] "As we have been shown mercy, we do not lose heart; [2] but we have renounced the hidden things of shame, not walking in craftiness nor adulterating the word of God, but by the manifestation of the truth commending ourselves to every conscience of men before God." Here you are dealing with God. You are re-nouncing hidden things. Such an inner operation comes out of the transforming supply of the Lord, the Spirit.

When we are under the transformation of the Lord, the Spirit, there is an inner operation that causes us to deal with God and be dealt with by God. That operation includes the death operation of the cross over our being. A song on the death of Christ from Song of Songs expresses it well:

> On the mountain till the daybreak
> Linger I, Lord, thus with Thee,
> May Thy all-transforming Spirit
> Saturate me thoroughly.
>
> I will get me to the mountain,
> Willingly would get me there.
> All my self fore'er forsaking,
> One with Thee, O Lord,
> Thy death to share.

The words of this song impress us again that the operation of death is an operation that proceeds from the Spirit.

Death operating touches two sides of our being

We have to see that when death operates, two sides of our being are touched. Our outer man is touched, and our inner man is touched. The outer man is crippled and feels helpless, but simultaneously in our inner man we are supplied to relate to this crippled outer man. We pass through the throes of the outer man's decaying strength, and the result is a greater sense of need for God every step of the way. God operates in our being to renew our inner man so that we become a person with a new dispositional essence.

When death operates, your soul gets troubled — your soul is affected in many different ways (cf. 2 Cor. 4:8-9). You are passing through all the environmental dealings. Passing through them is part of death operating. Now what matters is how we relate to what we pass through — whether or not we go to *our* Gethsemane. For example, driving down the street in the middle of a troubled soul, you start to have a Gethsemane of your own. Death is working, and you can feel intimidated by the strength of your own will. You can feel your own stubbornness. You feel it. You know it. You know the struggle. It is your will seeking to assert itself above God.

What you feel is the outer man decaying. What you feel is death operating to terminate the self of your soul-life. The self gets exposed through environment. Its rebellion comes to the surface. And now it is there to deal with, not in the strength of ourselves, but in an utter dependency upon God. Inwardly you are contacting God. You are touching the Spirit, saying "Abba!" and from within, there comes a prayer that says, "Not my will."

The Lord Himself became the embodiment of child-like dependency when death was working the strongest in His own soul. In the middle of His troubled soul — in the middle of His natural life and reactions to the outward environment — He prayed, "Not My will." That means He was feeling the intimidation of His own will. He felt the temptation of a proposal — "Father, would You save Me from this hour? Father, is it Your will that I escape this?" He felt it. But He counteracted His soul-reaction with His spirit-reaction to the Father's will. Death operated in Him. By not loving His soul-life unto death, He multiplied Himself as the one grain of wheat into multitudes for eternity.

In the same way, all of us pass through real things. All the trials in our lives are real. It is all real stuff. Real rebellion gets manifested in our soul. Real unhappiness surfaces in our outer man. There is real troubling and sorrow within. Thank God for all the real stuff, because death operates in it all. With that operation the outer man is decaying and the inner man is being renewed. This is more than encouraging. This is the way it works. This is the way death operates.

The dispositional result of death operating

In 2 Corinthians 1:8-9 we see the result of death operating in our being. It is a dispositional result. There is a change in our essence. In verse 8 Paul says, "For we do not want you to be ignorant, brothers, of our affliction which befell us in Asia, that we were excessively burdened, beyond our power, so that we despaired even of living." Because of the pressures, Paul was despairing even of life itself. He continues in verse 9, "Indeed we ourselves had the response of death in ourselves, that we should not base our confidence on ourselves but on God, who raises the dead." There is the key — "that we should not base our confidence on ourselves but on God." God let

Paul go to the depths of despair so that there would be no way out in himself. "We despaired even of life" for one grand reason — that death would operate to so weaken this outer man with its capabilities and its abilities, to affect such a change, that our trust and confidence would not be based on ourselves but on God. This is dependency.

Then listen to how Paul talks in 2 Corinthians 3:5: "Not that we are sufficient of ourselves to account anything as from ourselves; but our sufficiency is from God." To have no confidence in ourselves and to not account anything as coming from ourselves are manifestations of a dispositional change, of a wrought-in dependency.

Paul again expresses this dispositional change in 2 Corinthians 4:7 when he says, "We have this treasure in earthen vessels that the excellency of the power may be of God and not out of us." It is all of God and not of us. So what happens is dependency. You are drawing the supply of the Spirit from Another life. This is the evidence that death has operated — dependency upon God.

The Outer and Inner Man's Experience of the Cross

The outer man's experience is the operation in trouble. Consider the nature of trouble. There is trouble by reasonings rising up in your mind (Luke 24:38). There may be trouble by knowing you will deny the Lord (John 13:38—14:1). You have denied Him before and you are going to deny Him again. But the Lord said, "Don't let your heart be troubled." He said this immediately after He told Peter, "You are going to deny

Me. You are going to deny Me three times." Then He added, "Don't let your heart be troubled. You believe in God. Believe also in Me." And then He said, "Peter, when you are turned again, strengthen the brothers" (Luke 22:31-32).

The inner man's experience of the cross is this turning again. It is the survival of a living faith inside of us that keeps coming back after we have been dragged through the mud and feel ourselves contaminated. You come back with a faith that turns again. The Lord said to Peter, "When you are turned again." The Lord had prayed for him that his faith would not fail. This means there is ability to come back on the heels of the sorrow and bitterness of our soul when our outer man has been shredded into pieces. The confident Peter had a soul that was shredded. Death operated. That is the way it operated. It operated to humble the man. But the Lord could say, "When you are turned again, strengthen the brothers." This is encouraging for all of us.

The operation in trouble

The New Testament reveals that there are many ways our soul can be troubled. The following are a few of them: troubled by "words" (Acts 15:24); troubled by "some," refer-ring to distracting persons (Gal. 1:7); and troubled by things or persons that affect us (2 Cor. 7:5-6). Why do these things happen? It is for death to operate. It is for us to be reduced once again, to see that in ourself we cannot do anything (John 15:5). We need Another life.

learn this paragraph

The operation in being put to death

The operation of death in Romans 8 is expressed in verse 36: "For Your sake we are being put to death all day long; we have been accounted as sheep for slaughter." In other words, we don't choose what puts us to death. All the environmental problems just put us to death. Your husband is a nail, to nail you right to the cross. Or your wife is a nail, to nail you right to the cross. Her look is a nail right into you. You were just put to death. And you feel that death, you feel your hostility with the files of past offenses behind it. And you feel like you want to pull the files out and start reading them. All this comes to the surface. You feel it and you want to say it, so you reason, "Well, I don't want to be a hypocrite. I had better say it. I don't want to be false." But we are not talking about that. Some people think, "Well, I don't want to be a hypocrite so I am just going to let it out." But it makes a huge difference if you don't let it out, if you don't murmur. Just don't murmur. It is there, but you just do all things without murmuring, because it is *God* who is working in you. So just say "Amen."

The operation in desperate situations

Second Corinthians 4:8-9 describes what it is like to be in desperate situations. You feel like you are actually not going to make it. I have been through many of these experiences over the years where there have been environments, situations, troubles, and I felt like we were right on the brink of a disaster. That was death operating. It operated in feelings that the environment had gone over our head, that we couldn't handle it. But it all caused us to say, "Lord, thank You. You are over all. Let that die in me which needs to die, that I could live by Another life."

"Persecuted, but not forsaken. Cast down, but not destroyed." Paul experienced all these things, but somehow he kept coming through. Because he was bearing about in his body the putting to death of Jesus, the life of Jesus was made manifest in his mortal body.

We have seen that the inner man's experience of the cross is *turning again* — that is, coming back with a faith that will not fail. It is praying through and crying "Abba, Father!" all the way to the willing spirit.

The context of the inner man's experience of the cross is the very thing the outer man is passing through. Death operates in us. Is death operating? It is not just inwardly saying "Amen." It includes a context for you to say "Amen." And the context is the outer man weakening, decaying, and being exposed.

When this is happening in the church, when God is operating in this way, life comes to the church — "death operates in us, but life in you." It is life for our homes, our families, our work — all our situations. Oh, may more of this kind of life spring up on the earth. When we see the golden countryside with its harvest, we will know that many seeds have fallen into the ground and died. Oh, may the Lord renew our minds and give us right thoughts concerning the cross.

10

THE CROSS AND THE NATURAL LIFE

Two gates, two paths, two groups, and two destinies

In Matthew chapter 7 the Lord confronts us with the possibility of entering one of two gates, living on one of two paths, being with one of two groups, and having one of two destinies. These possibilities are defined as the wide gate and the narrow gate, the broad way and the constricted way, the many and the few, and destruction and life. It is possible as a believer to have an experience on either of these two ways, or roads. These two ways represent two kinds of inward pathways.

One pathway is a strict experience inwardly with the Lord — an experience that is confined and restricted to the realm of the Spirit, and that has no other point of reference (Gal. 5:25). It is an experience in which you do not know how to do anything apart from the realm of the Spirit (Rom. 8:13). You refer everything to the spirit (Rom. 8:4). You will not think apart from the Spirit (Rom. 8:5-6). You will not decide apart from the Spirit (Acts 16:6-7). You have no life apart from the Spirit (2 Cor. 3:6). You have no existence moment by moment apart from the Spirit (Rom. 8:14). You are on a constricted way, eliminating everything else but the spirit (Rom. 7:6).

The other pathway is the broad way, which has room for many other things. It has room for all the mixture and the impurity of our self. It has room for our mind, our thoughts, our opinions, our concepts. It has room for tolerating our reactions and our emotions. It has room for grudges, it has room for resentments, it has room for jealousy. It has room to let a lot of time pass while allowing these things to remain. And it also has room for our will, our choice, our way. This is the broad road.

We can see these two paths. One is broad and roomy inwardly. You have a lot of room for your self, a lot of room for your flesh. But on the constricted way there is no room for anything but touching the spirit, turning to the spirit (2 Tim. 1:6-7). On the constricted way there is this basic dealing of the experience of the cross. And this cross is experienced in the Spirit (Rom. 8:13-14).

On the constricted way we must be confined to the experience of the cross in the Spirit. This was the Lord's way. He is the Forerunner. He is the One who cut the way. He already traveled this path. Hebrews 12:2 speaks of the Lord as the One who, for the joy that was set before Him, endured the cross and then sat down on the right hand of the throne of God. This means He traveled a pathway, and on that pathway He endured the cross. Surely all the way from His birth, through His human life, to Calvary, He endured the cross. So we can see the Lord as the pattern, as the model, as the One who was the Forerunner cutting the way. And now His life enters into us, and we, by the Spirit, must go this same way. We must travel the same way in spirit for the experience of the cross on this path of life.

"It's either profound or not found

There are four aspects related to the cross on the path of life: first, the need for this experience of the cross; second, the provision for this experience; third, the dangers to this experience; and fourth, the divine procedure to experience the cross.

THE NEED FOR THE EXPERIENCE OF THE CROSS

Adam before the fall

In Genesis, even before man fell, in his state of innocence, he needed to be regenerated by the life of God. As a "living soul," man was positioned in the garden to both receive and live by the life of God, signified by the tree of life (Gen. 2:7, 9). Adam was not to live by *his own* knowledge of good and evil, in an independent way; but he was to live wholly dependent upon God by eating of the tree of life (John 6:57). We might think that Adam, being created upright and innocent (Eccles. 7:29), was automatically a developed and transformed person. But as H. C. G. Moule comments, "We are not to assume that [Adam's] moral state, or his mental, was of *developed* excellence" (*Outlines of Christian Doctrine*, p. 165).

The first Adam was made a living soul. For Adam to have become a fully transformed man, he needed to live by the tree of life. This meant he was not to live by mere knowledge in his soul, but by the divine life in his God-formed spirit (Zech. 12:1). So even Adam in his pre-fallen state was not to live by his natural life, but by the life of God signified by the tree of life. If he had lived in this way, he would have realized the full reality of the image of God.

The first Adam failed, but Christ as the last Adam was incarnated and then fully brought humanity into its complete expression as God's image (Col. 1:15). He uplifted and saturated humanity with the Father's life. He did this by not living by His own soul-life, even though it was sinless. Because He was a real human being with real human feelings (Rom. 8:3), His soul was troubled (John 12:27) and sorrowful (Matt. 26:38) while passing through trials; yet He never took His soul as the source of His living. He always lived by the source of His Father in His spirit (John 8:29; Matt. 26:41). In this way He kept His natural life in the place of death. Then Christ as the last Adam, with His perfected humanity, became a life-giving Spirit (1 Cor. 15:45). Now His God-man life is available as the Spirit for us to drink of and live by (John 7:37-39). The cross with the effectiveness of His crucifying life is now in this Spirit.

A soulish body

In Romans 8:13 Paul reveals the need for the experience of the cross: "For if you live according to the flesh you are about to die; but if by the Spirit you put to death the practices of the body, you will live." Here the experience of the cross in the realm of the Spirit is for the specific purpose of putting to death the practices of the body. Notice that Paul does not say "the practices of the flesh," but "the practices of the body."

In order to better understand what Paul is referring to when he uses this unique phrase, "the practices of the body," we need to know the significance of "a soulish body." First

Adam, in the beginning

Corinthians 15:44 says that there are two kinds of bodies — a soulish body and a spiritual body. The soulish body refers to the body controlled by the soul, or the natural life. It means our earthly, physical existence is determined wholly by the soul. Thus, it is called a soulish body. The first man Adam was made a living soul. He had all the needed faculties for God's image, but he was still natural and soulish. When Adam was created by God he had a soulish body. He had yet to realize an existence in a spiritual body, that is, a body controlled by the spirit. Such an existence could only happen by the process of Adam living according to his God-formed spirit and eating of the tree of life (Rev. 22:14). By living in this spirit-life realm moment by moment, he could become spiritual and transformed. He could bear God's image, with its full content and essence. He would not be existing merely with the *framework* of a spirit, soul, and body, but he would have the *content* of God Himself filling his whole being.

So we can see that in the beginning man was made with a body. He was a living soul. This is what is referred to as a soulish body. When Paul speaks in Romans chapter 8 of putting to death the practices of the body, he does not mean only the negative, lower, fleshly, sinful practices of the body. Those practices are quite obvious. Many times when we talk about putting to death the practices of the body, our realization is limited to evil things such as fornication, uncleanness, and drunkenness, that is, the grosser forms of the flesh. Surely because of our fallen state, these are included. But Paul does not limit the practices of the body to the things of the flesh. By calling them the practices of *the body,* he is including the soulish body. The soulish body is an all-inclusive phrase. It refers not only to our physical body, but also to our soul with its mind, emotion, and will. Everything that is in our natural makeup is part of the soulish body. Even though the practices of the body may not be "sinful" in the sense of committing so many outward sins, they are still natural. We may be good, not practicing evil things, but we are merely natural.

We have existed in our natural life, growing and developing from birth through childhood and teenage years into adulthood. Also developing in this time have been the practices, or the habits, of our natural life. The practices of our body include the total history of our human existence, with its patterns, habits, natural tastes, and natural preferences — all of which have been developed through culture, education, and training. Also, everything that has formed our concepts — all the things that have gone into the totality of our human living — are part of the practices of our body. These practices are not related merely to the fornicators and the drunkards. They apply to the most sincere, upright, moral, ethical person who is doing his best to live a good life. These practices embrace every man in his natural state, and everything good that man would do from the source of himself. They include feeding the poor and other kinds of philanthropic endeavors. They include speaking a kind word and doing good deeds for people. They even include giving your body to be burned (1 Cor. 13:3). All this activity out of the source of the natural life profits us nothing. It is the practices of the body. So this phrase, "the practices of our body," takes in the totality of what we are naturally.

The burden in Romans 8 is not only that man in his sinful state would be justified, but also that man in his natural, soulish state would become a son of God conformed to the image of His Son (v. 29). Man would not just be forgiven, but transformed, saturated, and fully permeated with God's element. For this process to go on and reach the goal requires that we live a life led by the Spirit to put to death the practices of our natural life. This putting to death is not applied merely in a general way. It is applied to practices — specific habits, specific patterns, specific things. The word *practices* is plural, emphasizing all the specific practices of the natural life. By the experience of the cross on the path of life, we are transferred from the source of our natural life to the source of God Himself.

Perhaps we have never had such a realization. Our thought of the cross is only this: "I should not do the evil things. I should not lie, I should not steal, I should not be involved in those kinds of things. So I take the cross, I experience the cross, for my evil flesh." But it is not only those things that need to be put to death; it is also our goodness, our training, our self-confidence — all that has been built up through worldly principles, human philosophy, and the value systems that originate from man's wisdom. This is all our natural life.

Everything that has come from the self-life, including its birth, training, and development, must be put to death. This was Paul's vision. In Philippians 3:4 he said that if there was anyone who should have confidence in the flesh, he should. But he had come to the point of having no more confidence in the flesh. Then he enumerated the things of his natural life —

his birth, his history, his training, his enthusiasm, his zeal, his religion — everything. He counted it all loss on account of Christ, on account of the excellency of the knowledge of Christ Jesus his Lord (v. 8). That means he was not in the realm of being merely a good man. He was in the realm of being found in Christ, with God's essence. Oh, brothers and sisters, we must have an uplifted vision of what God is after. Otherwise, this experience of the cross will not be appreciated by us. We must have the vision of God's goal — that He does not want good, natural men. He wants men who are saturated and permeated with Himself through transformation and conformation. This is what God is after.

The cross changes our essence and impression

The real significance of Paul's burden is that we would be led by the Spirit to put to death the practices of the body because we are just natural. We can be "a good brother" in the church over the years, but still remain natural. We may be good, we may be moral, but there is a natural essence that proceeds from us. What is natural has a definite taste and sense, and it leaves an impression, not even by our words or by our outward doings, but by what we emanate. The impression and the taste we emit is definitely not that life-giving. So others have an involuntary, automatic reaction to us if our natural life has not been under the dealing of the cross.

When the natural life is being dealt with, there is a real transformation going on, even to the extent of transfiguration. This is what the Lord Jesus experienced in Matthew chapter

17. The Greek word *metamorphoo,* rendered "transfigured" in that chapter, can also be rendered "transformed" (Rom. 12:2; 2 Cor. 3:18). Thus, in Matthew 17 the Lord was being transformed before them, and there was an essence, even a beaming out (v. 2). This was because He was permeated. In the same way, there is an essence, a fragrance, with us when we are being transformed.

Paul even identifies us as a fragrance in 2 Corinthians 2:15. He says, "For we are a fragrance of Christ to God in those who are being saved and in those who are perishing. To the one we are the savor from death unto death, and to the other the savor from life unto life." Like Paul, when our natural life is under the dealing of the cross, we are a fragrance of Christ not only to God, but also to others. There is an essence with us.

That essence that leaves an impression with others is an indicator of how much the natural life has been dealt with. For example, if we have dealt with our own thoughts about ourself, our essence will tell it. However, if we do not have the fragrance of Christ, but instead emit something that produces in others a kind of aversion to our person, this is an indication of something undealt with in our being. It could mean that the view we have of ourself is inaccurate. We may have the view that we are wonderful, we are the best, we are number one. We prize ourself. Just by holding that view and keeping it, even though we would never speak it, our natural thought, our thought centered in ourself, is not inwardly crucified and dealt with by the Spirit. As a result, we give off an odor, we give off an impression.

Many times we do not even realize the impression we leave because we are just sunk in ourself. We are sunk in our soul. Our soul and spirit are not divided, so we are just living out the self. The natural life remains because there is no dealing of the cross over how we view ourself, how we think about ourself. We may not be evil or sinful, but we are inwardly cherishing thoughts about ourself. This is something of the natural life.

The undealt-with natural life

Now let us look at Moab in Jeremiah 48. We have to realize that Moab was a country just on the outskirts of Israel. By the end of Jeremiah chapter 44, Israel and Jerusalem had been fully judged by God, and the last two tribes had been carried away into captivity into Babylon. Jeremiah had spoken many prophecies and many words concerning Israel, judging the whole nation. Of course, strictly speaking, his prophecies were directed toward the southern kingdom, composed of the two tribes of Benjamin and Judah. The northern kingdom of ten tribes had been taken into captivity earlier by Assyria. So these two tribes remained in the south.

Jeremiah was there in the south prophesying through all of God's judgment, and we know that his words were strong concerning Judah and their condition. And not only so, the description is also there of God's judgment upon the ten tribes in the north. Eventually, the two tribes were also taken away into captivity. That was all under the judgment and hand of God. Because of Israel's rebellion, their sinfulness, their own way, their natural thought, God came in and judged them, taking them into captivity. This was God's love and God's favor toward them, because He was dealing with them and judging them in order to lead them back to Himself.

After chapter 44 Jeremiah's prophesying is no longer toward Judah and Israel. He now begins to prophesy to all the foreign nations surrounding Israel — those nations that had gone untouched and undealt with. Moab, on the outskirts of Israel, had been watching God's judgment on Judah, but had not itself been judged and dealt with. So Moab was just an undealt-with country.

This is the context of Jeremiah 48:11, which says, "Moab has been at ease." The Hebrew word here for "ease" means secure, rest from trouble, undisturbed by ill fortune. Moab had been this way "from his youth" and had "settled on his dregs." The dregs are also known as sediment. In the process of wine being purified, the sediment, or dregs, go to the bottom. Normally in the purifying process, wine is poured from one vessel to another until the dregs, which produce a strong odor, are gone. But in Moab's case, the sediment was settled there, with its strength of smell. So Jeremiah prophesies, "Moab has been at ease from his youth; he has settled on his dregs, and has not been emptied from vessel to vessel, nor has he gone into captivity. Therefore his taste remained in him, and his scent has not changed" (v. 11).

Moab was like wine that had not been poured out and purified. This means they had not been judged and dealt with, but instead had avoided all of God's dealings and escaped God's judgment. Because of escaping God's judgment and dealing, they had settled on their sediment, with its strong, unchanging scent. And their taste stayed with them. This means that if we escape God's dealings over our natural life, if we escape turning to the Spirit and dealing with and judging the self, the end result is that we have an odor, an impression, and our taste is still the same.

Our burden should not be the gaining of more knowledge or the improvement of behavior or the correctness of our living. But our burden should be that our scent would change, that our life-essence and impression would be different. We do not want to settle in our soul, in what proceeds from our life by nature; but we want to be continually purified to have something more of Christ. So we realize that our need to experience the cross is not merely for the flesh to be dealt with, but also for that which proceeds from the natural life.

Concerning Moab, Jeremiah 48:12 says, "Therefore behold, the days are coming, says the LORD, that I shall send him wine-workers who will tip him over and empty his vessels and break the bottles." This means God's judgment will come. The Lord will come in with environments. He will come in to deal with this Moab who has settled and has had no change.

The hidden rock that will stop God's economy in our lives is related to the natural life — our culture, our habits, our nationality, our race, our education, our preferences, our tastes. All these things make up our natural person. It is absolutely the natural, undealt-with self that causes a wrong smell in the church life. We may have the same old smell coming from us year after year, and be saying the same old things and giving the same testimonies. Why are we still the same? It is because we have been at ease from our youth. We have cherished our natural self, our natural opinion, our natural life. Our natural life has been undealt with. We have skirted around God's dealings by which He has tried to break this natural life. Yes, we are still in the church life, but we have escaped God's dealing in our environment, so our scent is not changed. Thus, our burden is that the Lord would not leave us to ourselves, but would make us desperate to no longer be a natural person, living according to the practices of our body with its habits and ways. May He never leave us to ourselves, but may His loving hand be heavy upon us for the breaking of this natural life.

We need to experience the cross for the dealing with our natural person. Do you not want your scent to be different? your taste to be different? Do you not want the impression that you give to be the fragrance of Christ? You cannot make this up. You may have a good behavior outwardly. You may stay away from sin. You may stay away from all the worldly things. Yet if the natural life is still undealt with — if you are living in views about yourself, living in your reasoning mind, living by right and wrong, living in your culture, your natural thought, your preference, your taste, your cliquishness, your likes and dislikes, your habits — in all the practices of your body — you will still have a strong scent.

Your scent is strong in whatever is undealt with in your being. If your mind is undealt with, the impression others are left with is that they meet a mind; they do not meet Christ. When you are going to fellowship, when you are going to consider something together, the impression is that a mind is there, thoughts are there, reasons are there, logical thinking is there, rather than Christ. Or, if you meet a saint whose natural emotions are undealt with, you meet emotions. They may be nice emotions, they may be lovable emotions, they may be likable emotions, but you meet emotions and not Christ.

Brothers and sisters, we need to be transformed, to be made sons of God having God's element. For this we need the experience of the cross. This is, undoubtedly, what Paul is mainly referring to in Romans 8:14 when he says, "For as many as are led by the Spirit of God, these are sons of God." This leading is the leading of the Spirit. He is leading us moment by moment to identify the practices of the body and to put them to death (Rom. 8:13). Apart from the Spirit, we cannot identify anything in a proper way. We must realize that only by the Spirit can we put to death our natural life, and only by the Spirit can we be led to identify what to put to death. We must be able to identify the practices of the body by the Spirit. So we see that the leading of the Spirit includes not only the act of putting to death, but also identifying what is our natural life.

Our saturation and touch with the Spirit causes us to have this wonderful leading, this leading to the practices. Have you caught some practices in the last twenty-four hours? That is a sign of how much you are in the Spirit. If you are not in the Spirit, you may feel that you are wonderful and have no need of anything, just as the lukewarm church in Laodicea had no sense of need (Rev. 3:14-22). But we have to see that if we are in the Spirit, the leading of the Spirit is the leading to the practices of the body. We did not realize how natural we were until we began to get to God, touch the Spirit, and have real contact with the Spirit. Then we were led to apply the cross in our experience.

The divine life has been installed into our spirit. Now we are in a wonderful procedure, passing through our days dealing with this natural life and bringing this humanity into a continuous state of being transformed and ultimately conformed to the image of the Son — fully into God. Hallelujah! We are in this divine procedure in which God has not only forgiven sinners, but He has provided for those forgiven sinners to become sons of God who bear His image and express Him. They are fully transformed by being led again and again to put to death the practices of the body in order to be a living expression of Christ.

THE PROVISION FOR THE EXPERIENCE OF THE CROSS

.9. 09

It is by being led by the Spirit that we by the same Spirit put to death the practices of the body (Rom. 8:13-14). This shows us that everything has been fully provided for us. There is a full provision for this experience of the cross. We have seen the need for it, and now we will see the provision for it. Again, the provision for the experience of the cross is just the Lord's life as the Spirit. He fulfilled everything in the flesh, and He preserved it in the Spirit. And now He has installed that fulfilled, preserved life into our spirit, and as the Spirit He is also supplying it continually for our experience. So the divine provision for the experience of the cross is fully realized in Him. This life of putting to death was lived out in His flesh, then became the Spirit, was installed into our spirit, and is now being supplied to our inward parts.

Romans 8:13 reveals the divine provision for this experi-

by the Spirit =
the provision

ence of the cross. It is found in the phrase "by the Spirit." This shows us that the experience of the cross is supplied to us by the Spirit. Every aspect of the inward operation of the cross is provided to us by the Spirit. Paul gives more utterance to this in 2 Corinthians 4:10: "Always bearing about in the body the putting to death of the Lord Jesus." This means Jesus has so mingled Himself in my being that there is an inclination within me to put to death. And that inclination to put to death is the putting to death of Jesus, which is the provision of the Spirit in my being. From the supply in my contact with the Spirit, I not only identify the practices, but I have the inclination within me to put them to death. This inclination in me is the putting to death of Jesus that was fulfilled in His flesh, preserved in the Spirit, and is now installed in my spirit and supplied to my inward parts. So now I have the desire to put to death the practices of my body — "Lord, I hate my natural life. I hate the soul-life. I hate its attachments. I hate its natural ways" (cf. Luke 14:26-27). This is the bearing about of the putting to death of Jesus.

In the putting to death which is supplied to us, there is the element, the provision, of the proper feeling of weakness in yourself. For the cross, we need to be weak. But the weakness we experience is not a natural weakness, but we are weak in Him. In 2 Corinthians 13:4 Paul says, "For though He was crucified out of weakness, yet He lives by the power of God. For we also are weak in Him."

Out of His weakness, Christ experienced the cross. And now we are weak in Him. This means His weakness is supplied to us to experience the cross. We may think of ourselves as being so weak, but natural weakness is not in the experience of the cross. To be weak in Him is to experience Christ's feelings of weakness within our being, related to our natural life. It is an absence of trust in the ability of the natural life, or soul power. So Paul could say that we are weak in Him. Hallelujah! "Oh, Lord, I want to be weak in You!" But, if we are weak in ourself, we fall on our face. We are discouraged. We are condemned. This is all weakness apart from the Spirit. Weakness apart from the Spirit does not avail for the cross. Only the weakness that is supplied in the Spirit, which is the real feeling of inability in yourself, brings us into the experience of the cross.

This same spiritual principle is defined by the Lord in Matthew 5:3: "Blessed are the poor in spirit." To be poor in spirit means that you have nothing. You are a beggar. You cannot do anything. You are just that way in the realm of the spirit. You are not morbidly depressed in your self because you are weak in your flesh, but you are in spirit having the proper feelings of your own inability and your dependence on Another life. This means we experience a state of inability within our being that makes us so weak in ourself. But this weakness is the weakness that is focused in God Himself as our source, as our power, as our life. Paul says this at the end of 2 Corinthians 13:4: "For we also are weak in Him, but we shall live together with Him by the power of God toward you." So even this feeling of weakness and lack of trust in our natural life is part of the supply, the provision, for the experience of the cross.

We have seen these two points: the need for the experience

of the cross, and the divine provision for this experience, which is the bountiful supply of the Spirit of Jesus Christ (Phil. 1:19). This Spirit supplies our inward parts at every stage, at every juncture, to identify the practices of the body, to furnish us with the sense of inability and weakness and of having no trust in ourself. At the same time, He fills us with a trust that is focused in Him for the full supply to resurrect us and to bring in resurrection life.

It is a privilege to experience the cross, because we are ushered into a divine procedure of experiencing both the feelings of weakness and the actual putting to death. This experience is all Christ from beginning to end. Praise the Lord! It is marvelous to see such a provision. You never again want to be experientially outside the spirit (1 Cor. 6:17). The experience of the cross is altogether Christ as the Spirit reenacting Himself, as it were, again on the earth through us — the many sons who are being brought into glory. The way we are being brought into glory is by being led by the Spirit to know the cross operating in our lives. It is by this that we are the genuine sons of God.

Feb. 16

THE DANGERS TO THE EXPERIENCE OF THE CROSS

Self-introspection

We must warn of some dangers to this experience of the cross. The first danger is self-introspection, that is, looking at the self with the self. Self-introspection is the self examining the practices of the body. It is the self trying to figure out what needs to die in me. It is the self analyzing my experience. Self-introspection is definitely a big danger when we are pursuing the experience of the cross. Here we must realize a divine principle: If you are not in the Spirit, do not analyze, do not introspect about what needs to be put to death in your natural life. This kind of self-analysis just leads to something that is full of accusation and condemnation. If we are accused and condemned over this matter of the cross, it is most likely that we are just in self-introspection.

We should not analyze the self by the self or with the self. The only One qualified to touch the self in any way is the Spirit. Do not dare to touch the self apart from the Spirit. To do this is suicide, spiritually speaking. For example, some have followed the teachings of the Mystics of the past in an outward way. After reading of the experiences of Madame Guyon, Thomas á Kempis, and others, people have picked up certain of those experiences in an outward way and tried to deal with the self by the self. This is nothing but asceticism. So we must see that we should not handle ourself with introspection. This is spiritually dangerous.

No contact with God

Another danger is having no contact with God. It is not safe, spiritually speaking, to try to experience the cross without having contact with God. To experience the cross apart from contact with God is to fall into asceticism. This is what Paul opened up to the Colossians, especially in chapter 2, verse 19: "And not holding fast to the Head, out from whom all the

Body, being supplied and knit together by means of the joints and bands, grows with the growth of God." When we hold the Head, the Body does not grow with a false growth, with human behavior, but it grows "with the growth of God." There were some in Colosse who were not holding the Head. They were not contacting Christ. They were not seizing Him, they were not laying hold of Him. As a result, they were not growing with the growth of God.

Then Paul says in verses 20-23, [20] "Therefore, if you died with Christ from the elements of the world, why, as though living in the world, do you subject yourselves to ordinances — [21] do not touch, do not taste, do not handle, [22] things which are all for corruption in their using — according to the commandments and teachings of men? [23] These things indeed have an appearance of wisdom in self-imposed worship and humility, and severe treatment of the body, but are of no value against the indulgence of the flesh." Here Paul warns strongly against involvement in any kind of dealing with yourself by ordinances and little inner rules — touch not, handle not, taste not.

You may hear a saint testify in a church meeting about a genuine dealing with the Lord concerning some kind of food or drink, or some kind of clothing. And you may take that word right into your mind and go back home thinking "touch not, taste not, handle not." Your conscience is bothered because you heard it and now you have knowledge about it (1 Cor. 8:7). You think to yourself, "If I am going to follow the Lord, I had better not touch that or handle that or wear that." It is possible to live in this natural way. Paul warned the saints not to deal with themselves apart from the Spirit, apart from holding the Head. Only by holding the Head, only by seizing the Head, do we really experience the growth of God. Otherwise, we are just in a natural realm. So we must have contact with God for the genuine experience of the cross.

THE DIVINE PROCEDURE TO EXPERIENCE THE CROSS

Touch the Spirit to focus the self

We have spoken from Romans chapter 8 about being led by the Spirit to the practices of the body. In the same chapter we can also see our need to touch the Spirit and focus the self. The self, or the natural life, could never be focused apart from touching the Spirit. This is the way to focus the self — it is by being one spirit with the Lord, joined to Him, experientially enjoying Him, and then looking at your self. It is not looking at your self with your self and by your self, but looking while you are in contact with the Spirit, crying "Abba, Father!" The only way to look at your self is by merging with the Spirit, being one with the Spirit, being one with Christ. You are *with* Christ, looking at your self. This is the *only* way to look at your self. This is the real experience of the cross in the Spirit — to focus the self, to judge it, to put it to death, to condemn it by focusing it in the Spirit. Most of the time we are looking at our self from our self, analyzing our feelings without any light. We are not focusing the self with the Spirit.

From Romans 8 we see that we need to focus the self by the Spirit. This focusing happens by our touch with the Spirit, crying "Abba, Father" (v. 15). Then we get the witness that we

are children of God (v. 16). And we also have the consciousness that we are heirs of God and joint heirs with Christ (v. 17).
This means we are altogether mingled with Him. And then in
this same experience, we are suffering with Him. We are not
suffering *by ourself,* but *with Him.* That means we are with
Him against the self. We are with Him against the flesh. Being
in the spirit in this way is the divine procedure to experience
the cross.

Walk by the Spirit and catch the self

In Galatians 5:16 we have another principle related to the
divine procedure, which is, walk by the Spirit and catch the
self. Paul says, "I say then: Walk by the Spirit, and you shall
by no means fulfill the lust of the flesh." You will by no means
fulfill it because you catch it. It begins in you, but you catch
it; and then you are led by the Spirit to put it to death. Walk by
the Spirit, be submerged in the Spirit, let your entire way of
living be by the Spirit, and you will by no means fulfill the lust
of the flesh.

Because we are in the Spirit, we catch the flesh, we catch
the natural life, and we put it to death. But apart from the
Spirit, we will never catch anything. Everything will escape
us, and we will live out the natural life. For example, we may
talk on and on, covering the world, the weather, the sports, and
more. We get very involved, not catching a thing. But when
we get into the Spirit, we start walking by the Spirit, and our
whole life is immersed in the Spirit. Then we start catching all
of our natural talk and natural interests.

It is in walking by the Spirit that we will not fulfill the lust of the flesh. Not fulfilling the lust of the flesh implies that the lust is there and it is warring against the Spirit (Gal. 5:17). It may even begin to rise up in me, but it does not get fulfilled because I am walking by the Spirit, and I can catch it, identify it, and crucify it (Gal. 5:24-25). So this is another principle of the divine procedure for the experience of the cross — walk by the Spirit and catch the self.

Seek the things above to divide self and Christ

In Colossians 3:1-2 Paul says, [1] "If then you were raised together with Christ, seek those things which are above, where Christ is, sitting at the right hand of God. [2] Set your mind on things above, not on things which are on the earth." Now pay careful attention to verse 3: "For you died, and your life has been hidden with Christ in God." There are two you's here — the "you" that died and the "you" that is hidden with Christ in God. Then verse 4 says, "Christ is our life," and verse 5 says, "put to death." This putting to death is related to our members which are on the earth, beginning with the more gross forms of sin in verse 5 and continuing into verses 8 and 9: [8] "Put off all these: anger, wrath, malice, blasphemy, foul, abusive language out of your mouth. [9] Do not lie to one another, since you have put off the old man with his prac- tices." The Greek word here for "practices" is the same word used in Romans 8:13. In both places it refers to specific things.

This putting to death, or putting off, is the result of a procedure. What is that procedure? It is seeking the things which are above. In that seeking, something begins to happen. The "old you" and the "new you" get divided. The new you is the part that is hidden with Christ in God. The fact that it is "hidden" implies that you do not begin in such a clear way. You need to be exercised to seek the Lord. And in the seeking there comes a dividing between earth and heaven, between you and Christ, between what is of the self and what is of the spirit. This all happens in the seeking.

In the seeking, things get clear; and then you can set your mind. Your mind can be set because there is something to set it on. This is all experiential. In the past we may have taken the words, "I am raised with Christ, and I am seated with Him," in a mere doctrinal way. But now we see that it means getting to the Spirit and seeking the Lord. And this seeking is present tense. It means to continually be desperate to get to the Spirit. And in that desperateness, do not be satisfied merely with generality, but dig out that which is hidden — the hidden part.

Your life is hidden with Christ in God. This implies that experientially we get a dividing between the "you" that died and the "you" that is hidden with Christ in God. Based upon this procedure of seeking and setting your mind on the things which are above, Colossians 3:5 says, "Therefore put to death your members which are upon the earth." So the cross issues forth from this glorious procedure, this framework and atmosphere of seeking, setting, and getting divided. Again, this is all one divine procedure — getting to God, getting to the Spirit, getting to the realm where our mind is on things above.

Depend on the organic union to crucify the self

Galatians 5:24-25 says, [24] "And those who are Christ's have crucified the flesh with its affections and lusts. [25] If we live in the Spirit, let us also walk in the Spirit." To live in the Spirit is to be in the enjoyment of and dependence on our organic union with the Lord. This means that if we live in the organic union, if we live depending upon the supply — if we live in that realm — let us also walk in the Spirit. To walk is to take a specific step, which is simply to crucify some passion or lust, something of vainglory in the natural life (v. 26). So it is by turning to and depending upon the organic union that we put these things to death.

Turn to the Lord to renounce the self

In 2 Corinthians 3:16-18 Paul is turned to the Lord, beholding the Lord, and being transformed by "the Lord Spirit" (lit.). And based upon this he renounced "the hidden things of shame," which refer here to all the ill motives (4:2). He renounced the things of the natural realm by getting to the Spirit, by turning to the Lord and beholding the Lord. So Paul was dealing with himself by the Spirit.

Draw near to God to discover the self

James 4:8 says, "Draw near to God and He will draw near to you. Cleanse your hands, you sinners; and purify your hearts, you double-minded." From this verse we again see that the divine procedure is to get to God, to draw near to Him. And when you draw near to God, He draws near to you; and then you can deal with Him. You deal by the Spirit and with the Spirit.

Praise the Lord for this divine procedure! From beginning to end, the divine procedure for the experience of the cross is altogether a matter of the Spirit. Get to the Spirit, touch the Spirit, seek the Spirit, open to the Spirit, and let Him saturate you. Then you will be able to identify the self, to have a dividing of soul and spirit. Every step is altogether an experience of the Spirit. By the Spirit we can come to grips with this natural life and deal with all the undealt-with things in us.

We all should have this deep sense about ourselves: "Lord, what about the impression the saints have of me? Is it life-giving? Or do they meet my mind, my emotion, my will — my undealt-with natural life?" In his book *The Release of the Spirit*, Watchman Nee says that it may be good to ask some who are close to us and trusted, what their impression is of us — not of our behavior, but the impression we give others. And open to the Lord, "Lord, I open to You for Your dealing by the cross with all of my natural life — my view of myself, my self-love, my reasoning — with everything that keeps this natural life whole and intact. Lord, expose it in Your light."

We keep coming to the Spirit so that we can enjoy a life of completely putting this natural life to death, that we could be conformed to the image of God's Son. This is God's economy — that He would have real sons by this procedure of our being led by the Spirit to discover the practices of the body, one after another, and put them to death. Then we become living, and our taste is life, our smell is life, and we are changed. Oh, may the Lord grant us much mercy to take the path of life in this way so that the natural life might be dealt with by the cross.

11

THE OFFENDED SELF

The sum total of the Christian life is in learning how to remain in our inner union with the Lord. This inner union was established in us through regeneration. When we remain with the Lord through all the storms and varied experiences in our lives, there is an inner blessedness. This blessedness is known only to those who remain in the place of abiding. In John 15:4-5 the Lord says, [4] "As the branch cannot bear fruit of itself, unless it *abides* in the vine, neither can you, unless you *abide* in Me. [5] I am the vine, you are the branches. He who *abides* in Me, and I in him, bears much fruit; for without Me you can do nothing."

When we remain in Christ, in that position of abiding, we can sense that inner blessedness. There is a portion called "blessedness," and it is connected to the unchangeable state of our inner union with the Lord. This blessedness is that inner happiness, that inner joy, which comes from abiding in Him.

The inner blessedness and being offended

In Matthew 11:6 the Lord says, "Blessed is he who is not offended in Me" (lit.). That is, "Blessed is he who is not offended in his union with Me, or in relationship to Me." Here the Lord is speaking specifically about John the Baptist. But the way He says it — "blessed is he" — includes all of us. It not only applies to the disciples at that time, but it also opens up a crucial factor in our own experience with the Lord.

When the Lord says, "Blessed is he who is not offended in Me," He connects an inward state of blessedness to our abiding in Him *while* He handles us, *while* He allows circumstances over our lives. We know that nothing is an accident in the life of a child of God. As His children, we are living under the mighty hand of God. There is one purpose over all of us. God has an ongoing goal over us year after year, month after month, day after day, even moment by moment. That goal is His Son — that we would enjoy His Son and be conformed to the image of His Son, that His Son would be manifested in our mortal flesh so that we could utter with Paul, "For to me, to live is Christ" (Phil. 1:21).

It is in the context of this goal that the Lord says, "And blessed is he who is not offended in Me." In your union with Him, in your relationship with Him, in how He is handling you, in how He is allowing things to be the way they are in your life, He speaks the word "blessed." This means "happy." The Lord uses the word "blessed" again and again in the beginning verses of Matthew 5. We call these verses the Beatitudes: "Blessed are the poor in spirit, blessed are those who mourn, blessed are the meek, blessed are the pure in heart, blessed are those who are persecuted for righteousness' sake," and so forth.

"Blessed" describes an inner state, an inner quality, of joy or happiness. Regardless of what is happening on the outside, on the inside there is an inner blessedness. This word "blessed" needs to sink deep into us because it is by this word that we see God growing in us and we see the enemy routed and we see the church emerging. Oh, that we could be persons entering into this blessedness.

The background of John the Baptist

To understand the significance of the Lord's words, "Blessed is he who is not offended in Me," we must consider the preceding verses in Matthew chapter 11. Verses 1-3 say, [1] "Now it came to pass, when Jesus finished commanding His twelve disciples, that He departed from there to teach and to preach in their cities. [2] And when John had heard in prison about the works of Christ, he sent two of his disciples [3] and said to Him, Are You the Coming One, or do we look for another?" The "John" referred to here is John the Baptist. He is the one who had said of Jesus, "Behold! The Lamb of God who takes away the sin of the world!" (John 1:29). This is the John who was the forerunner of the Lord Jesus. He was God's messenger, sent to prepare the Lord's way before Him (Mal. 3:1). Concerning John, the Lord said to the crowds, "What did you go out into the wilderness to see? A reed shaken by the wind?" (Matt. 11:7). No, they did not go out to see something so insignificant. They saw someone who was "more than a prophet," signifying that John was actually the fulfillment of prophecy.

John the Baptist was uniquely set apart in God's administration on this earth. The Gospel of John speaks of him so simply but profoundly: "There was a man sent from God, whose name was John" (John 1:6). So John the Baptist was the unique forerunner that God raised up. He was strong in the power of the Lord to face all the hypocrisy of religion and the opposition of the Jews. He possessed the boldness required to introduce the Lord and to point everyone to Him as the Son of God. John was this kind of person. When the Pharisees came to be baptized, John called them vipers and said, "Bear fruits worthy of repentance" (Matt. 3:8). So John was bold to speak the truth. The Lord Jesus gives a strong testimony concerning this one being God's chosen one (Matt. 11:7-15).

The Lord's handling of John

Apparently there was nothing wrong with John the Baptist. He was someone honored and dignified in God's administration. Yet notice how the Lord handled and treated him in Matthew 11 — He left John in prison, in a dungeon. According to historical accounts, dungeons were musty, dingy, infested places. While John was confined there in prison, the Lord Jesus was carrying out His public ministry. People were being healed. The blind were seeing. All kinds of miracles were happening.

John received reports from his disciples concerning the works of Christ. As he was hearing all these reports, he was filled with great expectancy that this One was the Messiah, the Son of God. And at the same time, his expectancies were rising concerning how this One should care for him. It was due to John's self-life with its expectancies that he began to reinterpret the Lord's purpose over his life.

Our self being touched and reinterpreting our life

Whenever God begins to touch our self-life — the part of us that gets offended, that gets stumbled — the Lord must get to the root of it by the cross. Otherwise, we will begin to reinterpret our life. What we once believed and held to we will let go of, and we will look for something else to take its place — some new hope. This is what began to happen with John the Baptist. No one had a more direct contact with Jesus in the flesh than this man. No one had a clearer revelation concerning Christ's person. John declared Him to be the Son of God and pointed everyone to Him. All of Judea was in a stir because of John's preaching about Christ. Yet it is this very man who began to reevaluate and reinterpret his whole relationship to the Lord because he was treated in a way that he did not expect to be treated. Thank God for this word, because it exposes how the self-life gets offended in even such a notable one as John the Baptist.

Elijah was another servant of the Lord who had the same problem of being offended. After Elijah had called fire down from heaven and had also destroyed the prophets of Baal, the wicked Jezebel was pursuing him to take his life. So there he was, sulking under a juniper tree and bemoaning that God was treating him this way (1 Kings 19:4). This again indicates that some of the strongest servants of God can be found in their self-pity. So our trust is not in man, not in ourselves, but in the living God.

Let us further consider John the Baptist. While in prison he sent two of his disciples to the Lord to ask Him, "Are You the

Coming One, or do we look for another?" We might wonder, "How could John ask such a question!" He would tell us, "Don't you know, I am nothing but dust apart from the Lord? Don't you know that for me to even pose such a question, there had to be something in me that was offended with Him?"

While John's mind was in that state of reasoning, he lost his blessedness within. Whenever our mind begins to reinterpret things and question what is happening to us and ask, "Do we look for another?" we lose our blessedness. Do you want another day, another environment, another husband, another wife, another set of children, another job, another house, another another? Do we look for another? Whenever we are looking for another instead of the direct hand of God, we lose our blessedness. We lose that happiness within.

John's environmental problem

John was in this state of having lost his blessedness. To his question, "Are You the Coming One, or do we look for another?" Jesus answered, "Go and tell John the things which you hear and see: The blind receive their sight and the lame walk; the lepers are cleansed and the deaf hear; the dead are raised up and the poor have the gospel preached to them" (Matt. 11:5). We would say, "Oh, don't tell John that! It will compound his mental agony." It would be like telling someone who is starving that everyone else is enjoying a feast, eating and drinking to full satisfaction. So John was in prison — deprived, suffering, and limited — while hearing reports of how much the Lord was doing for others.

John was the man who had been out in the desert with the multitudes coming to him. His ministry had revealed the Messiah to the whole Judean area. This ministry had grown so much that there were "disciples of John." That was part of the problem — John had his own disciples. In John 3:26 his disciples came to him and said, "Rabbi, He who was with you beyond the Jordan, to whom you have testified — behold, He is baptizing, and all are coming to Him!" John's disciples realized that he was losing his group because all were going to the Lord. To this John replied, "He who has the bride is the bridegroom." John was admitting that he was only "the friend of the bridegroom" (v. 29). So all these things had taken place and now John was in a predicament. The Lord had left him in prison.

The way the Lord chooses to deal with us

The Lord answered John's disciples, "Go and tell John the things which you hear and see: The blind receive their sight and the lame walk; the lepers are cleansed and the deaf hear; the dead are raised up and the poor have the gospel preached to them." The Lord could have added that those who were captives had been released (cf. Luke 4:18). When John's disciples told him all these wonderful things, he may have been thinking, "But, Lord, aren't You going to say something about me?" However, the Lord's message ended with, "Blessed is he who is not offended in Me," telling John that He was not going to take care of him the way He was taking care of all these others.

The Lord was saying, "John, yes, I am the Coming One. You do not need to look for another. But I have chosen to do things this way and to leave you there. And John, I am sending you a little message: Do you want to keep your inner happiness in prison — without My releasing you, without My doing something for you, without My performing some miracle to get you out of prison? I am going to allow you to stay there, but I want you to know something — Blessed are you if you are not offended now in Me."

The Lord's reply to John shows us that blessedness is in always remaining in our union with Him, under His mighty hand, which is over every one of our lives. When we stay in this union, we have no question about God's ways with us. We are not thinking that He has made a mistake over our environment in any way, outwardly or inwardly. Instead, we are letting our God-given environment drive us deeper into God. This is the testimony of the church life on the earth today — just a group of people saying, "Deeper in God I go." So the blessedness is in maintaining that inner submission to His hand and that absolute surrender to whatever He allows.

The Lord's environment

Continuing in Matthew 11, we see the Lord Himself as an example of one who maintained the inner blessedness in His environment by His absolute submission to the Father's sovereign arrangement. After commending John the Baptist, the Lord says in verses 18-19, [18] "For John came neither eating nor drinking, and they say, 'He has a demon.' [19] The Son of

Man came eating and drinking, and they say, 'Look, a glutton-ous man and a winebibber, a friend of tax collectors and sinners!' But wisdom is justified by her children." These verses show us that no matter what they did, both John the Baptist and the Lord as the Son of Man were rejected. So we can see that there will be things that offend others, regardless of what we do. Regardless of what path we take, there are enemies that come in this way.

Matthew 11:20 says, "Then He began to upbraid the cities in which most of His mighty works had been done, because they did not repent." This verse refers to the Lord's ministry. Then the Lord says in verse 21, "Woe to you, Chorazin! Woe to you, Bethsaida!" The Lord is pronouncing judgment upon these cities because they did not repent. Here we see that His ministry was rejected. The Lord Jesus Himself, under the Father's hand, had ministered to city after city and been rejected by all of them. Yet He was not offended with the Father. Rather He was full of thanksgiving and delight in the Father's ways.

The Lord answering His environment

Verse 25 says, "At that time Jesus answered and said, I thank You, Father, Lord of heaven and earth." Notice the phrase, "At that time." At what time? At the time everything was negative and contrary. At the time when everything was against Him. At the time when, naturally speaking, you would not utter a thanksgiving. At that time, Jesus answered and said, "I thank You, Father."

When you read the word "answered," you may wonder whom the Lord was talking to. In the preceding verses, He was not talking to anyone. He was going through the cities and they were rejecting Him. They would not repent. It was at this point that Jesus answered. What was He answering? Whom was He answering? He was answering His environment. He was answering what was being spoken to Him in His environment.

Brothers and sisters, we must this moment answer our environment just as it is. How have you answered your environment? How have I answered my environment? Our environment requires answers. We cannot remain neutral. We cannot just cope with environment. We cannot blame environment. There is no progress in God that way. Not only will there be no progress, but we will go deeper into the flesh, deeper into our mind, and deeper into Satan. So we dare not answer the environment in that way.

When the Lord answered His environment, He was answering all the rejection. And what did He say? "I thank You, Father, Lord of heaven and earth, because You have hidden these things from the wise and prudent and have revealed them to babes. Even so, Father, for so it seemed good in Your sight" (Matt. 11:25-26). The Lord uttered this in His humanity, after having a disappointing environment, an environment contrary to His expectation. The Lord answered with thankfulness from His inner being, saying, "Even so, Father, for so it seemed good to You." So the Lord kept His blessedness.

When we answer our environment under the mighty hand of God, and say, "You are sovereign, Lord. You have chosen to do it this way, for so it seemed good to You," our environment may not change. It may even get worse, but our blessedness increases. That inner happiness comes forth, and this is the church. It is this blessedness of living in the abiding, in God, deeper in God, that produces the reality of the church.

In Matthew 11:27 the Lord says, "All things have been delivered to Me by My Father." This shows us the Lord's absolute realization that nothing was an accident. He is saying, "This environment was delivered to Me by My Father. It is not accidental. It is not someone else's fault. It has been delivered to Me by My Father." Then He continues, "And no one knows the Son except the Father. Nor does anyone know the Father except the Son, and he to whom the Son wills to reveal Him." So the Lord lived under the consciousness of the absoluteness of God's sovereignty in what was delivered to Him.

Do we live this way? Do we have this consciousness in our daily life? As the light shines brighter and brighter in us, we begin making the connections of God's sovereignty in our daily life. We see our environments as opportunities to fill up the sufferings of Christ, to go deeper into God. It is a matter of seeing beyond the surface things to the larger view from eternity. In our environments we realize God is saying, "I want My Son formed in you. I want His life manifested in you. That is what matters in this universe. And so I am processing you through various environments, all kinds of pressures, all kinds of trials, in order that you would just go deeper into Me."

Bitterness or blessedness?

There is a blessedness that we need to maintain. We see this in the whole context of the Lord leaving John the Baptist in prison and speaking this word to him: "Blessed is he who is not offended in Me." That means, "Don't be offended by the way I have treated you, the way I have chosen to handle you, the way I have chosen to limit your situation." This is a very vulnerable point for us. We either get bitter or we get blessed, especially when we get hurt. When the self is hurt, when the self is offended, when the self is wounded, when something has happened and the self's expectation has not been met, we can either get bitter or get blessed.

When John the Baptist asked the Lord, "Are You the Coming One, or do we look for another?" he was saying, "I am looking for a Deliverer to come in and do something for me. I have an expectation." This was John's thought. But the Lord left him there in prison. And just at that point the Lord said, "Blessed is he…" He put the word "blessed" in John's situation. That means, brothers, when you come home from work and the house is a mess and nothing is done the way you expected it to be, you are on the brink of bitterness or blessedness. You can walk into the house with, "I thank You, Lord! It seemed good to allow this in order that You might enlarge Yourself in me — in order that I might enter into sympathy with my dear wife's situation and help her." This is Christ growing in us. He wants to be enlarged. This is what all our environments are for — to bring in more of this blessedness.

The larger picture

The messy house is about the larger picture — it is about Christ being formed in us. Indeed, everything that happens to us is about the larger picture. But we do not learn these lessons quickly or easily. It may take many failures and many experiences of eating the fruit of our bitterness and learning *that* taste versus the taste of life — the taste of blessedness and happiness within us. We see that the Lord's desire at these points is this blessedness — this inner happiness, this joy that is not dependent upon our environment. The joy is simply dependent on how I am relating to my God: I am thanking Him, I am praising Him, I am worshiping Him that everything is good in His sight. And I am content with my Christ. This kind of blessedness becomes the blessedness of the church because the enemy is routed in our relationships and the building of the Body takes place.

Taking His yoke upon us

After remaining under God's hand in His environment, the Lord then says to us, [28] "Come to Me, all you who labor and are heavy laden, and I will give you rest. [29] Take My yoke upon you and learn from Me, for I am gentle and lowly in heart, and you will find rest for your souls. [30] For My yoke is easy and My burden is light" (Matt. 11:28-30). This is the inner blessedness — the soul that is rested by the Lord. He says, "Take My yoke." What is the yoke? The context of these verses tells us: to "take My yoke" means to "take all the environments that I place over you." So the Lord is saying, "John, in prison take My yoke. Take what I have put upon you, what seems to be something you do not want, yet what links you with Me. I am going to link you with Me in this environment. Don't miss it. Don't look at the yoke. Don't blame the yoke. Take the yoke, and be linked together with Me under it. Now learn from Me. Just draw from Me, open to Me. Learn how to say, Lord, I do not know what I need. But You know what I need."

Blaming, or maintaining our inner blessedness?

We can live disgruntled, blaming, and hurting the rest of our life and go to the judgment seat of Christ with blame in our heart — blame for others, blame for what happened to us — and stand there and say, "Lord, why did You do this to me?" Or we can have boldness and joy and blessedness because inwardly we remained in the blessedness through our environments by saying, "It seemed good in Your sight, Father. Thank You, Lord." We can know if we are ready to be at the judgment seat by the way we are inwardly this minute. If you have inward blessedness right now, you are ready to meet the Lord. If you are blessed right now and you can say, "Lord, thank You! I delight in remaining with You in what You have given me," that means you are ready for the judgment seat. How encouraging!

But if within us there is something other than blessedness, we will be ashamed at the Lord's coming (1 John 2:28). The Lord says, "Blessed is he who is not offended in Me — in union with Me, in the way I have handled him, in the way I have dealt with him." Brothers and sisters, this is a very practical truth within the context of the church, because when we are together we will all be tested. This is true in any place on the earth, in any locality, in any grouping of saints. There will always be reasons for being offended. But that resounding word has to come — "Blessed is he who is not offended in Me." Then we go deeper into God. This is how to maintain our inner happiness.

In our experience, when we are offended, we may only deal with the cause of that offense. We search out the factor that is offending us and try to adjust it outwardly. We may live on this level for many years. As a result, there is an accumulation of offenses. Pretty soon it starts seeping through and others can smell it. Some of us may be "backed up" from many years of accumulated offenses. You may have the ability to keep up a good outward smile, but if your offenses are not processed through Christ and the cross, eventually the smell comes out.

4-27   ### What gets offended in us?

When I was a little boy, I used to impersonate a well-known singer. I was not the real person. I just pretended that I was that person. I tried to be like the real singer. We may do the same thing in trying to live the Christian life. For example, when we are offended, we outwardly pretend that everything is okay, but inwardly we are repressing our real feelings. We do all of this rather than genuinely opening to the Lord. We may get offended again and again. Eventually, no one can say anything to us because the result of our coping is that we are ready to explode. This state is due to the fact that we have never really dealt with God. Instead we are always outwardly adjusting ourselves or the situation.

We have to ask, what gets offended in us? What is it in us that gets offended, causing us to lose our blessedness? Notice your blessedness inside. Watch your happiness. Don't lose that. Maintain that. That is why the Lord said, "Blessed, happy, are those who are not offended in Me. Stay in Me and you will keep your happiness. But if you do not stay in Me, if you move a few inches into your thought-life and your reasonings about the other person, you will lose your happiness. It will just evaporate."

Being offended is a marvelous thing. It is a blessing in disguise. It is as if God is saying, "I am going to go deeper in you now." This is what being offended is about. What happens in your experience is that you learn to say, "Lord, what is in me that is getting offended?" If we can be offended, then we need to be offended. If we can so easily lose the blessedness, then we need to. By this the Lord exposes the *self* that is at the core of our being offended.

Just like John the Baptist, you may have your expectation and your idea and your view about the Lord. This is what gets offended. We have somehow accumulated a certain view about the Lord. We have a view about our life that is similar to the "American dream": We are going to have a certain job. We are going to have a certain wife. We have it all planned out. Then our life goes the other way, and we get offended with the Lord. We are stumbled. We are bitter. Then, like John, we start reinterpreting our whole life based upon an offended self.

Our expectations and being offended

Recently I read a book about how to have "the New Testament church." The author presented true principles from the Bible, including the matter of all the members functioning. Diagrams were also given for arranging the chairs for the meetings. The book described certain things that the New Testament church did, and it proposed that this is the way the church should be practiced today. This kind of word puts expectations into you about the way the church should be. Then you come to a church meeting with your expectations. You measure what you see by what you have read. For example, a brother gets up and shares for half an hour. This is longer than what you expected, and as a result you get offended. Or you may feel that there should be speaking in tongues. Your expectation is that in the New Testament church there should be speaking in tongues with interpretation in every meeting. But then you may come to a meeting and there is no speaking in tongues. So your expectation is not met.

This is the case with so many of us. We have hidden views that we do not know about until something happens and we get offended. John the Baptist had his view of the Lord — "Are You the Coming One, or do we look for another?" In the same way, we may ask, "Is this the church, or should I look for another?" It is so good to expose this realm and to release Christ — to give Him freedom to walk and live among us so that He can be manifested through us.

Being offended and going deeper into God

We can see that this is what gets offended — our views and our thoughts. So let an offense bring you deeper into God, to tell Him, "Lord, grant me to not live according to my rigid expectations, according to the way I think things should be. I want to be in You — the 'I AM WHO I AM.' I want to know You as the living God." In our relationships in the church — in the meetings, in the serving, in functioning — we are in touch with God. We do not have another expectancy. Our one expectancy is God Himself.

The Lord must deal with the source of the self's expectation. So take your offense, and like a detective trace it back to its source. You will discover that the source is a self that has a certain view. It is this self with its view that got offended. It is the self-life. Then just say, "Thank You, Lord, for showing me that I am a person set in concrete." Some of us live in concrete, but God is not set in concrete. God is water! He is flowing water. We are like concrete. Our minds are set like concrete. Our views are like concrete. But God is a living God.

Being offended and the stones in our heart

Matthew 13:20-21 says, [20] "But he who received the seed on stony places, this is he who hears the word and immediately receives it with joy; [21] yet he has no root in himself, but endures only for a while. For when tribulation or persecution arises because of the word, immediately he stumbles [is offended]." These verses describe a person who received the word. But the word could not take root because there were stony places in his heart. This means we may respond to a meeting, to a message, to the vision of the church. We may exclaim, "I have never seen God's eternal purpose before!" We can come out of that meeting filled with excitement and joy because this is really what we should be living for. Yet at the same time, there may be some hidden stones in our heart that we are not conscious of.

But eventually the trials come, the pressures come, the persecution comes — a cloud comes over the church for a little period of time. These things test what you saw that day concerning God's eternal purpose. You discover that there is a cost to live one with Christ, and this cost exposes a stone in your heart. For example, the stone may be the love of money. But rather than deal with the stone, you adjust and fit yourself into what will keep the love of money as the center and driving force of your life. The result is that you interpret things according to this love in your heart. Apparently someone did something or said something that offended you. But actually, when you trace that offense it goes back to the hidden stone. You have not dealt with God over your money. Who holds your money? Who regulates your money? Who does your money belong to — you or God? So God touches the core of your being. And you surrender and say, "Lord, I have held on. This stone is in my heart. Apparently I am offended about something else, but actually the root problem is a stone." We deceive ourselves so easily. We are correcting things outwardly, when all the time our heart is stony.

Being offended and moral problems

In our experience over the years, division in the church life has arisen from time to time. Certain issues would come up concerning something about the church life. But eventually, when we got into the situations, it was discovered that the persons who were speaking the most divisively had closets filled with skeletons of sexual perversions and things in their lives that were not dealt with by God under the cross. They apparently had a problem with another saint. For example, they interpreted something a saint said in the wrong way and got offended. But actually, hidden in their own life was a perversion, a moral, sexual problem. Because this was characteristic with divisive persons, eventually I realized the flesh is a network (Gal. 5:19-21; Col. 3:5-9). Enmities over here are networked with fornication over there. This means that in our experience there cannot be even one area of our life lived in the flesh, because it will affect everything else.

We know that money, sex, and pride are the three major things that cause the downfall of many Christians. There may be hidden stones in us of pride, ambition, self-exaltation — wanting to be something. These desires can even be fed by others' "charismatic prophecies" about us. For example, someone may prophesy that you are going to be "the Daniel" of this hour. Many believers have been ruined because of someone giving a prophecy that God was going to use them as the Daniel of their day. They lived their whole life under a kind of secret thought: "The world is waiting for me to one day step out on stage, and they will know that I am Daniel." May that thought not be in any of us. We are members of the Body, connected to the Head. We are in Him.

Being offended and our natural views

Matthew 13:54-57 shows us the relationship between being offended and our natural views: [54] "Where did this Man get this wisdom and these mighty works? [55] Is this not the carpenter's son? Is not His mother called Mary? And His brothers James, Joses, Simon, and Judas? [56] And His sisters, are they not all with us? Where then did this Man get all these things? [57] So they were offended at Him." These verses show that the ones closest to the Lord were offended at Him. They were totally in their natural view. In our experience this applies to our relationships in our own families, where we just treat one another naturally. Husbands and wives, you know how we can take each other for granted, how we can relate to each other in a common way. We acquire natural views about one another. We may also acquire natural views about the other saints in the church, and then our relationships are brought down to that level. If we are in our natural views, many times when things happen in the church we will get offended with a saint. Our offense is really due to our natural view, to knowing each other according to the flesh rather than according to the spirit. But when we live in the new creation, where old things have passed away and all things have become new, we respect each other as saints in Christ.

Being offended and our traditions

In Matthew 15:6 the Lord said that the Pharisees had made the commandment of God of no effect by their tradition. This shows us that if we have a traditional mind, traditional thinking, we cannot correspond to God. Then we also find out in verse 12 that the Pharisees were offended with what the Lord had said. Why? It was because of their tradition, because of something settled in their being. We also, like the Pharisees, can trace our offenses to our traditions.

Being offended and a crossless life

In Matthew 16:23 the Lord spoke to Peter, "Get behind Me, Satan! You are an offense to Me." The enemy had come to Jesus through the soul-life of Peter, through his good, reasonable mind. Concerning the cross, Peter told the Lord, "This shall not happen to You!" In other words, Peter was harboring Satan in his soul, in his mind; and his natural view came out through his advice to avoid the cross. What gets offended in us is our natural view of the Christian life. It is a crossless view, a view that says the cross is not our appointment.

Some have come to me over the years, offended with what others have done to them, saying, "But they did this to me. They said this to me. And it was not righteous. It was not proper. It was improper." To these remarks I have said, "Let us stop for a moment. Look at the Lord Jesus. Was anything proper that was done over Him by the Pharisees and the Sadducees? Everything done against Him was the most unjust, the most improper, the most insidious insult to His Person. It was full of deceit. *But that was the cross.*"

What is the cross? The cross is not a nice package with a pink bow, beautifully wrapped, appealing to your sight. The cross does not come that way. It comes with a crooked stick. It comes with something that is against us, something that is unjust. Yes, unjust. This, more than anything else, is what tests the self — having something unjust happen to us. We vindicate and defend ourselves. This is the level we live on, rather than seeing the larger picture — that this injustice has happened in order to plunge us deeper into God and to cause us to repudiate this self, not allowing it to make one more decision in our life, not allowing it to be the source of our living. I am a man under authority. I am a man under a Head. And life and peace in my spirit is the deciding factor. That blessedness and that happiness is right here in my bosom, and I know when I have it and I know when I don't have it. Sorry, mind, I don't have the blessedness right now. So I am going to interrupt all this thinking by calling on the name of the Lord. I am going to open my mouth and praise the Lord. I am going to maintain my inner blessedness.

Brothers and sisters, the Lord is walking to and fro throughout the earth (Zech. 6:7). His eyes run to and fro throughout the whole earth (2 Chron. 16:9). We are all being tested for the sake of the earth. We are not on the earth for ourselves. We are here for the whole Body of Christ. All saints everywhere are for the whole Body. Their experiences are for us, and our experiences are for them. Today the Lord wants to connect us all, so He is processing us through the cross right where we live. He is doing it in the details of our daily life. Our experience of Christ is for the whole Body. Oh, it is wonderful to keep the inner blessedness. There is nothing like the blessedness of abiding.

12

INWARDLY APPLYING THE CROSS

A practical question that arises about the subjective experience of the cross is, How do I apply the cross? What does it mean for me to experience the cross and apply it in my everyday problems and situations? We know that the Lord wants to give us a transfer out of our self into the spirit to live Christ. This means not to live out of our self as the source, but to be transferred subjectively to live one spirit with the Lord, just to live Christ and to live out from Him as the source. The way this transfer is effected is by our experiencing the cross. So we must answer this practical question of how to apply the cross.

We have considered the outward aspect of the cross by which God comes to us through the sovereign environments He allows day by day, even moment by moment. He measures out things that cause us to experience cycles of death and resurrection so that we would be transferred more and more out of our self and into the spirit. The Lord allows the environments to come, as Paul declares in 2 Corinthians 4:11: "We who live are always delivered to death for Jesus' sake, that the life of Jesus also may be manifested in our mortal flesh." On the one hand, we are handed over to trials, environments, and all kinds of situations. On the other hand, we need to match those environments with the inward application of the cross by the Spirit in our spirit.

The single most important factor needed to live a life of inwardly applying the cross is vision. What do we see in relation to our experience of the cross? What is our vision? Without vision, our subjective experience of the cross will be greatly frustrated. We may be seeking to apply the cross in an ignorant way. So most importantly, we need to have clear vision in order to be a person inwardly applying the cross.

In Acts 26, Paul was before King Agrippa testifying about his whole life and about the Lord's appearing to him to make him "a minister and a witness" of the things that he had seen and the things that the Lord had yet to reveal to him. At the time of this appearing, the Lord said to Paul, [17] "I will deliver you from the Jewish people, as well as from the Gentiles, to whom I now send you, [18] to open their eyes and to turn them from darkness to light, and from the power of Satan to God, that they may receive forgiveness of sins and an inheritance among those who are sanctified by faith in Me" (vv. 17-18). This means Paul *saw* something. And from that day on he lived under this vision, so he could testify before Agrippa, "I was not disobedient to the heavenly vision" (v. 19).

What do we see? What is our vision? What is our revelation? Without vision, there is no proper incentive to apply the cross, and there cannot be a real application of the cross in its full significance. Thus, to experience the proper subjective application of the cross we must be filled with heavenly vision.

Let us consider the Lord's own vision in relation to the cross in Hebrews 12:2: "Looking unto Jesus, the author and finisher of our faith, who for the joy that was set before Him endured the cross, despising the shame, and has sat down at the right hand of the throne of God." This means that for the Lord's application of the cross in His daily life all the way to Calvary, the single most important thing was His vision of the joy that was set before Him. He saw the throne. He saw the Father's eternal purpose. He saw the consummate goal — the holy city. This was the joy set before Him. It was as if the Lord was on a course, looking down that track to the end, toward the goal. He was looking at the finish line. He saw the throne of God with all the overcoming saints with Him (Rev. 3:21). He saw Himself seated there with a Body incorporated into Himself, conformed to His image, satisfying the Father's pleasure for eternity. This was the joy that was set before Him. Based upon this vision, this heavenly goal, He endured the cross.

Without vision we do not endure the cross, we do not apply the cross. That is why to fellowship about the cross is even foolishness to some believers. It is because to the natural or soulish man the things of the Spirit are foolishness (1 Cor. 2:14). Paul says that, to some, the word of the cross is foolishness (1 Cor. 1:18). Therefore, to talk about the cross and the Spirit's application of the cross may be ineffective apart from the vision of God's goal and the meaning of our human existence. We need to have the proper sight in order to endure and apply the cross, to deny the self, to take up the cross, and to follow the Lord.

The vision of God's economy

All the passages in the Epistles related to the inward application of the cross are filled with the vision of God's economy. In Philippians 3:14 Paul says, "I press toward the goal for the prize of the high calling of God in Christ Jesus." Here Paul was pressing toward something that was before him as a goal. That means he was filled with vision. He was not running in vain, aimlessly, but he was pursuing toward the goal. He saw what all his environments were for. And in verse 15 he urges the saints to also have this same kind of mind — the mind to gain Christ.

Then in verse 18, Paul contrasts the mind to gain Christ with another kind of mind: "For many walk, of whom I have told you often, and now tell you even weeping, that they are enemies of the cross of Christ." This means that some who were professing to be believers were actually enemies of the inward application of the cross. In verse 19, Paul further describes these enemies of the cross: "whose end is destruction, whose god is their belly, and whose glory is in their shame — who set their mind on earthly things." This means they had no vision. They were merely living on the level of the earth, in their self-centeredness, interpreting everything from an earthly perspective, rather than from the vision of God's economy.

The enemies of the cross, who are on the level of earthly things, are in contrast to a person who is filled with vision. Paul defines the vision of God's economy in verses 20-21: [20] "For our citizenship is in heaven, from which we also eagerly wait for the Savior, the Lord Jesus Christ, [21] who will transform the body of our humiliation that it may be conformed to His glorious body, according to the operation by which He is able even to subdue all things to Himself."

To be a person under God's economy is to be one who lives according to the divine destiny over his whole being, which is to be completely conformed to the image of God's Son. Even our bodies will be conformed to the body of His glory. Paul was under this vision of God's economy. We need the clear vision of God's economy over our being in order to apply the cross. I have to see that my being — my mind, emotion, will, and body — has only one destiny, that is, to be saturated and filled with Christ Himself. By this saturating and filling, God becomes my portion.

Because my being has only one destiny — conformity to the image of God's Son — God is causing everything to work together to this end and goal (Rom. 8:28). So if I am a person who is clear about God's economy, I will readily apply the cross inwardly to anything that challenges that economy, anything of this self that has a controversy with the Lord. This includes the self in any relationship with any person. This includes my private life, my daily living. My stubbornness, my impulsiveness, my mind — anything in my being that opposes God — has to bow. It has to be terminated, because I am under the vision that my being has a destiny to be conformed to the image of God's Son. My god is not my belly. My God is God Himself.

Paul makes a very serious statement in Philippians 3:19 about those who are enemies of the subjective cross: Their "end" is destruction. The end of every person who is an enemy of the cross in this age is destruction and ruin. This means to "lose the soul-life." If we do not deny our soul-life, we lose it. And at the judgment seat of Christ we will not hear, "Well done, good and faithful servant." But as unprofitable servants we will be cast into the outer darkness where there will be "weeping and gnashing of teeth" (Matt. 25:21, 30). So the end is destruction for the enemies of the cross. But the end for those who pursue the cross is the prize of the high calling of God (Phil. 3:14).

The vision of the judgment seat of Christ

Whether we know it or not, we are all on a track and in a race. We are going somewhere. We are on the way to the judgment seat of Christ (2 Cor. 5:10). We are on the way to meet the Lord. This is the vision Paul had. That is why he was pressing toward the goal. That is why he was losing everything to gain Christ. He was pursuing toward the goal for the prize of the high calling of God. This means Paul was filled with vision. He was filled with the vision of God's economy over his being — to be conformed to the image of God's Son. He was filled with vision that he was on a pathway that would end at the judgment seat of Christ. Concerning his earthly life, he would "receive the things done in his body," according to what he had done, "whether good or bad." This means he would receive the reward or suffer the loss at the judgment seat of Christ. This is all the Word of God — the truth. And our vision is related to this truth. Paul was under this heavenly vision that incorporates God's goal, God's plan, and God's economy in the context of all the truth related to eternity and our destiny. He could say he was not disobedient to this vision. Filled with this vision, he readily applied the cross. Nothing controls our steps more than having a heavenly vision.

The problem today with many believers is that there is an absence of the vision of God's economy in their lives. They know they are saved. They know they are going to heaven. They know they are not going to hell. But there is little realization of God's goal to transform their whole being into the image of Christ. So consequently there is not much thought or fellowship about the cross. But God wants us as His people to see the heavenly vision, the revelation of His goal over our being. Then based upon this goal over our being, we apply the cross.

The vision of the meaning of creation

Experiencing the cross is very much connected to the vision we have of the meaning of creation. In Romans 8:13 Paul speaks about the inward application of the cross: "For if you live according to the flesh you will die; but if by the Spirit you put to death the practices of the body, you will live." Then following this verse about applying the cross, Paul brings in vision. What kind of vision? It is a vision of the whole creation expecting something to come forth. All of creation is eagerly waiting for the revelation of the sons of God (v. 19). Here creation is personified by Paul as stretching her neck toward an object of attention. Creation is crying out, as it were, for the redeemed children of God to be conformed, to be revealed as the sons of God, to express Christ. Thus, when Paul speaks about the subjective application of the cross, he speaks of it in the context of a vision of the meaning of creation.

All of creation came into existence as the setting for you and me to be conformed to the image of God's Son, God's Firstborn. So we need to see that the whole creation is waiting for our transformation, our conformation. Based upon this kind of vision, we apply the cross subjectively to terminate, to end, the old creation in our being. The self, the flesh, the soul-life, the world — everything that competes with Christ — must be terminated subjectively so that the Lord could be wrought into our being.

The single most important factor in the subjective application of the cross is vision. The question in all our trials is, What do we see? When you are tempted to talk back to someone in a way that would give vent to your flesh, what do you see in those moments? When you would like to strike out at someone — to either vindicate yourself or to say something in a cutting way — what do you see? What is your vision then? If our vision is on an earthly level, we will exchange words with our spouse and live out the self. There will be no application of the cross to interrupt what we feel, to not carry out what begins to boil within us. So without vision we are a person who does not execute the cross from our spirit over our self in that kind of situation.

But, brothers and sisters, many of our problems are solved very simply if we have vision, if we see that the meaning of everything is Christ — this Person gained by us subjectively. And the way we gain Him is by losing everything — losing our opinion, losing our heated reaction — not gaining it, but losing it. We lose our reaction by dropping it, by interrupting it. We are not suffering through it, but we are letting it be terminated. Just terminate it, gaining Christ in that moment. This must be our vision. If we are under this vision, everything is clear. You are clear about your marriage. You are clear about your job. You are clear about your problems. Because the Lord Himself had this vision before Him, He endured the cross, that is, He applied the cross. We have the same vision set before us, so in like manner we apply the cross in every situation.

In our experience this vision means that we learn to say, "Lord, I am here to be one with You, not to live out myself. Because I am under Your purpose and economy, I live one spirit with You for this self to be terminated. Thank You that I am on the pathway. I am running the race. I am headed for the judgment seat. All my daily life is going to be accounted for. All the exchange of words with my spouse is going to be accounted for" (2 Cor. 5:10; Rom. 14:10-12). The question in that day will be, How has the cross operated in your life? How much inward application of the cross has taken place to lose the self and to gain Christ?

Naturally speaking, to talk about the cross and losing the self may not sound so appealing. But we are talking about the cross with vision — the vision that our destiny is to be saturated with Christ. Under this vision everything becomes simple and clear. It is not mere doctrine to us. We see by vision that the destiny over our being is conformity to Christ. The meaning of everything is to gain Christ. This becomes the factor for us to deny the self, take up the cross, and follow the Lord to be constituted with Him. We need to be filled with this kind of vision.

HOW TO LIVE A LIFE INWARDLY APPLYING THE CROSS

Stirring up your spirit

The way to live a life inwardly applying the cross is by stirring up your spirit (2 Tim. 1:6-7). Stir up your spirit to renew the vision continuously in order to execute the cross over your self. This is exactly what Paul is saying in Romans 8. Let us consider verses 13, 14, and 15 together, looking first at their structure: [13] "But if by the Spirit you put to death the practices of the body, you will live. [14] For as many as are led by the Spirit of God, these are sons of God. [15] For you did not receive the spirit of bondage again to fear, but you received a spirit of sonship in which we cry out, Abba, Father."

The putting to death in verse 13 is the *result* of the leading of the Spirit in verse 14. That is, the leading of the Spirit is a leading to put to death the practices of our body. So verses 14-15 actually reveal to us what *precedes* the putting to death in verse 13. Thus in our experience verse 15 brings in verse 13. That is, the stirring up of our spirit by crying "Abba, Father" (v. 15) brings in the leading of the Spirit (v. 14), and this leading issues in putting to death the practices of the body (v. 13).

Renew your vision

You just consider, by the stirring up of your spirit you freshly renew the vision of *who you are*. And because this stirring up of our spirit is a continuous experience, Paul uses present-tense verbs to describe it. In Romans 8:15-16, we are *crying* "Abba, Father," and the Spirit Himself is *witnessing* with our spirit. Notice, the witness is that we are the children of God. And then Paul quickly adds in verse 17, "And if children, then heirs — heirs of God and joint heirs with Christ, if indeed we suffer with Him, that we also may be glorified with Him." In other words, out of that crying comes the sensation that you are a child of God, an heir of God, and a joint heir with Christ. And if you suffer with Him, you are going to be glorified together with Him.

This is vision coming to you instantly when you stir up your spirit. And it is vision with a consciousness — "What am I doing here arguing with my wife? What am I doing vindicating myself? What am I doing living out this flesh again? What am I doing here? O Lord Jesus!" You begin to stir up your spirit and get out of your reasoning mind and your fickle emotions. This is the vision of God's purpose and economy that comes by stirring up the spirit. Exercise and stir up your spirit. Call on the Lord. Cry "Abba, Father!" The result will be an instant and fresh consciousness of who you are in Christ and what you are doing here.

Execute the cross

Stirring up the spirit is the way to execute and apply the cross in our experience. If we do not stir up our spirit by crying "Abba, Father," the Spirit does not have anything to witness with. The Spirit witnesses *with* our spirit. "Our spirit" in Romans 8:16 is "the crying spirit" in verse 15. Therefore, His Spirit witnesses with our crying spirit. This means that *we* take the initiative to stir up our spirit, and then it is His Spirit that bears witness with *our initiating spirit*.

The witness that His Spirit imparts to our spirit is an inner testimony that we are children of God. This is a subjective consciousness that emerges within our being. It is a Spirit-produced consciousness of who we are. We are children of God with a destiny to be conformed to the image of His Son. We need that consciousness reproduced over and over again in our daily life. When we are passing through various trials, we need to have the instant knowledge of who we are stamped once again upon our consciousness. Simply taking the initiative to release our spirit with "Abba, Father!" will launch a consciousness in us of our destiny at that given moment, in that given situation. We are not mere earthly creatures. We are destined to bear the image of the heavenly (1 Cor. 15:49). The Spirit-produced consciousness in Romans 8:16 takes us out of our earth-bound view, our self-pity, our morbid introspection — all the different aspects of the self — and brings us into the fact that we are heirs of God and joint heirs with Christ to be glorified together with Him.

Praise the Lord that we have a spirit and that by stirring up our spirit we experience what Romans 8:13 describes. Paul says, "If by the Spirit you put to death the practices of the body, you will live." To say "by the Spirit you put to death" means that there is an aptitude toward the cross. It is an aptitude that is given to us, by the stirring up of our spirit, to put to death all the practices of our body. When we contact the Lord, enjoying Him, calling upon Him, we are stirring up our spirit of sonship. And with this spirit of sonship is the realization, "Lord, I just need more of Your element wrought into my mind, more Christ into my emotions, more Christ into my will." This is the kind of spirit we have. So the Spirit gives us an aptitude to apply the cross: "By the Spirit, you put to death." This aptitude comes out of stirring up our spirit. Thus, by stirring up our spirit, we continually refresh and renew our vision to live a life inwardly applying the cross.

Perhaps last week in your daily life, this vision was so clear. The consciousness of being a child of God with a divine destiny was ever before you. By the Spirit you put to death everything that surfaced in your being — not only your badness, but your goodness, your independent living, your living out of your own energy, your own strength. You just put it all to death. You said, "Lord, I am not going to live by my life today. Although I do not have a specific consciousness of sin or evil, yet, Lord, I have the possibility of living out of my self, out of my own energy. So by the Spirit I put to death my self-righteousness and self-confidence, and I reject living by my own natural life."

This vision may have been clear last week, but today the vision with its consciousness is not so sharp. We need the vision freshly renewed. It is not something that transpires once and for all, and then we are controlled by it automatically. In one sense, that is true; but in another sense, the vision needs to be constantly brought to the surface of our consciousness. This could be likened to having the power of a desktop publishing program permanently stored on the hard drive of your computer. On one hand, the program is always there. On the other hand, you still need to bring the program up on the screen in order to fully enjoy its benefits.

You may be in the throes of a situation where you find yourself perplexed, confused, and depressed. You do not know what is going on in your life. You are not clear about what the Lord is doing. You find yourself in the grip of anxiety. At that specific juncture, you need your vision renewed. You need a fresh realization that you are a child of God, an heir of God, and a joint heir of Christ. The Spirit needs to redraw on the screen of your heart that your destiny is to suffer with Christ and be glorified together with Him. You need a *present* life-consciousness that you are on the pathway of the cross which leads all the way to the throne, to sit with Him on His throne (Rev. 3:21). For this realization to be your experience, you need to stir up your spirit.

You do not need to live feeling that everything is wrong, and that all hope has vanished. You simply need to stir up your spirit to cry, "Abba, Father!" When you do, a fresh consciousness will begin to arise in you. A fresh realization of your destiny as a child of God will begin to take hold of you. Fresh vision will emerge, and you will be able to sort out things from God's viewpoint. This is the meaning of Romans 8:13-19. To stir up our spirit is to usher ourselves into inwardly applying the cross. This is the genuine leading of the Spirit mentioned in Romans 8:14. It is being led by the Spirit to put to death the practices of our body.

Coordinate your spirit with your environment

To inwardly apply the cross we need to coordinate our spirit with our environment. For this we have to look at 2 Corinthians chapter 4. In verses 10-11 we have both the outward cross and the inward cross. Verse 10 says, "Always bearing about in the body the putting to death of the Lord Jesus." This speaks of the inward cross. Then this inward cross is coordinated with the outward cross in verse 11 by the word "for": "For we who live are always delivered unto death for Jesus' sake, that the life of Jesus also may be manifested in our mortal flesh." The inward cross and the outward cross operating together is the "death operating in us" that produces "life in you" (v. 12).

In verse 11 we are handed over, or delivered, unto death. We may be handed over into weakness, into a trial, into insults, into misunderstandings — into being crossed out. We are handed over again and again to all kinds of outward environments. Just as the Lord Jesus was handed over to the smiters, to those who rejected Him — to all the environment that was sovereignly laid out for Him — so we also are always being handed over. So do not be surprised. This is our lot because we have a destiny and a goal — to follow this pathway of the cross, to enjoy resurrection life, and to be conformed to His image.

Verse 11 says that we are always being delivered over unto death "for Jesus' sake." The preposition "for" comes from the Greek word *dia* (διά), used here in the accusative case. It can be translated literally "because of Jesus." Thus, verse 11 would read, "For we who live are always delivered unto death *because of* Jesus." That is, He is the cause of all this. Because Jesus is hidden in our spirit, God's desire is to move Him out into our soul so that we would manifest Him, display Him, and make Him known. Jesus is not happy being confined to our spirit. He wants to spread out into our whole being. Yet because many times we do not take the initiative to pursue Him, we get handed over to a death situation — to an unhappy husband or wife, or to a disappointment. We are just handed over. This is because God is so desirous that Jesus be manifested in our mortal flesh.

This being handed over is the outward cross, and it must be coordinated and matched with the inward cross. Praise the Lord for Paul's testimony of his experience. He says in verse 10, "Always bearing about in the body the putting to death of the Lord Jesus." Now add to this the first part of verse 11 so that it would read, "Always bearing about in the body the putting to death of the Lord Jesus…for we who live are always delivered unto death." This shows us that Paul's whole life was a bearing about inwardly of the putting to death of Jesus. This putting to death is a lifelong process. It just continues. We are *always* bearing about. This means that gradually, throughout our whole life, the Lord is reducing us and simultaneously renewing us. And this is why Paul says in verse 16, "Therefore we do not lose heart. Even though our outward man is decaying, yet the inward man is being renewed day by day."

This verse indicates that we need to inwardly coordinate with our environment, which means we need to exercise our spirit of faith. In verse 12 Paul says, "So then death operates in us, but life in you." How does death operate in you? Death operates by your inwardly coordinating the inward cross with the outward cross. Thus, verses 10-11 result in verse 12: "So then death operates."

When does death operate? It operates when you are handed over to someone's long face and you want to react with self-pity or vindictiveness. But instead of carrying out your reaction to that long face, you inwardly touch the Lord. You stir up your spirit and do not agree with your kind of reaction. In doing this, your focus is immediately shifted from the person who gave you a long face to your own reaction to that long face. The fact that you could react in such a way is not Christ, so you are taken immediately out of the realm of right and wrong. You are not on the tree of the knowledge of good and evil. Your focus has shifted. The one thing that matters is that you put to death this self that would indulge itself in pity or hurt feelings. You put to death this thing that is not Christ, this thing that reacts in any other way than by turning the other cheek. This is how transcendent the Lord's life is which is to be wrought into our experience. If someone hits you on one cheek, then turn the other cheek to him — not in a coping way, but in a crucified way. Then you are living another kind of life.

You are not living just a "good" life, but a transcendent life (Matt. 5:39).

Thus, in the experience of coordinating with our environment, this outward cross must be matched with the inward cross. By this, a little more of the outer man decays, and a little more of the inner man is renewed. This is the proper vision for our daily living.

A spirit of faith for the realm of faith

This life is a life of faith. You are living by faith. You have a spirit of faith. That is why Paul continues in 2 Corinthians 4:13 by saying, "And having the same spirit of faith, according to what is written, 'I believed and therefore I spoke,' we also believe and therefore speak." This quote, "I believed and therefore I spoke," comes from Psalm 116, a Psalm about taking "the cup of salvation" and calling on the name of the Lord. So Paul's "speaking" in verse 13 is really a calling. He was calling on the name of the Lord, and his exercised "spirit of faith" brought him into the realm of faith.

In 2 Corinthians 5:7 Paul says, "For we walk by faith, not by sight." This is what vision does. When we exercise our spirit, we see the real situation from the view of God's economy — that we are in the process of transformation, and the life of Christ is being increasingly manifested in our mortal flesh. When you exercise your spirit, you get into another realm and you begin to live in faith. Our exercised spirit brings in vision, and vision brings in faith. The more vision we have, the more faith we have.

The faith expresses itself by contacting the Lord and applying the cross: "Bearing about in our body the putting to death of the Lord Jesus, that the life of Jesus also may be manifested in our body" (2 Cor. 4:10). How much do we inwardly coordinate with the outward environment? God arranges our environments. He hands us over to the exact environments we need — those particular ones for you and for me. Then He causes those environments to be matched at the right time with the inward application of the cross. This inward application of the cross is an exercise of our spirit of faith to call on the Lord, to get refocused from what is happening at that moment to what is happening in eternity, to what is happening in God's economy. Our focus is on what is taking place in the realm of faith and eternity. Our focus is not in the realm of right and wrong, what is due us, what we deserve, or how we are being treated. We get completely out of that realm into the realm of what is happening in relationship to God's economy — how much Christ is being added to us.

This is why Paul talks the way he does in 2 Corinthians chapter 4. In verse 17 he says, "For our light affliction, which is but for a moment, is working out for us a far more exceeding and eternal weight of glory." Then he adds in verse 18, "while we do not look." The word "look" comes from the Greek word *skopeo,* which can also be translated into English as "scope." It means a kind of looking or gazing with consideration or concentration. Thus Paul is saying, "while we do not concentrate on the things which are seen, but on the things which are not seen. For the things which are seen are temporary, but the things which are not seen are eternal."

What are the things that are seen? The things that are seen include someone's long, unhappy face. The things that are not seen are the riches of the divine life being added to your being by your believing right now that this long face is for God's eternal purpose of conforming you to the image of His Son. And this conforming happens by your outer man being reduced, losing its strength. More and more it is being crippled, it is being weakened. This old creation that defends itself, that lives itself out, that pities itself, is being reduced. And now, praise the Lord, while all this is happening, we consider, we concentrate on, the things which are not seen. This is vision!

This is how Paul talks — with vision. When he gets into the Corinthian situation and opens up the real state of things, he does not use small talk. He is speaking God's economy. He is speaking in a way of vision, in a way of coordinating all the outward, temporary things and making them work for God's economy. This is Paul's testimony, even when he speaks in 2 Corinthians 5:4: "For we who are in this tent [our body] groan, being burdened, not because we want to be unclothed, but further clothed, that mortality may be swallowed up by life." "To be unclothed" means to be in the state after death and before the resurrection. This was not Paul's desire. His desire was to be "further clothed" — to have what is mortal be "swallowed up by life," to experience full redemption, full salvation. Then in verse 5 he says, "Now He who has prepared us for this very thing is God." So we can see that Paul was fully under the vision of God's economy. Because of this, he coordinated his environment — he matched the outward cross with the inward cross.

In our daily life, many times we do not plan to experience the cross, but God arranges it by handing us over into death. Then we are inaugurated into bearing about in the body the putting to death of Jesus for the glory, the joy, that is set before us. Praise the Lord! To live the life of inwardly applying the cross, we need, first of all, to stir up our spirit, and second, to coordinate our spirit with all our environments.

Keep your consecration and fellowship fresh

For the inward application of the cross we need to keep our consecration and fellowship with the Lord fresh. There is no way to live this life without the fresh realization of our consecration and without fresh fellowship with the Lord. If we do not have this freshness, we lose the application of the cross. To see how vitally connected these are, let us consider Galatians 5:24-25: [24] "And those who are of Christ Jesus have crucified the flesh with its passions and the lust. [25] If we live by the Spirit, let us also walk by the Spirit." The phrase "those who are *of* Christ Jesus" in verse 24 implies ownership and fellowship. We belong to the Lord. This in turn implies consecration. We have a consecration of our being without reservation. One day we say, "Lord, every single member belongs to You. My eyes belong to You, my ears belong to You, my hands belong to You, my feet belong to You, my mind belongs to You, my emotions belong to You. Lord, I present myself."

We have been purchased by the blood (Acts 20:28). Now, based upon that purchase, the Lord legally owns us. But still

He does not force us. He waits for our consent. He waits for us to come to a point of seeing God's economy in our lives — that we are to be filled with Christ. For this economy to be effective in us requires our consent for God to take us over. This is consecration. It is a handing over of our whole being for Him to have the freedom to supply us, energize us, and so operate in us that all our members are willingly and exclusively presented to Him for His full occupation of our hearts.

Consecration means that we have no more rights, no more choices. It means that we are devoted and consecrated for the one purpose of saturation, conformity to the image of God's Son. It implies the pathway of the cross — the termination of the self, the flesh, and all that comes out of our self. This is consecration. A consecrated person inwardly applies the cross. But often we lose the freshness of our consecration. We may have consecrated to the Lord years ago, but what about today? Maybe we have backslidden from our consecration. We may have taken back our eyes so that we look at what we want to look at. We may have taken back our ears so that now we listen to what we want to listen to. But this is not the case with those Paul describes in Galatians 5:24. "Those who are of Christ Jesus" belong to Him, are consecrated to Him, and "have crucified the flesh."

A consecrated person is a crucified person

Every consecrated person is a crucified person. He is crucified to the flesh with the passions and the lust. And when we are consecrated, it means we apply specific crucifyings to the specific passions and the specific lusts. We inwardly apply the cross to those emotions in our being, those movements within us — the evil desires, the passions, the sinful stirrings, the unclean thoughts, the evil imaginations — that whole realm that Paul talks about in Galatians 5. This is to have our being drastically dealt with by the cross.

We need to inwardly apply the cross specifically to an evil passion toward some thing or some person. Apply the cross specifically to every individual lust that enters your being, that rises up within you. Those who are of Christ Jesus know that they do not belong to themselves. They are consecrated freshly: "Lord, I am Yours today. My mind is Yours today. My ears are Yours today." With this fresh consecration, you have consecrated the flesh with its passion and lust to be crucified.

Our consecration implies fellowship with the Lord. In our time with the Lord every morning we are freshly consecrating — "Lord, today, I give You myself. I love to touch You this morning, to have fellowship with You." This is a new day. We need to apply the cross today. So we need to have an up-to-date, fresh consecration and fresh fellowship with the Lord.

This is how to live a life inwardly applying the cross: by having the vision of God's economy, by stirring up our spirit, by immediately coordinating or matching our environment with the inward cross, and by being a person who is in the freshness of consecration and fellowship.

Do not rebel against God

To live a life inwardly applying the cross, do not rebel

against God. You say, "What do you mean, do not rebel? I am not rebelling." Every murmuring is a rebellion, and every reasoning is a rebellion. *Murmuring* and *reasoning* are two words that describe how we rebel against God and against the cross. These words are found in Philippians chapter 2, where Paul talks about the inward application of the cross. In verses 6-8 the Lord Jesus is presented as a pattern to us — as one who did not rebel against God. He humbled Himself, He emptied Himself, and became obedient unto death, even the death of the cross.

Then Paul applies this pattern to the believers in Philippians 2:12-14: [12] "Therefore, my beloved, as you have always obeyed, not as in my presence only, but now much more in my absence, work out your own salvation with fear and trembling; [13] for it is God who operates in you both the willing and the working for His good pleasure. [14] Do all things without murmurings and reasonings." This is the cross — to do all things without murmurings and without reasonings. This is how to inwardly apply the cross. But when we murmur or reason with the Lord's environmental dealing with us, we are nullifying the cross inwardly. This is why Paul gives us a most practical handle on how to apply the cross subjectively. Simply do not murmur and do not reason, because these are the two things that manifest rebellion to God and to His arrangement.

Consider the children of Israel in the wilderness. God arranged everything. He even brought them to Marah, where there was bitter water (Exo. 15:23). This He did not to punish them but to reveal more of Himself to them. But the children of Israel rebelled at Marah by complaining and murmuring. They did not know God's *ways*. They only knew His *acts*. But Moses knew God's ways (Psa. 103:7).

God's ways are how He treats us. He treats us with a spouse. He treats us with children. He treats us with in-laws. He treats us with a family. This is how God has treated us. These are God's ways in our life. So for us to murmur when God is treating us a certain way is an outright rebellion against God and His ways with us. To do or say things expressing our dissatisfaction, expressing what we do not like, is murmuring. Murmuring is just expressing, maybe even under our breath, our complaint. This murmuring and complaining — this kind of speaking — is rebellion. We have to realize that every murmur is a rebellion and is also escaping the cross.

The other form of rebellion is reasoning. Reasoning is intellectual rebellion, the rebellion in our mind. God does not give reasons. God just gives us what He wants to. Praise the Lord for the book of Job. Job eventually saw that God is God and that He does what He wants to do, how He wants to do it, and there is nothing to say. So when we begin to reason and question why this environment is happening, or why something else is the way it is, that is rebellion in our mind toward the Lord. We have to see that to live a life inwardly applying the cross, you just do not rebel. To not rebel means to do everything without murmuring and without reasoning. So you lose *your* speaking, you lose *your* reasoning mind, and you are left with your spirit. Praise the Lord! You are left with your spirit to apply the cross, to enjoy God, and to be renewed in the spirit of your mind.

Be detailed and specific with your members

Another aspect of inwardly applying the cross is being detailed and specific with our members. Paul expresses this in Colossians 3:5: "Therefore put to death your members which are on the earth: fornication, uncleanness, passion, evil desire, and covetousness, which is idolatry." This verse shows us that our members *are* fornication, uncleanness, evil passion, and evil desire. Our members here are not so pleasant. They are equivalent to fornication and uncleanness. These are what Paul speaks of as our specific members. And he tells us that we need to be specific, we need to be detailed, in dealing with these members. So we need to inwardly apply the cross in a specific way, in a definite way, to our members. In the inward application of the cross, these members must continuously be put to death.

Paul does not merely say in a general way, "Put to death immorality." He says, "Put to death your members." Then he specifically names them, beginning with "fornication." The Greek word here is *pornea,* from which we get the word pornography. This means put to death all forms of *pornea,* whether it is the outward act of fornication, or the mental act of imagining through pictures, magazines, and things the eyes behold. These are all forms of fornication. So we must inwardly apply the cross to all the lustful desires of the flesh.

The world is filled with all the things that stimulate the flesh — the television, the radio, the songs, the lyrics. Even the atmosphere in many worldly places is designed by the devil to ruin humanity — to make man useless to God and His purpose. It does so by causing humanity to become lower and lower in uncleanness, looseness, fornication — in all the filth that is filling the earth today. So let me say strongly that we need to exercise our spirit to be strict with everything immoral. Otherwise there is no way to grow in life.

Some may think, "Well, this kind of word is just for the unmarried." But this is just as much for the married as for the unmarried. The flesh does not cease at marriage. Lust does not stop, evil passion does not stop. It may continue in married life. That is why Paul said in 1 Thessalonians 4:4-5, [4] "That each of you should know how to possess his own vessel in sanctification and honor, [5] not in passion of lust [or, the lust of passion], like the Gentiles who do not know God." Possessing your "own vessel" can refer to possessing your own body, or it can also be understood as possessing your spouse. Even in a legitimate marriage relationship, Paul exhorted the believers to be sanctified.

We were not called to uncleanness, but we were called in holiness and honor (1 Thess. 4:4, 7). So this means we need to be specific to apply the cross to our members. Again, in Colossians our members are not spoken of as being our eyes, ears, or mind. Paul actually refers to our members as fornication and uncleanness. That is how constituted the flesh is with sin. So we must put to death these members. We must crucify them. Do not entertain the thoughts. When something starts, immediately interrupt it with your spirit. Allow your spirit to come out and put it to death: "Lord, I am in Your economy. I am not here being wasted in filth, wasted with my eyes, wasted in my mind, wasted in my flesh, giving my body to

uncleanness. I am not here for that. My body is to be sanctified. It is to be holy. It is Yours, and one day it is to be
conformed to Your glorious body." This is how to apply the
cross inwardly to our members.

How to Know When You Have Applied the Cross

You are living

One thing is guaranteed when the cross is applied in our
lives — we are living. Romans 8:13 says, "But if by the Spirit
you put to death the practices of the body, *you will live*." You
cannot help but live. So everyone that applies the cross is a
living saint. You cannot apply the cross and not be living.
Resurrection life is the spontaneous result of putting to death
the practices of the body. When you say "O Lord Jesus" to
your murmurings, to your reasonings, and you keep your self
in death, you keep your flesh in death, resurrection life will
burst forth spontaneously. You come to a church meeting and
you have a testimony. You talk with the saints and there is
genuine fellowship. You meet an unbeliever and you have the
gospel. You are just a living person.

This is how you can tell if you have applied the cross: How
living are you? If you are dead, if there is no supply, no life,
it may be that inwardly you have not coordinated with your
environment, you have not exercised your spirit. Or you have
allowed unclean thoughts to go by unchecked, undealt with,
so that your inward parts are defiled and you are deadened.
Thus, the way to know if you have applied the cross is simply

by your livingness. I do not mean that you are trying to behave in a spiritual way, but you are fresh and living. You are alive with God. This is the way you can tell the cross is operating in you.

The Body is happy with you

Another way you can tell that you have applied the cross is that the Body is happy with you. You may ask what this means. In Philippians 2:1 Paul says, "Therefore if there is any consolation in Christ, if any comfort of love, if any fellowship of the Spirit, if any affection and mercy, fulfill my joy." Fulfill my joy. That means "Make me happy." And how are you going to make me happy? "By being like-minded, having the same love, being of one accord, of one mind" (v. 2). To have this kind of oneness in the Body requires the cross.

Paul speaks of the Lord Jesus taking the way of the cross in Philippians 2:5-8, and then he applies this cross-taking mind to the believers in the verses that follow. He speaks of God operating in us both the willing and the working for His good pleasure. This all has to do with the inward application of the cross. And the way Paul would know that the saints at Philippi had inwardly applied the cross is that harmony would be among them, the flow of fellowship would be between them. This would make his joy full. This would make him happy.

Sometimes in the church life we have not made the Body happy because we have been so "crossless" in our experience. So the joy in the church is not full. The Body is a barometer. Are we making the Body happy? Is the joy full in the saints because of us? When the saints think about us, when they consider us, when they see our face, do they get happy, full of joy? This is a good way to tell whether we have applied the cross inwardly — do we make the saints full of joy?

Paul was saying, "Make my joy full. Encourage me. Fellowship with me. Bring some consolation to me. Make me happy." Such an atmosphere comes from the inward application of the cross. Make your wife happy. Make your husband happy. Make the brothers happy. How do you do it? By inwardly applying the cross to murmurings, to reasonings, to your views of right and wrong. Get out of the realm of the self and into the spirit. Be constituted with Christ, and the joy will be full in the church.

Others get affected

Finally, we can tell whether we are persons applying the cross inwardly by the effect our life has upon others. How much life do the saints receive from us? Paul says in 2 Corinthians 4:12, "So then death operates in us, but life in you." This means that Paul was affecting the saints with life because of the cross operating in him. When the cross is working in our experience, the result or the effect is life in others. So we can tell whether we have applied the cross by how much life is being supplied to our husband, to our wife, to our children, to the saints, to all the organic members of the Body. Those who are joined to the Lord, meeting together and being knit together, will be supplied with life. How do we affect each other? We can tell by the effect — others are receiving life, we are making the Body happy, and we are living.

Oh, may the Lord show us that we are persons with one destiny. And may we be under this vision of God's economy, under the vision of the goal of what God is after. This vision controls us every step of the way. Every reaction, every situation, is under the control of this vision. Everything is measured by this vision. It is brought under review by this vision. This vision controls us.

The Lord has opened up the vision of what everything is about. Now based upon this vision we have the incentive, we have the way, because of the joy set before us, to endure the cross. We apply the cross by stirring up our spirit, by drawing the cross out of our spirit, by bringing the vision freshly to our realization in the middle of our environment, by coordinating with our environment daily, applying the cross to whatever the Lord assigns to us.

We also apply the cross by being a person who is open to the Lord in a specific way at every juncture. We stop this self-life, this old creation. We say no to it. We do not walk in it, but we keep contacting the Lord, having God added to us even in our perplexity, even when we do not understand. We are not reasoning, not murmuring, but just gaining Christ. Then life becomes very simple, and the Body becomes very happy, and we become very living — this is the effect. And this effect of imparting life into the saints and of spreading this life to the ends of the earth comes as a group of people are enjoying God's economy by the inward application of the cross. May the grace of the Lord Jesus be with us to this end. Amen.

SCRIPTURE INDEX

New Testament

MINISTRY PUBLICATIONS

Other Available Books:

by Bill Freeman

The Supplied Life
A Daily Devotional • 409 pages

Spending Time with the Lord
A practical guide in learning how to spend
time with the Lord • 160 pages

God's Unconditional Love
The nature of God's love revealed
in the book of Hosea • 237 pages

Calling Upon the Name of the Lord
A study of the meaning, history, and basis of calling
upon the Name of the Lord • 149 pages

Our Common Oneness
A study in the book of Romans revealing
the oneness of all believers • 284 pages

The Kingdom Life
A study in the book of James showing the nature
of the kingdom life in our daily life • 227 pages

Hearing the Lord's Voice
A study of Scriptures related to hearing
the Lord's voice in our experience • 118 pages

Seeing and Feeling the Church
A study of Paul's prayers in Ephesians • 138 pages

The Church Is Christ
A look into the deep significance
of 1 Corinthians 12:12 • 238 pages

Vision in the Christian Life
The importance of vision in living the
Christian life • 99 pages

The Triune God in Experience
A study of the experiential emphasis on the
Triune God through church history • 391 pages

How They Found Christ — in their own words
The personal testimonies of Augustine, Luther, Calvin, Bunyan,
Guyon, Wesley, Edwards, Whitefield, Finney, Müller, Murray,
H. W. Smith, H. Taylor, Spurgeon, A. B. Simpson, and W. Nee
Edited by Bill Freeman • 201 pages

by Kirk Eland

Christ: the Christian Life
A step-by-step study of the basic truths and
experiences of the Christian life • Especially helpful
for new believers • 218 pages